WITHDRAWN
NDSU

THE LAND OF AFTERNOON

LEWIS SOWDEN

The Land of Afternoon

The Story of a White South African

McGRAW-HILL BOOK COMPANY
New York

DT
779.8
S68
A3

Copyright © 1968 by Lewis Sowden

All rights reserved
No part of this publication may be reproduced,
stored in a retrieval system, or transmitted,
in any form or by any means, electronic, mechanical,
photocopying, recording, or otherwise,
without the prior written permission of the publisher

Library of Congress Catalog Card Number: 68-24194
FIRST EDITION
59815

Printed and bound in Great Britain by
The Garden City Press Ltd
Letchworth, Hertfordshire

CONTENTS

Chapter			
1	The Long Afternoon	page	9
2	The River		19
3	The Mine		37
4	The Small Town		53
5	The Battle of Fordsburg		64
6	Slap-happy Years		76
7	The Great Gold Rush		86
8	Tambula of Vendaland		98
9	Time of Decision		104
10	At War		112
11	The Crucial Year		125
12	Enter Apartheid		136
13	The £20 Senate		147
14	The Treason Trial		155
15	In Parliament		162
16	Beauty and the Law		171
17	Race and Register		182
18	The Gathering Anger		187
19	Sharpeville Monday		192
20	Sharpeville Week		204
21	The Ugly South African		211
22	"The Polecat of the World"		217
23	U.N. and After		229
24	Exit		244

"... they came to a land
 In which it seemed always afternoon."

CHAPTER I

The Long Afternoon

It was an afternoon that lasted for fifty years, and we all behaved as though believing that it would never end, that it would last for ever.

The sunshine would never lessen. The day would never dim. And when the rest of the world was in darkness, we could go down to the shore and, like the people in a certain famous movie, play in the sea.

It happened that way in 1914 to 1918. It happened again in 1939 to 1945. People who came to us during the dreadful night of the Second World War gasped to see us enjoying our ease and comfort while the rest of the world was battling with a monster at its throat. After getting over their first shock, they accepted what they were offered of the good life, and they lay down to bask in the afternoon sun with us.

It had been like that for as long as anyone could remember—since early in the century in fact, which was a long way off; so why should it not go on like that ... on ... and on?

The land was wide and empty, and the skies were high and vast. When you went for a short trip overseas and hurried back from the cold and rain of Europe, you felt like flinging your arms wide to take in the great breadth of the sky, which was greater than anywhere else in the world. The air was clearer, the light was brighter and you could see further into the heavens.

Europe had its wisdom, its art, its culture and its traditions in which we ourselves had our roots. America had its wealth and its marvels. But Europe had its angers and unease. America was frightening. Was there anything better anywhere than our easy afternoon? Fifty years of Europe was not preferable to next summer in South Africa.

Our summers were long and, if you lived on the broad plateau of the highveld, seldom very hot. Our winters were short and never very cold. If a brush of snow came, you watched it melt in the sun and knew that tomorrow was spring.

Tomorrow was blossom time again. Tomorrow the fruit would be heavy on the trees. Tomorrow the fruit would be piled high on the greengrocer's tables in the shop round the corner. The day after, the vineyards of the Cape Province, lying between the two great oceans, would be sending us our grapes and our wine. The Garden of Natal would send us its bananas, mangoes, papaws and pineapples of tropical lushness. And after that we'd have the Transvaal orange crop piling up in the markets and shops of Johannesburg.

The Cape Province, stretching from Table Mountain northwards and eastwards, had its vines. The Eastern Province, washed by the warm Indian Ocean, had its great sheep farms and its wool. The Orange Free State, held between the Orange River and the dun-coloured Vaal, had its corn or maize. Natal had its sugar plantations. Kimberley was still famous for diamonds. And we in the Transvaal had our gold.

We had everything. Our gold mines went down six thousand feet to sea level and beyond. There was no bottom to them. They went sixty miles and farther east and west, and there seemed to be no end to them. The world needed our gold, was hungry for it, and there seemed no end to its appetite.

We had the greatest gold mines in the world and we had the people to work them. We had the black man. We had the black or Coloured man everywhere.

We let the Coloured folk work and get tipsy in our vineyards. We had the black men to tend our sheep and drag our bales of wool. We had the Indian labourers to work the sugar plantations of Natal. And we took the black men in hundreds of thousands from the Cape and Transvaal Reserves, from Basutoland, Swaziland and Portuguese Mozambique to sweat in the deepest mines on earth.

We had the black men in the home as well as in the office and factory. We had black women to look after our children; we had black men to do our cleaning, to work in our gardens and to keep them beautiful, to do our cooking, to serve at table, to bring us tea at work, to make our beds and wash our linen—while we went to play tennis or golf, sat at bridge or the movies, and let our swimming pools and bowling greens proliferate so that we could the better enjoy the endless afternoon.

Yes, we were a white aristocracy, and so we lived. Even the poorest of us, dirty, bedraggled and rolling in the gutter, belonged to the aristocracy if his skin showed white enough under the dirt. For every one of us who was white, there were four who were black or brown; but we were the aristocracy who had the power and the wealth, and they were the proletariat who had nothing but children.

And the black men were patient. That was the marvel of it. No matter what we did to them, they were submissive and passive. By law and by practice we confined them; we told them where they might live and where they might not live; where they might go and where they should be careful not to go; where they might work and where they might do no work; what they should do and what they should never aspire to do. We gave them shacks in the back-yard or shacks in the townships; or they had huts in the Reserves. And they stayed where we ordered them to stay.

We heaped all sorts of indignities upon them. We restricted their drink; we moved their homes; we separated the men from their womenfolk. And yet they remained patient. Sometimes we asked ourselves how long the black man would remain so abject. But we seldom stopped to think. It was enough that he was humble and servile, and raised his cap at us, addressed us as "boss", "Master", "Lord", and "Madam", and did the heaving and carrying while we sat sipping our drinks and giving orders in the long, long afternoon.

Even the Zulus, most warlike and proud of the southern Bantu tribes, were our servants. They had been in rebellion only a few years ago in 1906. Now they made good policemen and even better domestic servants. In the rich houses of

Parktown, Johannesburg, it was almost a symbol of status to have a tall bronze Zulu in a white suit to open the front door or serve at table.

All around us, in our homes, offices, factories, mines, we the white aristocracy were served by the cheap labour of the black man and woman, and we couldn't imagine how we could ever do without it. Every now and then someone in or about the universities protested that the black worker in industry was not getting a living wage. His earnings were below the breadline. To keep his family in food, clothes and shelter he had to let his wife brew illicit beer or do washing for the whites, and let his children go stealing.

The experts produced figures to show that on the white man's farms (where between two and three million black people lived) the black worker was earning only about £50 (then $200) a year, and on his own farms in the Reserves (where about the same number lived) he was earning about half. We of the white aristocracy were shocked for a day or two. But there was nothing to be done about it. The black man was only an unskilled worker; the white man's law prohibited him from becoming anything better; and no one was willing or able to change the white man's law that made the South African afternoon orderly, peaceful, quiet and restful.

For many years South Africa was a land without news. Happy is the land without a history, and happier is the land without news. There couldn't be any news.

Boer and Briton had made peace in 1902, ending the South African War. In 1910 the four provinces of the Cape, Transvaal, Orange Free State and Natal, had come together to form the Union of South Africa and build a new South African nation. Men like Louis Botha and Jan Smuts were at the head of affairs. They were both Boer generals who had fought the British long and hard. But South African politics was something made by the Boers, and the British were content to leave it in their hands, as long as they themselves were left with commerce and industry and the arts of playing games and making money.

For as long as anyone could see there was going to be peace in South Africa, thank heaven, and peace never makes news. After the storm of the South African War the world seemed to have lost interest in South Africa, to be bored with its internal quarrels and ready to forget them. As a young man I used to find that both puzzling and irritating. In the papers you could read news of Canada, India, Australia, all the countries of the Empire and the Commonwealth, and of America; but little news from South Africa ever splashed into the world headlines. Unless it was about sport ... when we sent a team of rugby football players to Britain or New Zealand, we gloated over the prowess of our big brawny men on a far-away field, our battlers with the ball grown stalwart under the South African sun ... and all white of course.

Or there was an animal story ... when a hippopotamus, named Huberta by the newspapers, started to wander against all the habits of her kind through farmlands and gardens of the eastern parts of the Cape Province, her doings were chronicled in the British newspapers every Sunday. When she was shot dead by an angry farmer, an outcry went up in the land against the destroyer of this plentiful source of South African publicity.... Publicity, publicity! That is what we wanted, but, alas! it was such a happy land—a land where only the animals made news.

There had been the rebellion, of course. When war broke out in Europe in 1914, the Boers saw their chance to revenge themselves against Britain now that she had her hands full elsewhere, and commandoes under die-hard generals took the field again. But Botha sent other commandoes against them and suppressed the Boer rebellion with Boer troops. Then he organised a South African expedition for the conquest of German South-West Africa, and giving the Allies their first success demonstrated how Britain's enemy had become her staunch and grateful friend.

South-West Africa was conquered in a mood of ebullience, which continued when next year Smuts tried to repeat the success in German East Africa. But here the Germans had greater resources, the country was more difficult and the German commander, Von Lettow Vorbeck, more elusive. The victory was slower and more costly than in South-West Africa, and less spectacular.

Going to London, Smuts joined the Imperial War Cabinet, and the picture of the Boer War leader now in the highest councils of the Empire angered the Boers in South Africa as much as it engaged the imagination of the world.

After the war and the death of Botha, the government was headed by Smuts, a man of steel-blue eyes and cold reserve. The miners' strike of 1922, which became the Rand Revolt, cost twice as many lives as the conquest of South-West Africa and led to Smuts's defeat in the 1924 elections. Even in Opposition he remained the dominant figure on the South African scene, and the world saw South Africa in his image.

When you travelled overseas in Europe, on a voyage that was as much a status symbol as a holiday, and you suggested to friends that all was not well in South Africa, that the black people lived in subjection, voteless, voiceless and confined by the Pass Laws and the Colour Bar, they looked incredulous. This was the land of Smuts, was it not, Smuts the great democrat? Would Smuts allow a state of servitude to continue within the South African democracy? It was too much to explain, when a man was on holiday, that the South African conception of democracy stopped short of colour—or otherwise, what would become of the South African afternoon?

It was not always a placid afternoon. The slump of the early 'thirties sent a cold wind blowing from across the Atlantic. Could it be that Americans would no longer want our diamonds? Thank heaven for the gold mines of the fabulous Rand! Then Britain went off the gold standard and the foundations shook perceptibly.

Could the world dispense with gold? The fear did not last. No matter what the nations did with their money, no matter how much paper they printed, they still needed our South African gold, and more and more of it. Explain it how you might. The gold shipments continued to Britain and America, and under Fort Knox, Kentucky, they stored away the gold that had been dug from under Johannesburg, Transvaal.

The recruitment of African labourers from the back-blocks was intensified. Between 300,000 and 400,000 black men were working in the mines. That meant there was work there also for 30,000 whites, and the flow of gold would continue. Moreover, as factories grew in the urban districts, the African labourers began flocking to the towns to earn the money they could not earn on their own eroded farmlands in the Reserves.

It was a most fortunate arrangement. Whatever the white man wanted to do, he had gangs of black men at his call willing to do the hard work for him, ready to live in a shack and work in the white man's kitchen, garden, office, mine or factory. And he was happy to do it all for about a sixth or less of what the white man next to him expected to be paid. If anyone objected to the inequality of such a dispensation, the answer was that the black man knew no better, and was used to no better. His needs were few; he was not civilised, and it was incongruous to apply to him such terms as "cost of living" and "a civilised wage". He knew nothing of these things, and to teach them to him was the worst kind of subversive activity.

If the whites wanted to build roads, they would place a white foreman in charge of a gang of twelve Africans to show them where to throw the stones, to pour the sand and to spread the tar. If they wanted to build a house, they would get African labourers to carry the mortar and bricks so that a white man could lay them and trim them. If a white man drove a lorry or a truck, he would have two black men to do the loading and unloading. If he planted a tree, he got a black man to dig the hole.

That was the way of life that continued throughout the 'thirties and the years of the Second World War, and not all the bombs of Europe could disrupt it. The possibility of a Nazi victory alarmed everyone but the Boers (or Afrikaners, as they now called themselves), the majority of whom were ready to welcome the Germans as distant blood brothers.

The possibility that gold mining might be hampered caused general anxiety. There were some troublesome men in Washington who were inquiring whether, while the West was fighting for survival, the mining of gold was really necessary.

They even sent envoys across to see for themselves. But to everyone's relief they decided that gold mining was desirable—and so also, a year or two later, was the mining of uranium.

Victory in Europe, and then victory in Asia, meant that the South African way of life—as arranged by the white man—was secure. Or so it seemed. New gold deposits were discovered. British investors poured hundreds of millions of capital into the country. The years ahead would be boom years. Immigrants in the thousands were coming from Europe to share the good life.

Then Smuts, a man who saw things on the horizon but stubbed his foot on a stone, lost the 1948 election to the Afrikaner Nationalists' cry of "Apartheid!". . . Two years later he was dead.

I was in London at the time, and I attended the memorial service in Westminster Abbey. An Oxford professor, shaking my hand, observed sadly, "It's the end of an era for South Africa." He was wrong. The era—and the afternoon—still had a decade to run.

In 1960, the British Prime Minister, Mr. Harold Macmillan, came to South Africa at the close of an African tour. Speaking to the assembled members of both Houses of Parliament at Cape Town, he talked of the winds of change that were moving through the African continent. It was a wise speech, a statesman's speech that looked into the future with prophetic perception.

I listened to him on a little radio next to a morning cup of coffee (made by a Zulu cook) in a house on the sunny northern slopes of Johannesburg, and I was elated to think that there were still British statesmen who could talk with daring and dignity, unafraid to face the challenge of the future. But among South Africans there was resentment that Mr. Macmillan should encourage changes in Africa by drawing attention to them and talking of them so plainly. For in South Africa the belief persists that you prevent undesirable happenings by turning your back on them, and you can exorcise unfriendly spirits with silence.

A shiver went through South Africa (and the Johannesburg Stock Exchange), but as yet only a shiver. There was a law on the Statute Book making Communism illegal. Political movements among the African population had been harassed and frustrated. (They were soon to be banned.) It was true that in Central Africa new black states were being torn out of the old colonial empires. There were rumblings just across the border in the Rhodesias. But the share market rode high. The new 15-storey blocks, including a new building for the Stock Exchange, were gleaming in the harsh Johannesburg sunlight. And it was wrong for a statesman from Britain to warn the cosy three million white population in South Africa that the wind was changing for them—even if it was true. Indeed, it was doubly wrong of him if it was true.

Two months later came the massacre of Sharpeville, when more than seventy African men and women died before a ten-second burst of firing from a squad of frightened white policemen. This was no revolution. It was not even an uprising. The crowd of men and women were only demonstrating against the much-hated Pass Laws. But the police panicked and knew only one way of defending themselves.

That short sharp volley sent a wave of horror through the world. But it also struck fear into the white population of South Africa. They had not been fired on; and none of them had been killed. Moreover, the few thousand demonstrators (less those left on the ground) had scattered in seconds, thus showing the futility of challenging the white man's authority. Yet the whites knew that the Sharpeville shooting would rouse the Africans as nothing had roused them before. The Africans would not forget and would seek their revenge. The whites knew that the battle was on with black Africa, and in their hearts they trembled.

That afternoon, as the dismal messages kept coming in from Sharpeville, a group of staffmen stood in one of the inner offices of the *Rand Daily Mail* in Johannesburg, passing the telex slips from one to the other. At last someone standing near the window spoke.

"All this, on such a lovely afternoon."

And it was a lovely afternoon. A typical late summer

afternoon which flushed the city in a broad mellow sunlight.

I went up to the window. "But the afternoon is over, boys ... The afternoon is over."

The thought had come to me that instant. I hadn't fully shaped it myself before speaking. Yet I was sure they understood.

"The afternoon is over." By the look on the men's faces I could see that the thought was echoing round the room.

CHAPTER 2

The River

It had started for me with a postman's knock one Saturday morning in a street in Manchester. The postman always called on Saturday with letters from South Africa, and the one he brought this time was thick and heavily stamped. Printed papers came to light as my mother tore it open in the little parlour beside the fuchsia at the window.

Next Monday morning in the Waterloo Road school I was an object of special interest. I was the boy who was going to Africa, and the woman teacher to whose class I belonged felt she had to pay some extra attention to me and Africa. When the headmaster, Mr. Sharples, came round, she pointed me out as the boy who was soon going abroad... to the Dark Continent. She made me feel rather lonely. I stood up sheepishly, but was glad when Mr. Sharples merely nodded and went on to the next class.

But the teacher hadn't done with me. She felt it was up to her to tell the class all about Africa, and she started at once. She told us that there were parts of Africa that were hot, dry and entirely without water. "And where," she demanded, "do you suppose the people get their water from?"

We all faced her with blank expressions, I a little guilty, feeling that I ought to know. When no answer was forthcoming, she supplied it herself, and I swear this is what she said: "They get it from water melons."

No one stopped her to ask where they got the water to grow water melons with, but no one was particularly impressed. We were much more interested in black policemen who carried letters in cleft sticks (as illustrated in our reading book) and in black boys who sat at school under palm trees (also illustrated). I pictured myself sitting next to a half-naked black boy in a desert sprinkled with water melons.

In the years that followed I was to eat many melons and never without remembering their prodigious water-yield. I was never to see a policeman with a cleft stick. And I was never to have a black schoolboy sitting beside me in class or indeed within miles of me.

In our kitchen in Manchester, in a house we shared with another family, there was a large picture hanging on the wall. It was entitled "The Great Boer War" and it purported to portray an engagement on a South African hillside. There were puffs of smoke in the air, and there were dead men lying on the ground. Count as I would, the dead on both sides seemed to be equal, and seeing that the British had won the war that was not a little puzzling to me.

Other things puzzled me about this Africa, where my father was waiting for us beside a river on top of a mountain —or so it seemed to me. But how could there be a river in the desert of Africa, and how could one live at five thousand feet or, as someone pointed out, a mile high? No doubt all these things would soon be made plain.

The ship that sailed with us from the Thames was crammed with emigrants, most of whom were bound for Australia and New Zealand. As we neared Cape Town I heard that only about a dozen passengers were leaving the ship, and that was more matter for puzzlement. In Table Bay the voyagers gazed in awe at the mass of the mountain, and a man who took a quick run ashore returned with an ecstatic description of the beauty of the country. "There are trees in the streets. ... There are trees!"

Yet all but a handful of the passengers preferred to look at Africa from the ship's rail and to travel on across the Indian Ocean to the other edge of the world.

For thirty hours a long train carried us north-east from Cape Town, through the vineyards of the Cape Province, through the dusty desolation of the Karroo that stretched from horizon to horizon, and then into the grassveld of the Transvaal. For the first and last time I rode uncomfortably in a ricksha through the dusty streets of Johannesburg. And then a horse and cart took us north through the refreshing grassveld again for nearly two hours.

Was this the mountain top? Incredibly I was assured that it was... and so into a valley, to a large corrugated-iron house standing amid bluegum trees—and of course the river.

It was not my idea of a river. When first it was pointed out to me from the verandah of the house, all I could see was a bridge where the road dipped and turned, and dark patches which stretched away in the ravine on either side. They told me that the road was the road to Pretoria and the dark patches were clumps of trees and bush. They looked almost black in the sunlight, and I could not understand how anyone could call that a river.

When I went down to the stone bridge, I stood at the railings and looked over the side. Below me were broad, yellow banks of sand and away at the edge was a slow trickle of water little more than a foot wide. I could have jumped across it had I wished. I kept asking myself how un-riverlike could a Transvaal river be.

The first day I went fishing with Japie, our Coloured servant, we squatted on grass behind a thick growth of reeds. I stepped out to get a closer look at the water and fell in up to my neck. Japie dragged me out spluttering and led me home. I dripped water all the way, and he just laughed.

Japie, barefooted and clad in torn shirt, patched breeches and floppy hat, was unusual in this part of the country. Here the people were either white like my family and the other families I was to discover in the district, or black—Bantu, African, Kaffir—like all the farm labourers. Japie was half-caste, yellowish-brown, and if you asked him where in the world he came from, he would smile darkly and pull the floppy hat further down his head.

They called the river by a name that I had never heard before, the Likkewaan, which no one knew how to spell and which was not the official name of the river anyhow. But the Likkewaan it always remained for me. Miles away it flowed into the Crocodile, which flowed into the mighty Limpopo, which finally emptied itself into the Indian Ocean.

It was here that I first got to know the country, the wide grasslands of the highveld, where the only trees that grow are those planted by man, and the only hills are the stone-topped koppies.

At the Likkewaan I first met the Boers or Afrikaners. Later, when we moved to the mine, I came to know the black people —the natives, the Bantu, the Africans.

And later still I met the Coloured people, the light brown half-castes, the people to whom Japie belonged, and I came to know them too in the small town.

But first let me tell of the Likkewaan.

The house on the hillside, which looked straight down towards the river, had four rooms and a kitchen. The broad verandah, which shielded us from the hot sun, was screened with grenadilla creepers. I remember the heavy fruit hanging like green pom-poms from the meandering stalks, but I don't remember ever eating any.

In the back-yard, there was also a large mulberry tree, the fruit of which was luscious and plentiful. In the summer—one long gorgeous summer—the soft juicy berries stained the ground black, and those we picked stained my hands for days with indelible red.

Fifty yards below the house, and fronting the road that curved past it, was the shop—and that was the reason for our being there. Who in the world could have thought of putting up a shop in this empty countryside where, from horizon to horizon, you could count only three houses apart from our own? It was an Englishman, who had stayed behind after the Boer War. He had bought a few acres of land carved out of the adjacent farm and put up a squarish brick building with a lean-to verandah in front and a low-roofed shack behind for a servant. He had stocked it with canned foods, flour, tobacco, biscuits and an assortment of clothing, and waited for customers.

When the customers did not come in sufficient numbers he

had to sell out. And that was when we came along. My mother had a round-faced cousin-of-sorts, Morris, who had a lean wife, Mary, and who had developed a craving for living in the country. They said they were tired of town life and the rattle of tram-cars past their door. So they bought the shop, the house and the few surrounding acres from the Englishman and had visions of living off the land, the country customers and the townsfolk who came at the week-end to picnic beside the river.

My father became Cousin Morris's partner because his own business had failed, but he had certain assets that neither the Englishman nor Morris commanded. He knew the language of the Boers—Afrikaans, the South African form of Dutch—without which it was difficult to make any sort of progress in this part of the country. In fact that was one of the reasons the Englishman gave for his failure. "Can't speak the *taal*—the lingo. Want to be friendly ... Can't make contact ... What's the good? You'd think we were still fighting the Boer War! We gave 'em the country back ... gave 'em their language ... gave 'em money ... You'd think they'd want to be friends now. Not they! Sold me the bit of land I wanted. But you think I can do business with them? Not me! Not an Englishman! Perhaps you ..."

The shop had proved unable to support one Englishman, and how it was going to support two Jewish families—well, no one seemed to have worked it out properly. Living was cheap in the country, and that was a formula expected to cover all deficits. As for me, I could see nothing but a lovely life ahead, with only school as a dark intrusion.

Every Monday morning I climbed sullenly into the trolley and Cousin Morris drove me to a bleak, red-brick Government school at the shabby end of town. Dick the horse took ninety minutes to pull up the ridge to Johannesburg, so I arrived late at school and always blamed it on the horse. I hated the school and I hated the boarding house (in a block where big mining houses now front the clouds) where I stayed five days a week. The florid woman who ran it was a distant relative of my father's. Every Friday evening she would don her finery, make up her hair in an enormous pile, and preside at top of table over the soup tureen and the fish. I was only told of this. I never saw her. Immediately after school on Friday I would take up my stand at the street corner waiting for Dick and Cousin Morris to take me back to the river, grieving over every minute they made me waste in waiting.

Head in wind, Dick the horse took only fifty minutes to run us home and he snorted as he felt the country air in his nostrils. I snorted too. For me, going home on Friday was like returning to heaven every week-end—a heaven where I walked barefoot and wore a floppy hat like Japie, and went paddling in the river with him (fortunately in the days before it became infected with bilharzia). I could talk to Japie and tell him how much I hated the school and the boarding house, where he sometimes picked me up on a Friday in place of Cousin Morris. "And don't you dare keep me waiting next time," I scolded him.

In this heaven of mine, where the sun always shone and the river always gurgled, we got milk straight from the cow and eggs and meat from the poultry in the yard. Cousin Morris was the Boss; my father was also a Boss, and I was a Kleinboss (Small Boss). The boys and girls around us were the chocolate-brown natives on the farms, and even biscuit-coloured half-caste Japie was never more than a Boy.

Japie was our houseboy and our shop-boy. He lived in a shack somewhere near the store-room; for food he had mealie meal and the left-overs from the table; his cash wages were £1 a month, perhaps thirty shillings; and he considered himself as well off as he could expect to be in the white man's world.

It was a way of life to which the white man coming from "the Old Country" or the Old World, took to as naturally as breathing. After a time he began to wonder how he could possibly have continued living in any other way.

The three houses we could see from the front verandah stood at the points of a triangle. To the left and west was Koos van Staden's, to which a footpath ran directly from us and through a barbed-wire fence. To the north and across the river was the house of his brother, Martinus van Staden, standing on a hill. And to the right, also across the river, lived an English family, Gittens by name, their house partly hidden by trees.

Koos was our nearest neighbour. In fact our few acres had been cut out of his farm, and though he never said anything about it, I always had the feeling that he resented it. He was stocky, hard-working and sullen, and when he came to the shop he entered with a stiff "Good day", and departed with a stiffer "Good afternoon".

His brother was lanky, easy-going and something of an idler—much the nicer of the two.

He liked us and we liked him. One day, over a cup of tea in the shop, he turned to me and in a sheer burst of friendship said, "Loo, my seuntie ... ek sal jy 'n roer maak ... (Loo, my boy, I'll make you a gun)."

"A roer! Jy kan a roer maak?" I was picking up the language fast. "You can make a gun?"

"Ja! Jy sal sien ... (Yes, you'll see)."

I looked at Martinus, whom I already regarded as a crackshot, with a new admiration.

The odd man in this bend of the river was Gittens the Englishman, except that we of course were the oddest of all. His wife, a spare smiling woman with grey eyes, explained to us on her first visit—I think she came to buy some calico —that her husband had had a good job in an engineering workshop on the mines, but he had a craving to go back to the land, and there was nothing to be done about it. So here he was growing maize, peanuts and pumpkins, and she hoped it would turn out well ... but who could tell?

Cousin Mary, who had straight black hair and was taller than her husband, listened sympathetically and nodded. "These men! So he'd rather be a farmer than an engineer!" She had at once promoted him engineer.

"Yes," said Mrs. Gittens, tacitly approving the promotion.

"You can understand a shopkeeper wanting to go on to the land, but an engineer!"

Mrs. Gittens sighed. "That's how it is." The children were at school in town, and she could have them home only at week-ends. Yes, these men!

She brought the children to tea with us on the very next Saturday afternoon. The girl, Stella, was the elder. She was pretty and we approved of each other at once. The brother, Roy, was noisy and covetous. He sat at the table gobbling Marie biscuits. He dipped them into his tea and stuffed them into his mouth, till Stella slapped him and told him not to be so greedy. He just laughed, and his mother quietly drew the tray of biscuits beyond his immediate reach.

I told Stella I was going to get a gun, a real gun. She didn't believe me. I said Martinus van Staden was making one for me. She didn't believe that he could. In my heart of hearts I didn't believe it either, but I would never have admitted it. Martinus had said a "roer", which was undoubtedly a gun. And no one could deny that the Boers were clever with guns. I would show it to them in due course.

For days after that, whenever Martinus turned up at the shop, I looked in his hands for that gun; but there was no sign of it. One day impatience got the better of my manners and I asked him, "Waar is my roer? ... Where is my gun?"

He nodded. "Dit kom, my kind, dit kom ... 'n bietjie geduld ... a little patience, heh?"

He had it with him the very next time he came. He took it from under his arm-pit and said, "There's the gun I made you ... How do you like it?"

I took it in astonishment and excitement. It was not a gun in any modern sense. But I knew at once what it was. I had seen illustrations in schoolbooks.

"It's a crossbow," I exclaimed. "A crossbow! ... With arrows! ... Does it shoot?"

"Of course it shoots. Would I make you a gun that doesn't shoot?"

It was made of wood, about eighteen inches long, with a groove of about half its length or more for the arrows, which were made of reeds. The trigger was a peg screwed into the side and operating an elastic bow-string.

He offered to demonstrate, and placing the crossbow along

his forearm, shot an arrow about twenty feet. It was thrilling. I took the bow from him and pointing my arrow in a higher angle sent it somewhat farther. Martinus was delighted to see how pleased I was. I tried it out all over the place.

Next week-end I showed it to Stella and Roy. They agreed that though it wasn't a gun, it was something quite interesting, and it worked! We were standing then under the willow on the Gittens' side of the river, and I shot an arrow across the water, from one sand-bank to the other. Roy had to wade calf-deep to retrieve it.

"You couldn't shoot a bird with it," he said, as he handed it back.

I wouldn't admit it, so merely looked doubtful.

"He doesn't want to shoot a bird with it," said Stella indignantly.

"No," I said. "I wouldn't want to shoot a bird," not believing a word of it.

"I would!" insisted Roy.

"Horrible boy!" said Stella.

A few days later it was our Coloured man, Japie, who showed me the crossbow in its proper light. Though he had never been to school in his life and couldn't read, he taught me, not my first lesson in history, but the first lesson that I remember.

He had been eyeing me and my harmless arrows for some days. At last he came out with it. "I can make you a better one than that."

"You can't!"

"I can, and I will . . . if you like."

"Go on, then. Do it!"

"You'll see."

It didn't take him long either. The very next day he brought me a longbow that made my crossbow look no more than the outmoded toy it was.

It stood as high as my shoulder and was made of a supple twig that you could bend double.

Japie placed a long arrow against the string, pulled it back and next moment sent it flying over the bluegum trees.

This was exciting indeed. I took the bow from him and

shot an arrow almost as high as his. At once I had to acknowledge the superiority of the longbow—as medieval generations had done before me—and I sent arrow after arrow flying to the tree tops.

Japie looked on with unconcealed pleasure to see how he, the barefooted half-caste, had done so much better than the white man. He even considered a suggestion for improvement. The arrows were light. They lost direction at the top of their flight and then often got stuck in the branches, so we could not retrieve them. Eventually we tipped the reeds with short nails taken from boxes. That did it. The arrows flew in a regular curve and at the end of their flight turned over and dropped almost vertically to the ground.

Japie chortled with pleasure to see the success of his handiwork. "Tha's good! What I tell you! Tha's better! Tha's champun, hey? Champun!"

He'd got the word from me. "Yes . . . champion!"

I left the crossbow lying about. He laughed to see it so completely superseded. But I was a little sorry, and when next Martinus van Staden came to the shop I made sure that the longbow was out of sight.

Now on the Likkewaan River that battle-piece which had hung in our kitchen in Manchester often came into my mind. That battle might have been fought here on the rising ground facing us across the river. So I tried to fit the people I knew into the artist's scheme, and for the life of me I couldn't do it. I could not see the Gittenses and the van Stadens on that battlefield killing each other.

Gittens I had come to know as a mild-spoken man who went about his farmyard always sucking at a pipe. He was another of our steady customers for tobacco, the only thing we sold with any regularity. I once watched him mending a part of one of his ploughs. His attention was concentrated on that mis-shapen piece of metal as though nothing existed beyond—except of course his pipe. He would never want to kill the van Stadens, and neither the light-hearted Martinus nor his serious-minded brother Koos would want to kill him.

... No, they never met, except fortuitously at the store, and then briefly.

They were very polite to each other. Did that mean anything? They always stood at opposite ends of the counter—Gittens at the tobacco, Koos at the rolls of calico even though he wasn't a bit interested in them. He would shy straight off to that corner after a stiff greeting at the door, knowing from the horse tethered outside whom to expect within.

They never discussed anything except the lack of rain, and their wives never met. For that matter I don't remember ever seeing the van Staden women at the store. Mrs. Gittens, yes, but neither of the Mrs. van Stadens. I once saw Mrs. Gittens ask Koos how his wife and the baby were managing "in this cruel dry weather", and I saw her disappointment at the curt reply.

All Koos van Staden was interested in was selling his crop of yellow clingstone peaches in town, and when he had done that he took his brother's crop away in his ox-wagon—Martinus was no salesman—and he disposed of that too.

When I saw him passing the store on his way out, whip in both hands, I longed to accompany him. I thought a two-day ride behind a span of oxen, helping with the chores on the way, ought to be an adventure. But my mother wouldn't hear of it, and Koos was only mildly interested in the suggestion. I felt sure that if it was Martinus going to town, he would have welcomed me and would have persuaded my mother to agree.

It was Martinus who taught me what a likkewaan was, on a morning I went shooting with him.

He loved sallying forth from his farmstead on the hillside, leaving his wife on the verandah scolding after him. We all knew that she scolded him. He told us so himself and I once heard her at it.

"There you go again! All you want to do is go roaming in the veld with a gun and that ... that ..." (I knew she meant "that Jew", Morris, of course, but I thanked her for not saying so...) "... What will become of us, Martinus? What will become of the land and the oxen and the children? What will become of us?"

When he kept cleaning his shotgun and seemed deaf to appeals, she tried another tack.

"Does Koos do it? Does Koos go roaming in the veld, leaving his wife and his home and his . . . ?"

"No, not with that wife," he muttered.

He sauntered away, I at his side feeling rather guilty, he trying to get her voice out of his ears. "Oh, these women, they don't understand what a man wants out of life. Can I help it if it doesn't rain?"

He would call in at the store for some ammunition (Cousin Morris never refused him, and that was usually when I joined him) and then go tramping over the countryside in search of a hare or some small buck. That morning we took a path alongside the river where it broadened out into shallow pools and straggly bush. We hadn't been out more than half an hour or so when Martinus stopped, put a hand out to hold me back, then raised his gun and fired.

I saw something writhing in the tall grass ahead. "What is it? What is it?"

He ran forward and I followed. The writhing creature was like an enormous lizard at least six feet long, half of it an angry beating tail. "Look out!" shouted Martinus. "It's a likkewaan! He can kill you with that tail."

He had filled the reptile's hide with shot and the wounded creature was making for the river. But we headed it off and dispatched it with stones aimed at its head, which was small and narrow. It was dead within a few minutes and lay there, a flabby mass.

"A likkewaan," he repeated. "Quite a big one too. In English an iguana, heh? But for me a likkewaan. Take it away. Take it home."

"But it's yours."

He scoffed. "Of course not! What will I do with a likkewaan? No use taking it home to my wife. She'll want something better than that. Take it."

He walked off with his gun in his hand and left me standing beside the dead likkewaan. I was not a little scared to be

alone with it; but I had no choice. After prodding it
with a stick to make sure it was quite dead, I took it by its
tail and dragged it away. All the way home I kept looking
over my shoulder in case I should be followed by another
come to take vengeance. If that had happened, I'd have
dropped it and run for dear life.

Eventually I brought the likkewaan home in triumph, and
when I presented it to Cousin Morris he was as pleased as
though he'd shot it himself. He kept it on display for hours,
showing it to anyone who came by, rolling it over on its
back and pointing out the peculiarities of its anatomy.

"See there. It's a male. And what a male!"

By the end of the day he regarded himself as an expert
on likkewaans. Next morning he spent more hours stuffing it
with dry grass and herbs, and finally he placed the hideous
thing, more hideous in death than in life, in a corner of the
front verandah, where he could show it to visitors.

Then one day someone said that likkewaans were unlucky.
Someone had also said that likkewaan skin was good for
rheumatism. No one was interested. But unlucky? That was
different.

"Do you hear, Morris?" demanded Mary. "Is that all we
need here now—an unlucky likkewaan?"

She called to Japie. She was sure the Coloured man must
be an expert on these matters. "Japie, is it true? Likkewaans
are unlucky? You can tell us."

Japie hesitated. He looked darkly from his master to his
master's agitated wife. "Yes, Missis... I think maybe I did
hear something like that. Of course I can find out for Missis
if likkewaans is unlucky."

"That's enough. No need to find out. If a likkewaan is
unlucky alive, how much more unlucky is a dead likkewaan!
Do you hear, Morris? And you had to go and stuff it!"

That was the end of it. She'd been against it from the
start; no friend of likkewaans in any condition. Next day the
stuffed iguana had disappeared, and if Morris was regretful
he tried not to show it.

A few days later, going to call Japie, I caught a glimpse
of what looked very much like strips of likkewaan skin

hanging in his shack behind the shop. He saw me looking at them from the doorway and at first he was taken aback. Then he laughed. "Yes, Kleinboss.... Some people does liking it for rheumatics. And why not? So I selling them."

I looked round at his shack... a monkey's tail, some claws and bones, a fur cap. One day, I reflected, Japie was going to set up business as a medicine man or herbalist, and with him I said, "Why not?"

We laughed like anything. After all, I owed him something for pulling me out of the river.

That picture I remembered from Manchester never seemed to fit anywhere into our life on the Likkewaan River. And yet gradually a pattern was emerging, although I could not be aware of it then, a pattern I was to find over and over again in South Africa.

The van Stadens had a father, a man who could not have been more than middle-aged, but who seemed old to me. He wore a trim beard, and he rode a wiry Basuto pony. He used to ride over from his farm a few miles away, hitch his horse to the verandah pole at the shop and then walk up with Morris and my father for tea at the house.

Old Mr. van Staden—we never called him anything else—talked to my father in Afrikaans, and Morris intervened in a mixture of Afrikaans and English. Old Mr. van Staden had three themes, the weather, his sons and the blacks. The weather would surely come right whether one prayed for it on Sunday or not; his son Martinus would learn to work harder; but he wasn't so sure about the blacks. That was the theme to which he kept returning.

"Keep a look-out, my friends. We must always be on the watch for a black rising. There is unrest in the country, unrest everywhere...."

I used to look out through the window to try and see where it was.

"The kaffirs get too much these days and they're always wanting more.... The week-end, Sunday, is the time to be careful. Be on the watch, my friends. Don't be caught. Look after yourselves and don't trust them...."

Those were usually his last words as he rode away—leaving Morris, my father and the women looking seriously at each other and wondering whose side Japie would take in an emergency.

I spoke up boldly for Japie. "He's not one of them. He says so! Japie's our friend. He's part white and he's all right." I was told to hold my tongue.

I tried to imagine what I would do if there was a black rising. Morris had a revolver and his shotgun, and he showed us once that with his revolver he could shoot across the river. Would that be enough to stem a black rising? I looked round for a heavy stick. I even consulted Japie about one and he laughed.

Old van Staden usually came to warn us before a public holiday. "Take care! ... On holidays the blacks get drunk. What should blacks do with holidays? It's the white man's holiday anyhow..."

And there was one holiday I had special reason to remember, though not the reason Old van Staden gave.

The holiday was Union Day, May 31, anniversary of the formation of the self-governing Union of South Africa in 1910. It was a holiday for Boer and Briton, for two old enemies come together in friendship at last to form one nation. So I was told at school.

One Union Day morning I rummaged among my books and there I found two little silk flags, each about eight inches long, which I had obtained in exchange for cigarette fronts, or it may have been soap wrappers—free gifts from the manufacturers. One was the Union Jack; the other was what was then regarded as the South African ensign, having both the Union Jack and the South African coat-of-arms.

I took the two little flags down to the store and tied them on to the verandah poles, feeling patriotic and public-spirited. There I watched them flutter prettily in the breeze and left them as a symbol of Anglo-Boer amity.

After lunch I went out to look at them again. There were

picnic parties at the river, and there were people loitering near the verandah. The flags were gone. There was no sign of them or even of the string that had held them. I thought I saw one of the men grinning, but I hadn't the courage to challenge him and swallowed my vexation. So much for the amity of Union Day! Can you tell people to be brothers and expect them to obey?

Instinctively I knew that our days on the Likkewaan River were coming to an end. It had been clear for a long time that the store wasn't paying and never would support the five people who had hoped so much from it. My father's knowledge of the Afrikaans language had been of little help; he had fallen ill with the disease that was to carry him off a year or two years later (oh yes, you could die of TB in sunny South Africa) and Morris had taken him to the Johannesburg Hospital, where he lay week after week.

The credit system that was the basis of business in the country was slowly breaking us.

When a Boer (the name means "farmer") drove in from beyond the distant line of koppies, we received him as a visitor. Japie was sent to the house to ask for tea or coffee, which Cousin Mary or my mother eventually brought herself. That was the way of the country. Your customer was also your guest.

Over two or three cups you discussed the weather, the crops, the cattle, their diseases and the children in that order. Two subjects you avoided—politics and money. Politics—because that was a sore subject on which you were sure to say the wrong things. Money—because you took it for granted that the Boer had none.

My father had carefully instructed Cousin Morris on the point. If you asked a Boer for money, he would feel persecuted, for he was always " 'n arme Boer" (a poor farmer). He might walk out there and then and you would never see him again.

When he placed an order, you wrote down everything ostentatiously in a large book and tacitly assumed that you would be paid after the next harvest, which would be in about six months' time or more.

When at the end of six months you suggested settlement of the account, the man looked hurt. "What's your hurry?"

Cousin Mary kept walking about with pursed lips telling anyone who came along, "Business is shlim, baai shlim."

She thought she was talking Afrikaans and ignored me when I tried to correct her. I told her the word was "slim" not "shlim", and anyway it meant "cunning" or "crafty". So she was in fact saying not, as she intended, "Business is very bad", but "Business is very cunning". But she stubbornly shook her head and muttered to herself.

"Business is baai shlim," she informed Martinus van Staden one morning.

He looked baffled, so I corrected her again.

She insisted. "Business is shlim, baai shlim." He winked at me.

Before we could leave the Likkewaan, however, great events were to rumble over the land.

The First World War came—to us on the Transvaal highveld an awful echo over the distances. A mounted policeman rode up to the store one morning and told us the news. At once it seemed that the world was in flames—Russia, Austria, Germany, France, Belgium, Britain, the whole world was at war, and instead of feeling safe and sheltered from it all on a sleepy little river in South Africa, we felt restless and eager for news, almost resenting the silence of the countryside.

The Boer rebellion came, and for days we saw nothing of the van Stadens. But we heard that Martinus was away (it would be he, not his brother) and had gone to join the rebel commandoes gathering in the south to strike at the old enemy now that Britain's armies were involved elsewhere. The advance of the Germans through Belgium seemed irresistible. "Like locusts," said the mounted policeman bringing us more news. "Like the march of locusts." To anyone who had seen a swarm of locusts that was a dreadful comparison. From the borders of German South-West Africa there were reports of Boers who had crossed to the enemy.

Martial law was proclaimed. Movement was restricted. The

roads were empty. School was forgotten, and I never had to explain my absence because I never went back.

General Louis Botha, the Prime Minister, a Boer himself, called out the Boer commandoes to quell the Boer rebellion, and that other grey-faced Boer, General Smuts, was with him. The word went out—the rebellion was wrong. "A contract is a contract." So all would be well. All must be well. "A konTRAK is a konTRAK" was the way the Boers said it, making it sound even more emphatic. But that was the last time we were to hear that formula in South Africa.

One rebel general was killed: another was drowned. The policeman rode up slowly with the news. The rebellion was suppressed and there was movement on the roads again.

That was when we left the Likkewaan River. They put my mother and me in the trolley, while my father, temporarily out of hospital, sat next to the driver.

The day we left, Martinus van Staden called at the store. Not a word was said about the rebellion or the part he might have played in it. Not a word about the war. He was home and safe, and so was his father, and that was all that mattered. So we shook hands all round, and Martinus van Staden, the bronze-faced Boer, remained in my mind as a man good to have had as a friend.

And so we went up the winding road that rose in humps towards the great Ridge of White Waters. For once I was out of sympathy with Dick the horse pulling slowly townwards. I wanted him to hurry. Where we were going the great gold reef lay—the mines, the city and the sprawling townships—and more than forty years were waiting for me like the pages of an opening book.

CHAPTER 3

The Mine

My idea of a mine was a hole in the ground. As this was to be a gold mine, it would be a hole with gold at the bottom, much like the pot of gold that was supposed to lie at the foot of a rainbow. They told me that was quite wrong, as one day I might see for myself. I didn't see it there, but once I went six thousand feet down the Simmer and Jack, the greatest gold mine in the world, and I stared into the jagged face of the gold reef where the almost naked black miners were crouching under the hanging rock. I was half-naked myself, and scared, and I saw nothing that looked like gold to me.

That did not, however, become my abiding picture of a gold mine. My mine always remained the Kleinfontein—Little Fountain—named after the original farm. There was a headgear (a tall scaffolding with turning wheels) against the sky, a heavy curl of smoke next to it, and beyond them a yellow-white mine dump.

These things formed my skyline, a couple of hundred yards away. In front of them stretched a white-washed wall with a burly black Induna—sub-chief, sergeant, foreman—sitting at the gate. Then the footpaths straggled across the dusty patch of intervening veld towards the shops in the road. That was the Kleinfontein and that was where we ended up after leaving the Likkewaan.

By some process of business that was quite beyond my understanding, my father had acquired a store in the Kleinfontein Road. He was well enough to work again and was hopeful. My mother was optimistic. A gold mine teeming with workers was a much better proposition than a bleak silent riverside where it didn't matter whether you had the door open or not.

The store was one of twenty or more that stood in a straight line facing the mine, and the village lay behind. That, of course, was the white people's village, where the white folk had their own shops and where a black man ventured hesitantly, if at all. The Kleinfontein Road was the black man's quarter where the mine labourers came in their hours of freedom. The white wall we could see from the verandah was the compound where they had their sleeping and eating quarters, all ranged round the compound yard. They came to the street as to their playground, to see the sights, to buy, to haggle and to eat when they grew tired of their rations. At the mine they were simply recruited workers, tagged and numbered, the raw labour on contract to the company. Here in the street they were free, at ease and eager to partake of the white man's world.

The store was the kind any youngster would be proud to be part-owner of (as I reckoned I had a right to consider myself), even though the stores in the street were mostly referred to with contempt as "the kaffir stores". But in those days the word "kaffir" had not yet become generally objectionable. People used it without knowing that it meant "infidel", and they still do, though polite folk usually remember to use "native", "Bantu" or "African" instead. At school we were taught about the "Kaffir Wars" of the eighteenth and nineteenth centuries, and that seemed as good a name for those ragged campaigns as any.

Today, South African gold mining shares are still listed overseas as "Kaffirs"—a curious survival I was once pressed to explain at some evening classes run for African adults in Johannesburg. (Such classes would be stopped now by the police.) No explanation I could give seemed adequate, and ultimately all I could do was to assure the class that the name was used only as a label by financiers who knew no better but who could be absolved of any malicious purpose.

It was really a wonderful store, much larger and better

stocked than the one at the river. To think how my father could have become its owner improved my opinion of him considerably. We sold everything from trinkets to tobacco leaf—not just packets of tobacco, but bunches of leaves that hung from the beams or were rolled into thick wads. The black mine-worker who came from the Reserves of the northern Transvaal or the Transkei in the south, from Basutoland, Swaziland or Portuguese Mozambique, came with nothing and wanted everything. The store was filled with the conglomerate smell of leather, soft goods, hardware and clothes, boots, mattresses and blankets, rolls of cotton print, silk shawls, sweets and snuff, cooking pots, beads, brooches and photographs of famous actresses in tin frames standing among the trinkets.

There was everything but food in our store, and there was no food because that was obtainable in the "kaffireeta" next door. When we first heard that word my mother was both bewildered and horrified. "A kaffir—what?"

It sounded very much like "kaffir-eater", and so it was. It was a "kaffir eating-house", shortened to "kaffir-eater" and then to "Kaffireeta". Nowadays they call those eating places "Bantu restaurants" or even, grandiosely, "hotela la Bantu". But in those days "kaffireeta" was the accepted word for the eating houses and a fluttering red flag over the door was the accepted sign for them, though no one could explain why.

There were several kaffireetas along the length of the street, and here the black man came to eat in the afternoon or at the week-end when his palate craved extra delicacies. He came in companies, striding long-legged across the grass, and he sat down at a metal-topped table, ordered thick dark soup with half a loaf of white bread, dipped and ate heartily. He could also order a sheep's head (they were cooked white and arrayed in macabre rows on the counter), or he could have a stew of entrails. And if he longed for a real savoury, he could get a tin of sardines or a can of bully beef, which he would eat straight from the tin, scooping up the fat with his fingers.

Oh, it was good to see the black man eat and enjoy his food! I used to stand at the doorway watching him, till my father got angry and ordered me away from the blacks and the smells. The place was indeed smelly and the food was not always quite fresh, but was apparently considered good enough for black miners. The kaffireeta was under regular inspection by a municipal health official, who must have considered the smells as normal and natural to that sort of establishment.

It was owned by a pot-bellied man, Mr. Ritz, who was no taller than I was. It never occurred to him or me that there was something comically incongruous about a man with his name running an eating-house for African miners, and I became aware of it only in retrospect when I was considerably older and was confronted with the forbidding grandeur of the Ritz of Paris and the Ritz of London. But there he was! Ritz of the Kleinfontein Road handing out dishes of dark soup and mugs of black coffee to bare-legged primitives —and enjoying it. Yes, enjoying it!

He used to come bustling in to our store. "Mister, mister . . . where's my red flag? Look at my red flag out there in the wind, all in ribbons! All in . . . I must have a new red flag, you hear! Up with the red flag, mister! Up with the . . ." but he had turned his back and was bustling out before my father could get the roll of red calico off the shelves.

His wife was as round as he was and pink-faced. She used to come to the kaffireeta in the afternoon, making her visit a kind of ceremonial affair. She seemed to think she owed it to the house to dress up. So she would do her hair high above her head, wear a low-cut frock with a necklace and pendant on her high bosom, and prop herself up behind the counter against a red-and-yellow advertisement for lemonade. From a high stool she surveyed the blacks at the tin-topped tables, and they, staring back at the sheep's heads and the stacked cans of bully beef from Chicago, stole reticent glances at the grand-looking white *Mafaza*.

But one day my mother, looking in at the door, saw her thus enthroned and was horrified. For one moment she stood rooted to the spot, and then cried out, "Mrs. Ritz! How can you! As God is with you . . ." My mother came of people who were on neighbourly terms with the Lord . . . "How can you, Mrs. Ritz, and you in your . . . !" She said no more but swept through the kaffireeta in a movement that carried her as on a wave of concern between the rows of tables and their abashed occupants and round the counter to Mrs. Ritz's side. Putting an arm round her, she almost heaved her off her stool and led her out through the back door, scolding her under her breath all the time.

I couldn't make out what all the pother was about. But I picked up the sense of it from what I overhead at the time and what my mother subsequently confided to my father. It appeared that Mrs. Ritz was going to have a baby, and it was dangerous for a woman in her condition to sit among black men, beneath their smouldering eyes and in such close proximity. Heavens! ... the baby might be born black!

When I understood that that was the reason for my mother's concern, I wondered why Mrs. Ritz hadn't known it herself. She was probably a very stupid woman (I had suspected as much) and very lucky to have my mother nearby to warn her—if, that was, the damage hadn't already been done.

My father scoffed at the idea. He "p'shaw'd" and kept on "p'shaw'ng". But my mother insisted that there was no need to take risks in such circumstances, and I felt sure she was right.

Surreptitiously I heard the story of a young woman who was about to have a baby and thoughtlessly wandered past a smithy where a man was chopping wood. She even paused to look, the insensitive creature! When the baby was born several weeks later, it was found to have a hare-lip. My father scoffed again when he heard this. "Grandmother's tales!"

But my mother argued that a woman should not take risks. Who could tell how hare-lips came? And Mrs. Ritz was not seen at the eating-house again, at least not for some months till after the child was born. The first time I saw it she had brought it to the store during an afternoon's airing, and I had a good look at it. I assured myself that it was white—as white as most babies were—and as far as I could tell with no sign of a hare-lip.

Pondos, Xhosas, Shangaans and Basutos were among the labourers who came thronging from the compounds on pay day, which was Friday, to spend their money in the shops and eating-houses of the Kleinfontein Road. The Pondos were the wildest-looking; the Basutos the most sophisticated; the Shangaans the most primitive.

The Shangaans were always addressed as "umfaan"—the word for a youth; but the others were either "madod" (young man) or "madev" for a man of years with a beard. No matter how big they were, and they were mostly lanky, the Shangaans were "umfaan". They never looked quite grown up.

They wore little more than a cotton vest and a loosely tied skirt made of light cotton material. It was coloured in a florid pattern and was called a "kaduncha". When the pattern was check, it was called a "macheka". We had them in piles on the counter, and the Shangaans used to come and try out a dozen before choosing one. They would sling it round the waist and secure it with a large safety-pin on the side. You could easily tell how they got the word "macheka"; but "kaduncha" remained a mystery.

One hot summer's day one of those umfaans was unconcernedly strolling down the sandy road in front of the shops with an auto-harp in the crook of his elbow. An auto-harp has three or four keys which give three or four combinations of notes. The day was sunny; it was sultry; he was barefooted and he wore his skirt flapping round his thighs but nothing above his waist. He strummed lazily on the harp as he walked, ringing the changes on those three or four chords, now and then stopping at a window to gaze at the shirts and trinkets, or possibly to admire his glistening torso reflected in the glass.

But a white policeman riding down the street on a bicycle did not admire it. He was offended by the sight of the half-naked minstrel, and as he approached him he was red with heat and indignation. Jumping from his bicycle he shouted at him. "Go and get yourself properly dressed you ... you ... stupid savage! Where do you think you are? At home in the kraal? When you come into town try and be civilised. Go inside somewhere and get yourself a shirt to cover that big black body of yours.... Go on! You spend your money on a silly harp, but you don't buy decent clothes. Go on, or I'll whip you off the street..."

The Shangaan came running into our shop. He hadn't understood all the policeman's bawling, but he understood enough, and he stood near the door trembling. He was not just terrified; he was ashamed. Suddenly made aware of his nakedness, in which he'd seen nothing wrong before, he tried to hide his body with his harp and crossed his arms over his chest.

My father produced a white cotton singlet and asked him how much money he had. Putting down his harp, he took out a purse from somewhere under his skirt and was able to scrape together enough in tickeys and pennies to pay for the covering of his nakedness. He drew on the singlet at once, took the harp under his arm and hurried away to the compound. He now had a shirt, but the music of his harp was stilled. The policeman, if he saw him again, must have been gratified at his success in thus fostering civilised decencies.

The Pondos looked the most outlandish because they stained their cheekbones with red clay, smoked long thin pipes and wrapped themselves in dull-red blankets that made them all look tall. My father said the Pondos had to be watched. They came along to "booga", to look, but often with an ulterior purpose.

Two or three men swathed in blankets, their faces just showing under flat straw hats, would stand at the window gazing steadily at the display within. Slowly they edged their way to the door, and then stood inside the shop immobile, turning only their heads. If you greeted them and asked them what they wanted, one of them answered, "Tina booga.... We look." That was a recognised form of entertainment on any afternoon—to booga, to see the sights.

The Pondos would rather steal than buy, and they could hide many things beneath their blankets. My father knew their ways and kept an eye on them. Sure enough he caught one of them in the act of slipping a boot under his arm. He crossed the floor, seized the boot from under the blanket and taking up a broom chased the men from the shop. They ran with their blankets flying high behind them, and one of the other Pondos—he had been a smarter operator—dropped the other boot of the pair as he jumped off the verandah. Then they turned round in the street and laughed heartily.

When they had done laughing, they returned to the store and bought the pair of boots they had tried to steal, or rather another pair like it, for the first had proved too small. (Not that that would have spoilt it for them. When they bought a pair of boots that turned out to be too tight, they rectified it by cutting slits in the toe.) When they had paid for the boots, they walked away happily cracking sweets under their big white teeth. Every customer expected something extra before he left, the *pasella* or *bonsella*, the bonus or lagniappe, and he usually got a fistful of cheap sweets from a box the shopkeeper kept under the counter.

The Basutos and the Xhosas (you pronounce the "Xh" with a click of the tongue if you can, simply as "K" if you can't) liked to wear white man's clothes or their version of it, and they loved to bargain. They would stand for an hour haggling over the price of a shirt, knocking pennies off, and were not satisfied until my father got angry and made for the broom. Then they knew they had beaten him down to rockbottom price, and they paid up in good heart.

As he wrapped up the shirt, they stood around talking amiably. If I happened to be there, they'd ask my father about me and where he'd got me. They would explode with "hau! ... hau!" when he said I'd come across the big water. He did it to impress them. So they stood and admired me with more "hau's!" and ended up by declaring solemnly that I was sure to become "lo m'kula boas k'lo kompon", the big boss of the compound. They could think of no higher station in life for a white man. And at the time neither could I. They must have regarded me as a youngster of great promise.

Someone else was amazed to learn that I had recently come across the sea. That was my teacher at the school in the village. In those days we were taught Dutch, the other official language, or High Dutch to distinguish it from South African Dutch or Afrikaans.

The teacher was a woman with a sun-tanned face. When she put a Standard 3 Dutch reading book in front of me and I read it off with ease, she was astonished. I had come from England, hadn't I? I was a "rooinek" from the land of "rooineks" or rednecks, who were notoriously poor at learning languages, especially Dutch. Yet here was a little rooinek who seemed to take to the language with ease. She scowled at me offended, resentful of my facility.

She was a woman with a mission. Her purpose in life was teaching the Dutch language and so preserving the identity of the Boer people in South Africa. In actual fact the Boers disliked Dutch as much as they disliked English, but she (or the Education Department) had not yet made that discovery.

When she looked at me stolidly and demanded, "How come you read Dutch?" I said that I had lived on a farm at the Likkewaan River. She had never heard of the Likkewaan River and she was still astonished at the amount of Dutch I knew.

I didn't tell her that even my mother could understand that Dutch reading book. When I read it out to her it sounded like Low German, and therefore like Yiddish. I didn't tell the teacher because she would have found that still more bewildering, if not offensive—another rooinek way of belittling the Dutch language.

There was another person at that school who was a man with a mission. That was the headmaster, Mr. Graham, an Englishman only two or three years out from England. His mission was to spread the British outlook, British thought and the British way of doing things. This of course made him a typical rooinek and imperialist, the kind of man who made the hackles of the Afrikaner rise instantly. But, oddly enough, he did not conform to pattern. Contrary to everything expected of rooineks, he was all for the teaching of Dutch.

He had also allowed himself to become tanned by the South African sun. Englishmen coming to South Africa feel they have to drink in as much sunshine as possible until they learn that the sun bites deep and one can have too much of it. But he was cheerful and not yet turned harsh by South African sunshine or politics.

With enthusiasm mounting in his eyes he would tell us (and our parents too whenever he had the chance) that it was good for folk to learn another language, and as Dutch was an official language of the country, that was the language to learn. "That's the way to be a good South African and a good neighbour. Learn the other man's language. Learn Dutch! It helps you with your own language to know another, and as you're living here, that's the right thing to do. Learn Dutch!"

They looked at him without comprehension, but he was undeterred by their indifference. "When I came to this country I didn't know a word of Dutch, but I began to learn at once, and"—when he came to this point his white teeth shone with gratification—"and within twelve months I was teaching the language. And I assure you I'm a better man for it, a better South African!"

English parents as they listened were mildly moved and urged their children to do their best. The Afrikaners on the other hand were mistrustful. They couldn't understand an Englishman who spoke up for the other language, and when he gave a short speech in Dutch they sniggered behind his back. They thought his pronunciation was odd, and so it was to their ears. He had learned his Dutch from a Hollander ("I went to the best teacher") and he pronounced it like a Hollander, and as Afrikaners disliked Hollanders as much as Englishmen, that was another reason for mistrust. He pronounced the word for bread more like "brode" than "brood", and the word for time more like "tide" than "tate", the South African way, and they could not bear the presumption of an Englishman suggesting that he knew more about the language than they did.

Graham was a patriot for the country of his adoption. And they couldn't tolerate that either. They regarded him as an out-and-out Englishman who really had no right to think of this country as his home. "We are South Africans," he told us, "all in it together, for the good of all." He would pause with mouth slightly open to see how the idea affected us. He gave it out with the fervour of an evangelist. "Not English, or Dutch, or Boer; just South Africans, all together..." To him that was an exciting thought, and he wanted us to be excited too. To the Afrikaner teachers and children it was just boring.

What Graham believed in, he believed in with his whole simple heart. The war in Europe was still on, and going hard for the Allies. He enlisted, went to France with a South African regiment and returned with the rank of captain. But by 1919 or 1920 Afrikaans was replacing Dutch in the schools, and his enthusiasm for the pure language of the Netherlands was even less acceptable than before.

In time he retired from teaching and went into politics. When I last heard of him he was fighting Afrikaner nationalism in the Transvaal Provincial Council, and they were fighting his English jingoism. He was a sincere man and no jingo, but I could understand how their mistrust and their own Boer patriotism might have turned him into one. His cheerfulness had gone hard and his ardour had turned to anger.

English and Afrikaners were rivals in class and playground, jeering at each other's mistakes and each gloating over his own victories. They combined in their opposition to the few Jews among them, and there was open merriment in the class when they could beat the Jews in the end-of-term exams. Sometimes they did, and sometimes they did not.

What looks odd, however, from the present ridge of time, is that there were English and Afrikaners in the same school and the same class. That was the rule then; but soon it was to become the exception. Soon the two-stream policy of General Hertzog and his Nationalists was to prevail, the earliest form of apartheid in modern South Africa. Nowadays it is called "white apartheid", the kraaling off of English-speaking children and Afrikaans-speaking children so that the Afrikaner could get his nationalism while young and unsullied by English influences.

But I went to school, and right through school, with English and Afrikaans children, and I was unaware at the time that there could be anything wrong in that arrangement. True, we learned Dutch as a second language and probably not very well either. But Afrikaans (the South African form of Dutch) was not yet recognised as a language and had practically no literature. Even our Dutch teachers (Afrikaners themselves) made fun of it and would pull up sharply anyone in the class who broke into colloquial Afrikaans during the Dutch lesson.

Afrikaans has a simplified syntax; it has replaced the word "we" with "ons" (us) making it sound like nursery talk to a Dutchman's ears; and it makes frequent use of certain Malay words introduced by the Cape slaves. The teachers of Dutch, having command of an old European language with an extensive literature, resented the intrusion of a local language that had as yet no literature at all or only the rudimentary beginnings of one.

Nowadays it is policy among the Nationalists to blame the British for the delay in the development of Afrikaans. But in the old Boer republics of the Orange Free State and the Transvaal before the Anglo-Boer War, Dutch (not Afrikaans) was the language used officially. After the war, the British agreed to the recognition of Dutch (and later Afrikaans) as the other official language. The Afrikaners themselves for long had little respect for the corrupt South African form of Dutch they had fathered, and they at first opposed its adoption in school and church.

The story is still told of the Dutch Reformed Church elder who stubbornly countered proposals to translate the Bible into Afrikaans with the argument that he had always read the Bible in Dutch, and the language that was good enough for Moses was good enough for him. Since then the Bible has been very successfully translated into Afrikaans, an achievement which is today the proud boast both of the Afrikaner people and the British and Foreign Bible Society.

For my own part, I resented having to learn either Dutch or Afrikaans at school. I wanted to learn French because of its great literature and its wide use in the world. By comparison there were few advantages in a knowledge of Dutch or Afrikaans, and I never took wholeheartedly to either of them. Nevertheless we talked both English and Afrikaans in the playground and sang songs in both languages. It was only the Afrikaner Nationalist politicians who afterwards decided there was something wrong in this, and began separating off

Afrikaners from English so that Afrikaans-speaking children need not have the contaminating sound of English in their ears.

It was in the Kleinfontein Road that I first heard of the Pass Laws, and I was to hear about them in all the years that followed.

If you asked anyone what was the purpose of the Pass Laws, the answer you got was that it was to keep control "of the kaffirs". It was commonly assumed that the black folk were by nature nameless, homeless, workless and perhaps even parentless. Without control they would run wild and vicious over the whole country. The Pass Laws gave them numbers and made them carry numbered forms which, it was believed, enabled the white authorities to curb their naturally lawless impulses. But no one could ever explain quite how it worked; the proof of the necessity of the system was to be seen in the hundreds of thousands of black men sent to jail every year for breaking the very Pass Laws that were designed to keep them out of jail—or so it seemed.

It was the same with the Liquor Laws, which prohibited the supply of alcohol to the blacks "for their own good", but had the effect of sending thousands to prison.

Our servant was a lanky Shangaan named Jim. That was the most common name for a black man, sometimes extended to "Jim Fish", the equivalent of "Jim Crow" in America. It was the name that most readily came to the minds of the officials when the "boy" decided to leave the Reserve up country and go to town.

To be able to travel he had to get a permit at the local Native Commissioner's office, and together with a permit he was given a European name or "name known by", his tribal name generally being regarded as unpronouncable, if not uncivilised. If he was not called "Jim", he might be called "Joseph" or "Zachariah" if he was a Christian, or simply "Sixpence" if he was a heathen and the official was in a flippant mood. When he found work in town, his employer would get him a service contract (known as the "Big Pass") and a monthly pass which had to be renewed every month for two shillings (known as the "small pass").

Any policeman could stop a black man in the street and demand to see the creased, soiled piece of paper that was his pass. If he was unable for any reason to produce it there and then, the policeman would take him off to the police station at once. He could also demand the man's "special pass", failure to produce which had the same consequences.

It was the special pass, "Special" for short, or "Spenchal" in the Shangaan's lingo, that introduced me and many young South Africans like me, to the operation of the Pass Laws. It was the oddest of documents.

Curfew time was nine o'clock, when a bell was rung at the police station. If our long-legged Jim wanted to stay out after curfew, or wanted to go visiting at the week-end in another district, he had to get a special pass, and for this he generally came to me. I would scribble a note in pencil on a piece of paper asking the police to "please pass bearer till 2 a.m.", and he would stuff it into a trouser pocket as he hurried out.

One evening he had neglected to ask for his Special, and some time after midnight he was making his way home warily, "looking hard for policemens", as he said afterwards. He almost evaded them, but fifty yards from his home lane he was stopped by a Zulu policeman, who soon discovered that he was Special-less and took him to the police station.

"I tell him, my home just here... My Baas just here, and my Kleinbaas, he's good to me... He write my spenchal..."

No pleas would avail. Jim was taken to the cells and next morning there was no one in the kitchen making the fire. An hour later, there was a Zulu policeman at the door. "Your boy in jail... no special, no money... ten shilling fine."

So my father went to the police station, paid the fine out of Jim's next month's wages and brought him home.

We scolded him for forgetting to ask for a Special, and I made some joke about his getting drunk or he'd have seen the policeman before he saw him.

He looked hang-dog and stoutly denied he'd got drunk. Even the policeman hadn't said he was drunk, which was true enough. He nearly outwitted that policeman. "Just here outside... One jump over the street and I'm home!"

He laughed, and my mother sent him to get his breakfast.

The black man's talent for laughter was like his patience; it seemed inexhaustible.

A few minutes later Jim was still quietly laughing while dipping his bread into a large mug of sweet tea. No one could say that our much-documented Jim wasn't happy.

The sirens of the Kleinfontein Mine hooted at four o'clock. "Chaiyeeli! Chaiyee-eeli! ... It has struck! It has struck!" We could sometimes hear the black miners coming off shift and shouting, "Chaiyee-eeli!"

But there was another "Chaiyeeli", the big "Chaiyeeli". It was the one that meant not just the end of the shift or the week, but the end of the term, and it came about every six months when another batch of miners had finished their contract with the company and they were about to leave for home.

They would be sent away in hard wooden coaches by railway, and on the way to the station they'd crowd into the shops to make their last purchases. Then they were gay, talkative and excited. They wore their red-and-yellow blankets flapping round them, boots swinging across their shoulders, felt hats crammed down over their woolly heads, tin portmanteaux in their hands and kit-bags under their arms. They were going home to their reed-and-mud-hut villages with all the dressings of civilisation, and they called in at the shops for their last adornments—another silk kerchief, another little mirror, another picture of Gladys Cooper or Ellen Terry to hang up in the hut or in father's hut.

They shouted, they laughed, they joked. My father filled their hands with sweets which they stuffed into their pockets or cracked between their strong white teeth. They shouted for their change and became impatient.

"Mlungu, mlungu! Lo stimeli...." Somehow in their language a train had been transformed into a "steamer" or "stimeli", and so they shouted, "White man, white man! Lo stimeli ... it waits for no man."

They were like schoolboys let loose for the holidays and many were not much older. They were leaving the white man's town and the mine and e-Goli, the white man's city. They were returning to their parched villages in the eroded Reserves where the food was meagre, the cattle were lean and the men grew old quickly. But it was home, where they had grown up in the sun and the sand, and where their women were waiting for them.

They had to hurry. They dared not miss the "steamer". They had to run to the station ... As they took their change and their sweets, they shouted joyfully, "Shlala kashle, mlungu ... Shlala kashle, 'nkos ... Stay in peace, white man. Stay in peace, master."

"Hamba Kashle, m'dod, hamba kashle ... Go in peace, young man. Go in peace. . . ."

They hurried away shouting to our Jim, "Shlala kashle. The white man's stimeli does not wait ..."

He laughed both with them and to himself, because he knew more than they did. He knew that when they got home they would tell their strange tales of the white man's world, and they would produce their hard-gotten treasures, a knitted shawl, a silk scarf, presents for the old folk. They would stay at home, eating and drinking, till the meal ran low again, the beer was not enough to go round, the bellies of the children became more and more distended, and their own bellies grew empty. Then they would have to start thinking of e-Goli again, the white man's City of Gold, which was far from home (though there was a lorry down the hill which would take them), but where a man could earn some real money again and get some strong food.

He knew what it was like at home, and he knew he would see them again.

CHAPTER 4

The Small Town

NINE miles east of Johannesburg the multiple chimneys of a power station rose beside a breezy bitter-water lake named after Queen Victoria. On the farther side of the lake there was a golf course, and on the nearer side was the town of Germiston which took its name from a Scottish village and its prosperity largely from the great Simmer and Jack gold mine. The mine had been founded by adventurous and hardworking Scotsmen in the 'nineties, and in due course the settlement that grew up nearby had a Caledonian Society, a pipe-band and a reputation for playing first-class football—soccer.

On its northern side, Germiston was the meeting point of the main railway lines from Pretoria, Durban and the Cape. This made Germiston, as the Town Council's publicity insisted, the most important railway junction in South Africa; it also made that side of the town irretrievably drab. Even drabber was the southern side, where some of the mine shafts had their headgears and dumps, and from where the dust blew naggingly on windy days. No one complained of the dust or the drabness. You couldn't very well complain of the gold that brought you your bread and butter and jam. All you could do was to put up a corrugated iron fence where the mine property ended. Someone had done that in the earliest days, and so this was where the main street ran—slap-bang up against the mines. It was called President Street, after President Kruger, which was only right considering that the lake was named after the Queen.

At one end, therefore, President Street led into the open

veld towards the lake, and at the other end to the Caledonian or Callies football ground. You went to the Callies on Saturday afternoon (behind a cluster of bars, beerhalls and ice-cream carts) to see the local team (whites only) beat all comers (or argue the reason why); and you went to the lake on Sunday, took a boat on the grey-blue water, had yourself photographed and pretended you were at the seaside (for whites only and servants).

This was the town where we found ourselves soon after World War I, when South Africa (much like the rest of the world) was preparing for peace, progress and prosperity—but especially peace. Boers and Britons had been at each others' throats less than a generation before; but in the World War they had fought side by side. Was it too much to expect them now to live side by side?

After the granting of self-government by Britain (as magnanimous an act of statesmanship as ever was) and the union of the four provinces in 1910, two Boer generals, Botha and Smuts, headed the government, and the English showed themselves willing to accept Boer political leadership. This fact itself discredited Botha and Smuts with many of the Boers, who couldn't understand magnanimity, and another Boer War leader, General Hertzog, had already broken away from Botha to form the Nationalist Party. Two years after the happy union, he started the two-stream policy that was to decree that for the next fifty years and more there were to be at least two nations in South Africa.

I remember a parliamentary election in Germiston when someone threw an empty beerbottle at the successful pro-Smuts candidate. But I remember another which was the prelude to the fall of a government. So Germiston, in spite of its cramped situation, was a place with possibilities.

It was a typical small town which outwardly proclaimed the composition of its population. The British were represented by their Anglican, Presbyterian, Baptist and Catholic churches; the Afrikaners by their Dutch Reformed churches (at least three); the Jews by their one synagogue; and the Africans by their Location of tin-and-wood shanties just out of town.

Everyone knew everybody's business and discussed it at the little municipal library, for whites only, next to the Town Office. Everyone knew who was going out with whom, which girls were of marriageable age, which girl was aiming too high, and which girl had stayed away too long on her holiday in the country. And soon every one knew that my father had left my mother just enough money to start a grocery shop on a corner in a back street, and I of course was the grocer's boy. That meant that after school hours I had to get behind the counter and do my share of running the shop.

It also made me an object of envy at school (for whites only). To the others in the class it seemed that I was doing a man's job and certain to be filling my pockets at the same time. To the sons of miners and railwaymen it seemed that anyone who ran a shop was wealthy, and anyone who worked in a shop need never be without cash. When they found that I was as hard up as any of them, they put it down to a streak of sheer timidity. One day, to prove that I could live up to their standards if I wished, I put a two-shilling piece into my pocket instead of into the till. But then I was afraid to spend it, knowing that that was the way to be found out, and there was nothing I wanted badly except books. On a Saturday morning I went along to a book-sale, but instead of buying the book I wanted, I stole it. It was a lesser work of Dickens, his *American Notes,* which I eventually found to be tedious and unenlightening. I don't think I read more than half. By now I had proved that I could be dishonest if I wanted to, and I could even steal, and there was no fun in doing either. So I put the two shillings back into the till, and I have never knowingly stolen a book since.

Working afternoons behind the counter gave me a view of human nature I could not have had anywhere else. I got to know the behaviour of the people who didn't intend to pay their accounts, who talked a lot, flattered and were too damn friendly. I learned to despise the women who paid their accounts grudgingly, and to be sorry for others.

There was one saddened wife who rarely raised her voice

above a whisper. When she paid her account on Saturday morning, she drew a line across her book at Wednesday and paid only up to the line. She said that if she paid for anything bought after Wednesday, it looked as though she was buying for cash, and she couldn't afford to buy for cash. We had to indulge her. Her husband was a phthisis pensioner; he had contracted silicosis in the mines, and she had to nurse a coughing husband and her dwindling pennies.

And I got to know the Coloured folk in Germiston. They were a people living in a sort of twilight, shunned or at most tolerated by the whites, and themselves shunning the blacks for fear of becoming submerged in them. They did not live in the out-of-town Location, of which they spoke with a horror exceeding that of the whites. The tumble-down Location, over which hung a permanent veil of smoke two or three miles along the railway line, was the home of the black folk—labourers, road-workers, scavengers and cleaners not attached to houses in the town, and also vagrants, thieves, loafers, skokiaan queens, shebeen keepers and prostitutes who, in the opinion of the whites, made up the bulk of the inhabitants.

Your own servant or houseboy lived in his shack at the back of the yard (next to the coal-shed), and if on a Sunday night or Monday morning he turned up at work looking dazed or fuddled, you assumed at once that he had been smoking dagga (marijuana) or drinking skokiaan in the Location and you scolded him for thus wasting his money.

You blamed other things on the Location. If a shop in President Street was burgled through a fanlight, it was obviously done by a gang of piccanins sent from the Location. If a man was waylaid and robbed in a lonely street at night, it was the work of loafers from the Location. Shoplifting was blamed on them. Police frequently raided the shacks there in the early morning for skokiaan and emptied canfuls of the liquor into the streets. And when your washing was stolen from the line on Monday afternoon, you went looking for it in the washerwomen's back-yard though you knew there was not the slightest hope of recovering it.

For the Coloureds to have lived in the Location or anywhere near it would have meant taking on a darker stain from the black folk and their way of life, and there was nothing the Coloured man dreaded more. He treasured his legacy of European or white man's blood as his dearest possession in a white man's world, and his constant aim was to conceal or remove himself from his darker legacy whenever he had the chance. If his hair was not obviously crinkled and his skin was not more coloured than sallow or olive, it became his ambition to try and "pass for white". He owed it to himself, his people and his offspring. And the number who "passed" was greater than anyone knew or cared to admit. But there were men in the Census Office who knew (and recorded) that while the Coloured population (despite a high natural rate of increase) remained constant, the white population in some districts showed accruals that could not be accounted for except on the theory of "passing". And if you took pains to scrutinise the people in backroom workshops, the passengers on trains and buses, you knew they were right. You began to wonder how white White South Africa was.

All this I learned only years later. When I was a schoolboy in Germiston I was aware only that the Coloureds lived in the back streets, or in the back-yards of the bigger streets like the lower end of Meyer Street where we lived. It was only a block away from President Street, which had the municipal offices, the library and the big stores.

Round the corner in a rambling corrugated-iron house lived the H. family... an old woman with daughters, sons, nieces and grandchildren. They were Coloured and all in all a lively brood. The liveliest of them all was Emily, the teenage granddaughter. She was as pretty as a chocolate box and knew it. She used rouge and lipstick, wore ear-rings, swayed on high heels and declared pertly, "We're really French, you know." She was the only one in the house who made such a claim. But she had got it into her little head that the French were dark-complexioned, and she being the lightest-skinned member of the family could very well claim relationship with them.

Emily made no secret of her determination to "go white". When she came into the shop on a Saturday afternoon, rustling in her satin and turning on her heel, ostensibly to buy some trifle, her real purpose was to display a French magazine she'd picked up somewhere and was now pretending to read. "A French story, you know ... Oh, very naughty, but clever! The French are like that. You have to understand them."

Or rather more discreetly she would refer to "Mr. ...." or to "John", a white man who was going to take her out—not the same as last week or the week before, but the one at last who would take her to the white side of town, some place "where you have to be white", and would make a lady of her. We might laugh at Emily and her affectations, but we knew she was determined to make the most of life.

I can still see her, tossing her little head. "We're French, Huguenots you know ... That's where we get our style. Huguenot descent ..." And she dwelt on the word "descent" as though it carried all her longings.

Emily was pretty. She was pathetic and eager. I hope she had her desires.

No one objected to the presence of a Coloured family in the street. No one cared. We all respected old Mrs. H., Emily's grandmother, who was small, round and friendly. She talked to the white women as an equal and had every reason to. From the whispers of the women behind my back —for women had the odd idea that if they lowered their voices, inquisitive boys became deaf—I gathered that she had taken care of many a white girl "in trouble" (she or some friends she had out of town) and had thus saved the honour of many a white family.

She ruled her own brood with genial authority, and when she bustled into the shop she was never put out by the presence of any of her white neighbours. They might move to the other end of the counter and leave her on her own. She talked freely and amiably. They would not dare to say a word against her. She knew too much about them. And when she left the shop, she gave them a broad-smiling "Good afternoon, ladies", to which they had to respond at their peril, "Oh, good afternoon, Mrs. H. Keep well now."

Hers was not the only Coloured household in the block. A few doors away, in some rooms along a verandah attached to a warehouse, a white man lived with a Coloured wife. Well, he talked of her as his wife, and no one would dare to question him about her. It was no one's business.

He was tall and fair, a strapping fellow who worked on the mines. She was light-brown, spare and narrow at the waist, and she dressed with a touch of Edwardian elegance. He often came into the shop to buy cigarettes and tobacco and she came to get her provisions; so we got to know both of them.

Perhaps I recall some sly remarks made behind their backs. "Fancy a fine-looking man like that taking up with a low-class . . ." But if a white man preferred to live with a Coloured woman that was his affair, and no one could interfere with them. And she was not low-class as far as I could see. She was good-looking and dressed well. The man was always well groomed. And the house—the verandah was as far as they could pry—their house was as well kept as any in the street.

Many of the white women hereabouts were slatternly, and often to be seen at their front doors shouting at their black servants. She employed no servant, but she was never otherwise than trim and self-possessed. So the neighbours contented themselves to referring to her maliciously as "the Lady —snff", but allowed their disapproval to show no further than that.

She often had friends round on Sundays. They were light-coloured like herself, but showed their lively temperament in their dress and talk. The man, smoking a cigarette on the verandah, seemed amused with them, but she only smiled amid their laughter.

When she came into the shop, she held herself erect, spoke softly and sometimes stayed a while for conversation. My mother addressed her by name, "Mrs. . . .", which I seem to remember rather pleased her. But I have forgotten it, remembering only the pleasure in her face and the way she did her hair upwards, to show of course that it was long and straight. My mother couldn't help noticing her affectations—"Always the lady, and why not?"

She liked making conversation with her. "That dress suits you, Mrs. . . . Did you make it yourself?"

"Well, I do a lot of my own sewing, you know. One has to these days, hasn't one? . . ."

She too was pathetic; but she was no longer confident. She was sad, and instinctively I felt she would never have her desires.

Best of all I remember the dignified, white-haired Boer lady, Mrs. L., who had the house across the road, a house with a thick hedge. She was tall but round-shouldered, could look severe if she wanted to, and talked a much better English than the average Afrikaner talks these days. Though she had lived through the Anglo-Boer War (which had scarred the koppies with trenches four miles away) she never talked about it, and she had seen too much to bear any grudges. She paid her little accounts scrupulously every Friday, and when she noticed my interest in books, she gave me one which she said she had found lying about the house. It was an English novel of adventure in the East, and when she heard later that I had devoured it in a night, she was astonished. She looked at me as though I had just bolted a meal and was sure that it could have done me no good.

Mrs. L. had a willowy daughter who was courted by a schoolmaster, a man who was considered to have excellent prospects. He married her in due course, and ultimately fulfilled his early promise by entering parliament (for whites only) as a Nationalist member. When last heard of he was drowsing on the back benches.

What looks significant at this distance of time is that the dour Mrs. L. did not mind living in a street where Coloureds lived across the road. And the future Nationalist Member of Parliament and protagonist of Afrikaans "kultuur" (culture) did not mind marrying into a family who lived in a street where Coloureds lived across the road.

Mrs. L. told us about a distant relative of hers, a young man called Jan, who was remarkable. He had matriculated at twelve, taken a university degree at fifteen, and become a professor at twenty-three. It all sounded prodigious, and though she told us about Jan more than once, we suspected that she had got her facts wrong somehow. But she hadn't. She was in fact telling us of the brilliant Jan Hofmeyr, who was soon to be the first principal of the University of the Witwatersrand, and later still a Cabinet Minister and General Smuts's right-hand man.

When I got to know Jan Hofmeyr, I never found the courage to tell him that I had first heard of him from his white-haired great-aunt when I was a part-time assistant in a second-rate grocery shop down a back street of "mixed" population. He wouldn't have minded. He was a man of understanding and ideals.

Nowadays, places like Meyer Street, Germiston, have been "cleaned up". No Coloured person would dare to put his foot in there except as a servant living in the back-yard. Coloured families like those of Mrs. H. (including Emily and her French magazine) would know that their home was out of town, as provided under the Group Areas Law. As for the biscuit-coloured lady, she and her white keeper would have been sent to jail under the Nationalists' Immorality Law which makes it illegal for white and non-white to live together, and even (in practice) makes it impossible for them so much as to be seen holding hands without being suspected of an illegal purpose. That's what "immorality" has come to mean in South Africa in the 1960s.

Now when the Nationalists insist, with the effrontery their spokesmen have acquired in proclaiming half-truths, that "apartheid" (separation of the races, segregation) is the traditional way of life in South Africa, I think of the white-haired Mrs. L. who was so kind to us—of the biscuit-coloured lady who was so genteel—and of the wrinkled old Mrs. H. who took in the unwanted babies of her white (and half-white) clients.

I think of the million-and-a-half Coloured half-caste South Africans, who live mostly in the western parts of the Cape Province, who love to dress up on Sunday, who want to get on like all good middle-class folk, and who look resentfully at the "Europeans only" coaches from which they are excluded on the railways. They have come into existence in spite of our "traditional way of life" and already number half of the officially white population. Would not a visitor who had never heard of our laws declare that the traditional way of life in South Africa was exactly the opposite of what the Government pretends it to be? And anyway, what price tradition that has to be maintained by laws, penalties and jails?

In the High School at Germiston we had some excellent masters. We had a Scotsman, John Duthie, who taught us English and Latin for the matriculation and made both sound exciting, living languages. He later took up law, entered politics, fought an election for the Labour Party against Jan Hofmeyr and ended up as a Labour Senator in the Upper House.

We had an Englishman who taught us history and tried to read some reason into the sorry tale of the Kaffir Wars. He also explained why the Africans and Coloureds of the Cape Province had the franchise and voted for Members of Parliament, while the same right was denied to non-whites in the rest of the country. This, he said, was part of the liberal tradition of the Cape, left over from the days of British rule and insisted on by the representatives of the Cape Province when the Union was formed in 1910. This was part of the Cape's culture and humanism, and the hope of enlightened men was that it would in time spread to the Boer provinces of the north.

When he said this, the Afrikaners in the class used to snigger behind his back.

And if we on our side answered their sniggers, sooner or later came the taunt, "You're only sticking up for Jack What'sis-name—ever seen his mother?"

I had seen his mother once at her home, and until I heard the sniggers in class, it had never occurred to me that she might be less white than anyone else.

Alas, alas! The sniggerers have proved the stronger. Within a generation, the African voters of the Cape were expunged from the roll and their white representatives were removed from Parliament. The Coloureds have also been taken off the common roll, for in the land of apartheid it was insufferable that whites and Coloureds should go and vote at the same polling stations.

And though the Coloureds still have their four white members of Parliament, the Nationalists make no secret of their abhorrence of this arrangement and of their intention to remove them also from Parliament in their own time.

How have the sniggerers eaten up our enlightenment!

CHAPTER 5

The Battle of Fordsburg

A LONE plane throbbing in the sky over the streets of Germiston brought us all out of our houses and shops to crane our necks upwards. A flying machine was still a novelty. No one could be indifferent to the marvel of it. We stood in groups in the roadway watching as it banked. "I hope someone takes a bloody shot at it!" muttered someone.

Presently the plane began to scatter red sparkles of light, and that was the sign for us to scatter too. This was martial law. Congregation of more than four or five persons was forbidden, and this (as the newspapers had informed us) was the warning for dispersal.

It seemed neither dangerous nor serious in that quiet small-town street. But it was both. Even as we turned to go indoors someone shouted, "Shoot the bastard down!" And someone else added gleefully: "He's in trouble! He's falling!" But he was wrong. I watched from a window and saw the plane banking again before it headed west and disappeared.

This was the 1922 strike, or rather this was what had begun as a strike. Now it was a revolt that had shattered order on the Witwatersrand from one end of the sixty-mile gold reef to the other, and people were calling it a revolution and a "Red Revolt".

Smuts was up from Cape Town where Parliament was in session. Smuts would settle the business—or would he? His train (so it was said) had been shot at on the way up—or was it his car? To the groups that had stood in the street and been ordered to disperse, that low-flying plane represented Smuts, and the muttered imprecations against it expressed

THE BATTLE OF FORDSBURG

the hostility that his name now stirred among the populace.

Yes, it was a miners' strike, a revolt if you like. And maybe it did have Moscow gold behind it. Who could tell? But it wouldn't have happened had Botha been alive, they said. Steely-eyed Jan Smuts had sat in Parliament waiting for the situation on the Rand to develop. And now it had developed so that only the guns could talk, guns and planes. That was the gossip among the people who came into our shop in Meyer Street. Smuts was on the side of the mine-owners, the great Chamber of Mines, and when they said in the street that they wished the aeroplane would crash, they really meant it.

It was March, late summer, and the loafers were abroad. They were the same sort of loafers, with the same sort of dirty faces and dirty shoes, as those who had shouted for Botha in 1915 when he had conquered German South-West Africa; and two years later had shouted for Smuts when he was chasing the Germans through Tanganyika. They had spent the intervening years, as it seemed to me, standing round street corners and bars, and I was sure they hadn't done a day's work in their lives. Now they were strikers, heroes of the Strikers' Committee, and they had come into their own. They were going about the town armed with sticks and ordering the shops to shut. They threatened to smash the windows of shopkeepers who showed any reluctance "to co-operate with the Strikers' Committee", and they had already broken a few.

Customers advised my mother to close before the strikers arrived. But she waited until two loafers (I knew them well by sight, for they used to cadge at the nearby liquor store) presented themselves in the doorway with cudgels in their hands and malicious grins on their faces. "Orders from the Action Committee to close down!" they shouted at my mother. "Or do you want us to break a few things first?"

My mother and I put the shutters up at once.

But strikers have to eat and even heroes come home for dinner. So while the striking miners were arguing at their meetings or drilling on the vacant lots near the railway line their wives came to our back door and filled their aprons with provisions. They were happy to get them and glad to pay for cash. In these circumstances there was no talk of "tick".

Meanwhile at the other end of President Street the wheels of the Rose Deep headgear were still, and if you walked further you could see the idle African miners sunning themselves on the grass outside the compound. They were idle because this was a white man's strike. The idea that black men might also go on strike was as unthinkable as that they could go down the mine without white overseers. So they sat in long rows on the grass, half-wrapped in their coloured blankets, contentedly smoking long pipes. They were men from Pondoland or Basutoland, and without regrets for their forced idleness they wondered what the white man was fighting about and why. Or perhaps they knew that they themselves were at the bottom of this dispute among the Abalungu, and it was for them merely to look on, pull at their pipes, and wait.

Smuts had been Prime Minister since 1919 and whether in or out of office was to place his stamp and image upon South Africa for the next thirty years. Unlike his predecessor, General Louis Botha, he was not an easy man to approach. This Boer was an aristocrat who found it difficult to speak to the common man. Botha was a Minister whom the farmers could consult over a cup of coffee in the Union Buildings, that edifice which Smuts had contrived to build at Pretoria out of the surplus revenues of the Transvaal when it went into the Union in 1910. It was and has remained the most beautiful building in the country.

The story has often been told how, when a deputation of farmers came to see Smuts when he was Minister of Lands (or Agriculture—for in his time he held almost every portfolio there was), they found it difficult to state their case to this visionary and went out feeling frustrated. But there was a secretary waiting for the ruffled farmers outside the office to lead them away to Botha, who would converse with them as Boer to Boer and make sure they left feeling understood and contented.

But Botha had died at fifty-six, weary of wars, politics and the wranglings at the Versailles Peace Conference. When Smuts took office he was almost immediately confronted with the threats and difficulties that beset men and governments emerging from victorious war. He had arrayed against him on one side General Hertzog, who always seemed to be grinding his teeth when he spoke in public and who was then moulding the Nationalist Afrikaners, the irreconcilables among the Boers, into a political force. And on the other side there was the English-speaking Labour Party, led by the straight-backed Colonel Creswell proclaiming trade unionism and socialism. Over them all hung the falling gold price. Together these forces ranged against Smuts spelled ruin to his regime.

Gold mining was the great sustainer of the South African economy—and still is. In 1920 the value of South Africa's gold production, at £6 an ounce, was about £50,000,000. By 1964 it had passed the £300,000,000 mark at £12 10s. an ounce and was the main reason for the strength of the country's reserves and treasury.

Before World War I the price of gold had been 85s. an ounce. It rose during the war years, but by 1921 had fallen to less than £5 an ounce. In many mines that were lifting low-grade ore containing less than a quarter-ounce of gold to the ton, the yellow metal at that price was hardly payable. Not for the first or last time, gold decided the destiny of party and government.

The Witwatersrand mine owners announced wage cuts. Worse still, they declared their intention to admit non-whites (or Coloureds) to certain classes of work previously done by whites. The white miners raised the cry of "cheap labour!" and went on strike unaware of the cynicism of their protestations.

There were 20,000 whites then working in the gold mines, together with 180,000 non-whites, who were excluded from all skilled work. The average pay of the white miner was seven or eight times that of the African who worked in gangs under white supervision. The gold mines had all along been developed on the cheap labour of the black man without the white worker showing any noticeable concern. Now he saw it as a pretext for rebellion. He was of course protesting not against the principle of cheap labour, but against the threatened cheapening of his own labour.

As the strike dragged on the miners grew desperate. There was at that time no legislative machinery for conciliation or the settlement of disputes. Parliament looked on helpless from Cape Town. That remark of Smuts about letting the situation develop would often be used against him. When he decided that it had developed to a point justifying Government intervention, it was already out of control.

The strikers had organised themselves into commandoes. They went drilling, marching and levying food supplies. The same two loafers came to our back door and meekly asked for a contribution. We filled their sack with six loaves of bread. Their story was that they were doing it all for the people's good. The blacks were sure to rise and then the whites would be grateful for the help of the Strikers' Commandoes. The same old story in a different setting! The mine owners were indeed preparing to send the black workers home to their country kraals if necessary. But the lanky men in blankets and *machekas* remained orderly in or about their compound yards, smoking their pipes in the sun.

The strikers raised the Red Flag and the strike openly became a workers' revolt. Defence Force Units were called up. Young men who had seen action in the World War were quick to don the uniform again. When the police fired on strikers their fire was answered. There were clashes on the ridges outside Johannesburg. A unit of the Transvaal Scottish regiment making for its parade ground on the East Rand blundered into a strikers' ambush and lost heavily. Two aeroplane pilots, flying low over Johannesburg, were shot by snipers.

Smuts called out the Boer commandoes and the strikers sent appeals to them to come over to their side. We heard the burghers were coming, and our Germiston loafers, now wearing bandoliers, cheered the news. For a time the issue seemed in doubt. But by now the cry had spread, "Moscow gold!" The Boers hated the spectre of Socialism more than they hated the mining companies (who bought their products) and they came sullenly to the side of the Government.

The strikers had their headquarters to begin with in the Trades Hall in Rissik Street, three blocks from the Johannesburg Town Hall. They occupied an imposing four-storeyed building fronted with classic columns. I was in town the morning the offices were raided by the police. The crowds were milling in Rissik Street, and when the police emerged from the building mounted men cleared a way for them through the mob. It was impossible from the street to see what had happened, but presently the story went from mouth to mouth that although no strikers had been taken, the police had found incriminating documents and paraphernalia, among them a black cap. It was not clear what the strikers' committee had needed a black cap for, but that item seized upon the imagination of the excited onlookers and suggested the most sinister speculations. That same day when I took the train back to Germiston, the warning was shouted down the corridor, "Keep away from the windows! They're throwing stones." So whenever the train passed open ground, we backed against the upholstery of our seats. There were no stones and I got home unscathed.

The strike leaders had already moved out of town, a mile or more westwards to the workingmen's suburb of Fordsburg, and set up headquarters in the Market Building. They had turned the place into a kind of stronghold, with trenches in the square, barricades in the street and a machine-gun on top of the Market Hall. They had turned the public lavatory into a block-house and they had cut the roads out of town. They had dug themselves in and set the scene here for the Battle of Fordsburg and the shabby climax of the revolt.

Troops of strikers massed at various places, and clashes with Government forces occurred at Benoni (twenty miles east), at Boksburg, Ellis Park sports grounds and other points on the outskirts of Johannesburg. In Fordsburg they were estimated to be 1,500 strong and determined on action. The rumour spread that they intended to march on Johannesburg and capture the Town Hall. It did not happen, but about a dozen or more years later when I wrote a play called *Red Rand,* I made one of the principal characters, a rebel, call for a column to march against the city by a roundabout route through the northern suburbs and take it by surprise. On the night of the second performance a man came to me during the interval and demanded how I knew of that plan of assault. I said I didn't know, but I had worked it out because this route into town lay open. "It's true!" he said, "and we wanted to do it. But they waited too long, damn them!"

They waited until Smuts had brought up enough troops to cow or subdue the strikers in the outlying districts and only the Fordsburg headquarters held out. Then Smuts announced his intention to bombard the Fordsburg Market Square. That was the best way of ending the fighting quickly and avoiding heavy loss of life. But first he ordered the evacuation of the district by the inhabitants. The attack was planned for Tuesday, March 14, and the inhabitants were warned by leaflets dropped from planes to be out before 11 a.m. They were told to make their way to the Agricultural Show Grounds across the ridge.

I was nowhere near it of course. But I saw the evacuation through another's eyes. My Cousin Morris had left the Likkewaan River, where drought, debt, the quiet and the Taal had proved too much for him. The Army had also taken his horse and left Dick's bones in the deserts of South-West Africa. Morris had sold his few acres to a smallholder and had moved into Fordsburg, where he was now among Tuesday's evacuees.

My Cousin Morris was an ordinary man. I was beginning to see that he was a little man too. But he showed me what the little man thought of Smuts when he recalled that Tuesday some time later, and showed me how he resented Smuts's military methods against a workingmen's suburb.

"You should have seen them running from Fordsburg that morning! It was bitter, bitter! ... Men, women and children in the cold. Whole families out in the street. It was still dark. Who could tell when the shooting would start? Could you trust anyone? ... Hand-carts, prams, bicycles, anything they could get hold of and anything they could carry. Food, blankets and bedding in case they couldn't get back. Who could tell how long it would take? All sorts of harmless people pushing up the hill, old people, women, babies... It was a terrible thing to do to them... A big man like Smuts should do a thing like that!... And what for?"

He might well ask what for. The guns opened up at 11 a.m. on Tuesday from batteries on the ridge and nearer town. We listened nine miles away at Germiston, and some folk said they heard the cannonade. They could have heard very little. It was all over quickly. Shells blew holes in the Market Hall. Shrapnel rained down on the buildings and barricades. When the infantry moved in after the guns, they were accompanied by a tank, which broke down half way. More infantry came in an improvised armoured train. There was hardly any fighting. Most of the rebels had scattered, and the rest surrendered in ragged groups. The suburb was deserted, and so was Market Square, except for a few dead. In the shattered Market Hall the troops found the bodies of two men, Fisher and Spendiff, who had preferred suicide to surrender.

So ended the Battle of Fordsburg and with it the **Rand Revolt**, which had cost the country 230 lives.

By now I was no longer a schoolboy. I was an undergraduate at the university and the revolt was an unfortunate interruption to the academic year, the opening of which had been delayed. The University of the Witwatersrand was new, having just burgeoned out of the South African School of Mines, and this was to be its first year of full university status. What a year was this 1922! And what a place was this for a university! Johannesburg still had a mining-camp or Wild West look about it—a town with dusty streets, verandahs sprouting flowered iron-work, and dirty-white mine dumps that closed the southern view. But the townsfolk had set their hearts on a university; the professors were gathering at the School of Mines near the railway station; and inspired by them a woman called Muriel Alexander (who had trained with Beerbohm Tree at His Majesty's Theatre in London) was planning to give Johannesburg its first Greek tragedy, a production of *The Trojan Women*. As she made notes on Euripides in her studio, she could watch the rebels massing in the street below. Whilst authority in uniform was clearing the strikers from the Trades Hall, authority in cap and gown was founding a university four blocks away.

The man who presided there was Jan Hofmeyr on the first step of his climb that would eventually take him to the top at Smuts's side. He was then in his later twenties and had been a Professor of Classics. He had a large round head, a thick neck to which his shirt-collar clung, and a patch of hair on one side of his face that stubbornly resisted the razor. Not much to look at, Jan Hofmeyr was nevertheless brilliant, and he came of an old Cape family that had been prominent in politics for fifty years.

So there he sat in a big, square building of classic design with a main entrance in Eloff Street. (It was the age of classic architecture in Johannesburg, following immediately on ornate and corrugated iron). His job was to build a university from scratch, and to begin with he did everything from enrolling students in January to examining Latin papers in October.

When I first stood before Principal Hofmeyr I was both disappointed and overawed to find what a prodigy looked like in the flesh. He glanced at my matriculation record and decided there and then that I was to be a scientist. Accordingly he planned a course for me in physics, chemistry and mathematics. That was the only time I ever allowed anyone to plan a course for me, and when years later Jan Hofmeyr discovered I was a journalist he was puzzled. I don't think he ever worked out how I had done it.

Behind the imposing pile of the former School of Mines there was a large rambling block of single-storey wood-and-iron buildings known as "The Tin Temple" and built originally in haste as temporary municipal offices. That was also marked out for dignity. Here most of the departments of the university were accommodated, in musty, stuffy rooms where professors nodded over their desks and then impatiently discarded their broad-sleeved academic gowns. Whatever those gowns might have been intended for, they served little purpose in the heat that came pounding through those corrugated iron walls.

Ordinary-looking in a crowd, Jan Hofmeyr was a different person when he mounted a platform. Then he acquired stature; he had a clear-ringing voice and a command of language that produced flowing sentences and rolling periods. He prepared his speeches carefully beforehand; he could be eloquent on any occasion; and he was much more impressive in English than in Afrikaans.

Among the students it was commonly accepted that Hofmeyr was marked out for even bigger things than the pricipalship of a university. "Hoffy", they would say in the common room where they wandered in between lectures, "one day—Prime Minister." He was regarded as the logical successor to Smuts... but his road was going to be both longer and shorter than people thought, and even Smuts's position at the head of the country was to prove by no means so secure as it seemed at the time his future lieutenant was knocking undergraduates into shape at the Tin Temple in Johannesburg.

Within a short time the Universitas Witwatersrandensis was ceremoniously bestowing its first degrees at a congregation of students, professors, parents and public in the Town Hall, and Smuts was to receive an honorary Doctorate of Laws. For half a day caps and gowns appeared in the verandahed streets, and people turned round to stare. They had never seen anything so outlandish before, and they accepted that this must be the way to start a university.

In the Town Hall, the students' song for the occasion was "The animals came in two by two", which they sang for the inaugural procession of the dons down the aisle.

While the orator recited Smuts's achievements in peace and war, the General stood gowned in red, his face grey and firm down to his pointed beard. He deserved well of his country; he had secured it many triumphs; he had saved the Rand from anarchy... but in the body of the hall there were also other thoughts. He had let the strike develop. He had bombarded a workers' suburb....

The orator read the list of battles he had fought. As he

came to the last, someone stirred in the hall near me and added sotto voce, "and the Battle of Fordsburg".

The white miners of the Witwatersrand had lost their strike, but the principle for which they had fought the mine owners remained and was to be strengthened in the years to come. Non-whites were excluded from skilled work, and that held not only for the mines but also for all the secondary industries which served them. That was the irony that emerged from the Rand Revolt and which neither Smuts nor the Chamber of Mines had power to alter.

And because they were barred from skilled work, non-whites were barred from skilled training; for who would train a man that could not be employed? And being prevented from doing work that would provide them with a living wage, Coloured and black men were forced to accept work that was paid for at a fraction of the rates paid to the white man working next to and over them. When the law applying to industry proved inadequate to protect the white man's privilege, the law was altered to make it adequate.

Licking their wounds, the miners were still determined to make Smuts pay for their humiliation and for the Battle of Fordsburg. A man can win popular acclaim in battle and then come home and lose it all by forcing a few thousand civilians to pack their bags and leave their homes for a morning to let the guns speak.

Two years after the revolt and its aftermath of trials and prosecutions Smuts had to fight a general election. And then the unpredictable happened. In 1922 the Boer commandoes had refused to join the strikers against Smuts. In 1924 the Boer Nationalists under General Hertzog made a pact with the Socialists under the British Colonel Creswell who could command up to twenty seats in the Assembly. Their sole purpose was to turn Smuts out of power and they did it.

Hertzog's Nationalists thought only of Boer survival. Creswell's trade unionists thought only of wage rates and maintaining the colour bar. Neither cared a scrap for Smuts's nation-building aspirations, which in any case looked to them too much like empire-building, and pseudo at that.

The pact defeated Smuts at the polls. Hertzog rewarded the Labour Party with three seats in the Cabinet, an experience from which it never recovered. From then on the Labour Party was a waning force in South Africa, eventually paying with its life for having allied itself to a rural land-owning party to whom the principles of labour-socialism, collective bargaining and trade unionism were anathema.

CHAPTER 6

Slap-happy Years

SMUTS, now in his fifties, was at the height of his powers. But he was a man made for office, not for Opposition, and to find himself out of the Government must have been deeply frustrating. Moreover, the Labour Party had played only a secondary role in his defeat. The people who had turned him out were his own people, the Boers, and that was particularly galling. He had always relied on his "oudstryders" (his old fighters) to stand by him; and they usually did. When Smuts arrived at a country town to open an election campaign or for some civic occasion, he was met by a column of his Boer War veterans on horseback, who would escort him to his hotel. The old fighters had not deserted him; they were simply getting fewer; and for the younger generation the aloof-looking Smuts, with his eyes always set on the distance, lacked appeal. When the new generation of Afrikaners were offered the choice between Hertzog's nationalism and Smuts's world view, or his imperialism as they preferred to call it, more and more of them chose "ons eie volk, ons eie taal, ons eie kerk" (our own folk, our own language, our own church).

Smuts was not yet the "Oubaas", the Old Master and father-figure he was to become twenty years later. While the British and the English in South Africa admired him for his great spirit, for the whole-hearted way in which the old guerrilla leader had become Britain's friend and a pillar of Empire in Africa, his own people resented him for the very same reasons and kept rejecting him. Though he relied on them, they kept on humiliating him. He lost his seat in the general election and another had to be found for him. It was

Botha's old seat at Standerton in the Transvaal, and in time he was to lose that too—and the next. He kept wooing them and they answered by showing that the more he was Britain's and the English-speaking voters' friend, the less he was theirs. When he crossed the Limpopo to offer Rhodesia partnership in the Union as a fifth province and the offer was declined they jeered. They regarded it merely as the failure of a manoeuvre to get more English votes.

In these circumstances Smuts sought the consolations of philosophy, and in his rambling old farm-house, "Doornkloof", outside Pretoria, he turned to old thoughts he had first essayed, as an undergraduate at Cambridge, in a study of the American poet Walt Whitman, and again in 1910 in *An Inquiry into the Whole* (both unpublished). Now he developed those theories of "wholes and Holism in nature", and in 1926 he astonished his countrymen with the publication in London of *Holism and Evolution*, a book in which the Boer soldier and statesman stood forth as a philosopher as well.

"Wholes are basic to the character of the world," he wrote, "and Holism, as a universal process of the evolution of wholes, is an ultimate feature of the world."

"Holism discloses the motive force behind Evolution..."

"The reflections embodied in this work lie far removed from the busy and exciting scenes in which most of my life has been spent; and yet both of them tend toward the same general conclusions."

"The League of Nations, the chief constructive outcome of the Great War, is but the expression of the deeply-felt aspiration towards a more stable holistic human society... The rise and self-perfection of wholes in the Whole is the slow but unerring process and goal of this Holistic universe" (*Holism and Evolution*, Macmillan, 1926).

Holism and Evolution—for a South African politician, especially one with any sort of dependence on the Afrikaner *volk*, that was a most unfortunate title and subject. The Dutch Reformed Churches, which stood four-square behind the Nationalist Party, held the whole idea of Evolution in abomination. They were fundamentalists, with whom the word of the Bible was the basis of knowledge, and they regarded evolution as the most offensive kind of godlessness. They could not stamp out the teaching of evolution in the universities; but they could restrict it wherever they had any say in the administration of a college or its staff. Woe betide the candidate for any teaching post, even in a science faculty, who when confronted with the inevitable question on his attitude to evolution, hesitated or gave the wrong answer. He need never apply for a teaching post again.

And here was the great Jan Smuts, the Leader of the Opposition in Parliament who aspired to lead the Afrikaner *volk* again, accepting the principles of evolution, preaching them and putting his name to a book on the evolutionary process. More than that. He was even suggesting that the writ of evolution ran in South Africa. The newspapers reported him as saying that in South Africa there was still "too much of the old divisions, but still the effort has been made, and you see today in South Africa the biggest problem facing us is being solved along Holistic lines". He had given his foes a stick to beat him with. But that was part of Smuts's trouble. He was not really a politician or a party man, and the stage of South African party politics was too small for him.

His own followers were both amused and bemused by the book. They doubted whether this thing called Holism would cure any of the ills of either Europe or South Africa, and they found it disconcerting to have a leader who showed so incorrigible a tendency to take a cosmic view. A man with a more confined outlook would have suited them much better. They doubted (entirely on hearsay) the validity of his philosophy and made mischievous jokes about his Holism. But they accepted the added stature that his work as a thinker brought him in a land, so ostensibly, of lesser men.

His appearances outside Parliament were not frequent, but when he spoke in public he dispelled the impression of a man sulking in his tent or nursing his wounds in his country home outside Pretoria. He was invited to speak at Oxford, and it was when he was leaving on one of his lecture tours abroad that I met him face to face.

I was then a junior on the staff of the *Rand Daily Mail*, the Johannesburg morning newspaper which was to claim a great measure of my days. It had been founded in 1902, when its first and brief editor was Edgar Wallace, later to become the foremost writer of crime and detective stories of his time. In the late 'twenties, the paper came under the editorship of Lewis Rose Macleod, a florid but hard-hitting Australian who had come to us from Fleet Street. He was a man who made his presence felt among those around him almost as a physical force. He liked the cutting phrase, good brandy, high society and a sob story. When he walked into the building, the whole staff became aware of his presence, and tension rose from office to office. He was that kind of editor. Among those who learned their craft under him, besides myself, were Douglas Ritchie, who during World War II became famous as Colonel Britton, the man who sent the "V" sign over the B.B.C.; John Cope, who in the 'fifties went into Parliament against apartheid; and John Barkham, who towards the end of World War II joined the staff of *Time* and later became book reviewer and columnist to the *Saturday Review*, New York.

Smuts had his critics even on his own side and suffered them ungladly. The *Rand Daily Mail* was one of them, showing itself critical of his leadership of the Opposition, and Macleod, much as he loved social prestige, declined to be drawn into that circle of awe in which Smuts's friends habitually moved. That was one of Smuts's failings. He inspired adulation and discouraged anything less. Newspaper criticism angered him.

My meeting with him took place late one evening on Johannesburg railway station—if a brief confrontation of a statesman and a junior reporter, and a reiterated monosyllable, can be described as a meeting. He was to join the train for Cape Town, where he would take ship for England. We knew that he would arrive by train from Pretoria and would have to wait for a while till his coach was hooked on to the main-line train for the south.

All efforts by our political and parliamentary correspondents to interview Smuts in Pretoria had failed. He turned his back on reporters and critics. So the newspaper threw in a junior to waylay him and get him to speak if possible at Johannesburg station. From Edgar Wallace, possibly, the *Rand Daily Mail* had inherited the unconventional or even irreverent approach. I was instructed to go to the station, confront Smuts and simply ask him to say something, if only a farewell message. Anything that Smuts said was news.

I made my way on to a crowded platform looking for the coach that had come in from Pretoria. I little fancied the prospect of having to push my way into his compartment. But I had to resort to no such tactics. My luck was in, I thought. I descried Smuts in an overcoat, head held high, strolling on the platform amid the throngs of passengers, porters and seers-off. He seemed far from the crowd, enclosed within himself.

I stopped him in his stride, and placing myself in front of him told him who I was and where from. At my mention of the newspaper his manner at once became frigid and his head took a somewhat higher angle.

As unprovocatively as I could I suggested that he might like to say something for publication before leaving for England.

"No!" he said abruptly.

I urged that there were surely some topics on which he would like to make a statement. Myself I hadn't the faintest idea what those topics might be, and I was wildly hunting my mind for just one little topic with which I might pin him to some words. But he gave me no chance.

"No," he repeated firmly, and "No" again when I showed a pencil "at the ready".

There was nothing to do but thank him and walk away.

Back in the news room I had ideas about writing a story of how Smuts said "No", but no one there wished to be as irreverent as that.

Some years later, in a different mood and a different world, I would remind him of this interview on the railway station, and he would laugh.

The land over which Smuts's uneasy spirit presided, though

it did not rule, was easy-going. Life was easy; the white man's work was well paid; and sport, which meant football, cricket and the race-course, was plentiful.

If you lived in the country towns, the principal preoccupation and, it was said, the principal output, was politics. If you lived in the cities, there was that thing called "culture" raising its head. There were visiting celebrities from overseas, Pavlova, Galli-Curci, to wipe out the angry memory of Paderewski who had played in the Wanderers Hall in Johannesburg and startled the pigeons. There were theatrical companies from Britain, Benson in Shakespeare, the Macdona players in Shaw, Sybil Thorndike as The Maid. The talkies were coming, and the youngsters who used to imitate Charlie Chaplin gave way to a new generation who insisted on singing like Al Jolson.

At entertainment, at sport, in education, South Africans of the 'twenties were little concerned with those reminders of apartheid that now prod them in their everyday lives. Non-whites—mostly Indians and Coloureds—came to the theatre to see the Cassons and the Macdonas, Pavlova and Shakespeare. True, they were mostly at the back of the house, but no one queried their right to be there.

Non-whites came to the football and cricket matches, and no one watched them to mark whom they cheered. Nowadays, if there is an overseas team on the field, British, French, Australian or New Zealand, that's the one they cheer—and the whites object.

At the university, then developing its campus two miles out of town, the concept of separate education for people of different skins was unknown. In our law classes I remember one or two Asian students (Japanese or Chinese) who today would have to receive Government dispensation as "honorary whites" to be admitted to a white university—if they were admitted at all. They sat on the same benches as we did; if anything we felt honoured to think that our young university could attract students from the other side of the world; the warrant of white separateness had not yet eaten into our education or humanity.

Living was easy because food was cheap. Milk was

threepence a pint anywhere; bread was 6d. or even less for a 2 lb. loaf; fish plentiful at 6d. a lb.; meat a shilling or thereabouts. (Now all these things are double or treble, and it seems you can't put the gold price up without eventually raising the prices of everything else).

Every man, from miner to magnate, had his African servant; and if there were growing children in the house there was very often a servant for them too. It was odd that in the land of the colour bar, no one objected to leaving his children in the care of a black or Coloured nurse. To the average white there was something unclean in the touch of a black man. He never stopped to think why it should be that way. It was certainly not in the colour; that would not wash off. It was a kind of defilement, and yet something to which he was drawn at the same time. There was some sort of release in it. Any white woman was willing enough to entrust her child to a black nurse girl, a primitive perhaps recently come from the kraal, who knew nothing of hygiene or child welfare, but who managed to make her charge deeply attached to her. Many a white boy or girl has grown up with the fondest memories of his black or Coloured nanny.

Life was easy even for the servant in his back-yard "kaya", for he had his food, a roof over his head, his master's cast-off clothing and his pound or two in cash at the end of each month. He was also learning the white man's ways and assimilating them at a speed which often surprised the white boss. Among the whites there was little desire to give the black man any education; there was even objection to it. There was a belief that education was in fact bad for black folk. It only produced "cheeky kaffirs" and gave them ideas beyond their station as cheap labour.

The white man refused to see that by taking black men and women into his house, his workshop or his factory, he was educating them whether he liked it or not. He was training them for organised living and absorbing them into his society and culture. If he was ever forced to consider that aspect, he did it with closed eyes. He would rather not watch the black man too closely. But the black man was watching him and was picking up his ways with remarkable rapidity. He was watching him at sport and discovering that if the white man could kick a ball around at the week-end, why! so could he! Passing the Germiston Location in the train, you could see a ragged mob shooting at goal, and someone reported that black nurse-maids at one of the hospitals had been seen playing tennis, which was something both astonishing and a little ridiculous. An African on a bicycle—that was acceptable. He was probably a "delivery boy"; one could label him. But an African on a motor-cycle? Now where in heaven's name had he got it? And what damn fool of a white man had licensed him? As for a native girl in tennis togs—that was something that evoked hoots of laughter!

There was no doubt about it, however; the black man was taking to sport in his own exuberant way, and there were people who approved. They said that the natives had to be given facilities for week-end recreation. Another fantastic idea! Did the natives need recreation? ... Well you couldn't deny the logic of it, and the black man knew it. He looked upon sport as the open door into the wide world of the white man.

In the 1920s, the African workers in the towns were already trying to organise into trade unions on the European model, and were throwing up spokesmen and leaders. Many of their organisers were fumblers and incompetents whom the whites refused to take seriously and whom most blacks were in any case afraid to follow.

Who, for instance, could take Clements Kadalie seriously? He led an organisation with a name abbreviated to "the I.C.U.", which as good as invited people to make fun of it. The letters stood for the Industrial and Commercial Workers' Union, and the man who led it was an African from Nyasaland (now Malawi). Kadalie was large, hearty and flamboyant. He was shrewd with the shrewdness of the primitive, but also with the confusion that often overtakes the primitive when first he finds his way into organised society.

The whites of course resented Clements Kadalie, his presumption in organising a Coloured union, and his suggestions

—they could hardly be considered as demands—that the black man needed more pay. But as long as the I.C.U. seemed so ragged an organisation and Kadalie himself so fantastic, they paid him little attention. They paid no attention to better men and movements like D. D. T. Jabavu, Z. Matthews, the African National Congress, the Joint Council of Europeans and Natives, and the Bantu Men's Social Centre in Johannesburg where a bland American, the Rev. Ray E. Phillips, presided and wrote a prophetic book, *The Bantu Are Coming*. So why should they bother about Kadalie? Even the Nationalists were content to snap and sneer from a distance.

The Joint Council used to meet in the draughty rooms of the Bantu Men's Social Centre—well meaning but doomed to failure as soon as it showed signs of getting anywhere. There I met Professor Jabavu, Dr. A. B. Xuma and other African elite. But Ray E. Phillips was suspicious of reporters —and me too to begin with—because he knew that the more the limelight fell on his work, the more difficult it became.

Kadalie had his headquarters in a tumble-down building at the western end of the city near the Indian market and the red-brick buildings of the Pass Office. There his lively followers would crowd round him on Sundays to listen to speeches in an atmosphere heavy with smoke and sweat, shout their slogans and sing "Nkosi Sikelela Africa" (God Save Africa) which has since acquired the status of an African national anthem. (Hear it sung by a crowd of Africans in the rhythms and harmony that come so easily to them, and you will know why.) The whites were resentful of this anthem too. They felt sure it must have a revolutionary purpose. But how could you object to anyone singing "God Save Africa" in a Christian country?

One of our senior reporters was detailed off to keep in touch with the I.C.U. on those sleepy week-ends when anything was news. He was a man called Hawtin who had spent some years in Rhodesia trying to grow tobacco and had little sympathy for men of the Kadalie type. He would sprawl with his feet on the desk next to the telephone, calling down the line and demanding to speak to "Native Kadalie".

His prejudices were well known to the other reporters, some of whom liked to provoke him.

"Why not try calling him Mister?"

"Mister be damned!... Call Native Kadalie to the telephone, will you!... Yes, I want to speak to Native Kadalie and hurry up!"

Not surprisingly Hawtin made little progress with Kadalie and the I.C.U. When I was assigned to covering the I.C.U. on Sunday, I found no difficulty in calling Kadalie "Mister" to his face. He was a big-headed, genial fellow and a good talker, who enjoyed leading his union in parades and demonstrations, but who, I had the impression, would never lead them anywhere.

On some Sundays he would hold a procession of his followers through the back streets of the city, ending up in a march down Fox Street past the mining houses and the Stock Exchange. Today such a procession would be regarded as sinister and subversive, to be prevented by stringent police action. But then the police merely looked on as at something mildly comical and unreal. And indeed it was.

There was Kadalie, wearing a black homburg and smoking a cigar, at the head of an untidy procession of a few hundred of his followers. They straggled down the western end of Fox Street towards his headquarters (which today without doubt would have been raided by the police and banned). As he walked he talked and gesticulated. His I.C.U. members laughed, shouted and sang in snatches.

Kadalie stopped talking only to puff and blow out clouds of smoke. When the cigar went out and had to be re-lit, he raised his hand, stopped the procession and waited for his nearest committee man to give him a light. Then he puffed hard, gave the signal and the procession moved on again.

That was the slap-happy aspect of African trade unionism in Johannesburg in the late 'twenties and early 'thirties—before the slap-happiness went out of it and anger took its place.

CHAPTER 7

The Great Gold Rush

THE men who headed the first Nationalist Government after Smuts had been jostled from power in 1924, were—like him—men who had fought in the Boer War. The men who fought the war were never so bitter as those who only learned about it at school. The men of Hertzog's administration were never so intransigent, violent or virulent in their nationalism as the men who twenty years later were to succeed to the control of the Nationalist Party. Moreover, Hertzog had three English trade unionists in his Cabinet, and his own nationalism was necessarily tempered by their humanism—up to a point.

When Hertzog decided that South Africa had to have its own national flag, he was eventually willing to compromise and agreed to a design which included the British Union Jack and the flags of the two old republics—the Transvaal and Orange Free State—as a composite centre piece. Hertzog headed the South African delegation to the conference of Imperial Prime Ministers in London and came back with independent and sovereign status for South Africa within the Commonwealth, with the King as head of state. Even Nationalist gatherings, hailing the victory of their Prime Minister (for which Botha and Smuts had prepared the way when they signed the Treaty of Versailles for the Union in 1919), were now willing to toast King George V as the King of South Africa.

At the same time, the Nationalists began sharpening their weapons. They started the separation of Afrikaans-speaking children from English-speaking children, by establishing separate schools for them. Though the resources of Afrikaans were still limited—literature, textbooks and technical vocabulary only rudimentary—they began to insist on bilingualism in the public services and refused promotion where a man's Afrikaans was considered inadequate. Where the situation allowed, they demanded equal and duplicated treatment of Afrikaans and English, so that a bus or tram-car going into town had to carry its destination in two languages—CITY/ STAD. Sometimes this produced odd results, as when a car park at a race-course displayed a sign MOTOR PARK/MOTOR PARK, the difference being only in the pronunciation—"motor park—mooter parrk".

Though the word "apartheid" was unknown at that time, General Hertzog's government began to hammer out its concepts with the Wage Act of 1925 and the Mines and Works Act of 1926. The first of these drew a line between civilised labour (the labour of the people living according to "the European standpoint" and to be paid for accordingly) and uncivilised labour (defined as that rendered by people living "as understood among barbarians and uncivilised peoples"). The second, usually known as "the Colour Bar Act", closed the skilled occupations to Africans, expressly limiting them to "Europeans, Cape Coloured, Mauritius Creoles and St. Helena persons". Skilled labour was therefore permitted to anyone but the natives of the land, who then numbered about five million in a total population of seven million. The socialists and trade unionists of the Labour Party looked on at the passage of legislation which condemned nearly three-quarters of the population in perpetuity to low wages, unskilled work ("kaffir work" as the white South African liked to call it) and a barbarous way of life, and apparently saw nothing wrong in it. It was difficult even for socialists to think of black labour as altogether human.

Smuts fought and lost another general election in 1929. At his own seat in the country town of Standerton, he was opposed by an able and ambitious young barrister, Oswald Pirow, a man marked for office by the Nationalist Party. A few years later he was to become Hertzog's Minister of Defence, and he was then to become known as "Bush-cart

Pirow" because of a plan he propounded for moving an army up to our northern frontiers in case of war. Troops would move in bush-carts drawn by oxen, which could be eaten when all else failed.

Twenty-four hours after the election there was no news from Standerton and ominous rumours were circulating. So I was told to get into a plane and fly there. I flew the 100 miles in a two-seater and got to Standerton in the dusk. I was just in time to see Smuts drive away in a large car, sitting bolt upright with a look of satisfaction on his stern face. He had won by 300 votes, a fair majority for those days.

By 1930 the price of gold had dropped to 84 shillings an ounce, and South Africa's gold output, not far short of eleven million ounces or about half the world production, was worth £45,000,000. That was a sizeable pot of gold to be taking out of the ground every year. It poured a steady stream of money into the Exchequer (for gold mining income was heavily taxed); into the secondary industries, which depended on the mines and the mining population; and into the farming population, which sent its products to town. That was the main reason for the low rate of income tax. If you really wanted to impress an Englishman with the amenities of life in the land of sunshine, gold, cheap labour and cheap food, all you had to do was to mention that the average man paid rather less than a shilling in the pound income tax, and that his wife could always have a servant.

And yet the future looked none too promising for the Land of Afternoon. The gold mines had been working for nearly fifty years. How much longer could they be expected to go on turning out that stream of gold from the ground? A gold mine, once it began to produce was a wasting asset. It would be kept working only as long as it could produce gold in payable and profitable quantities. Its life depended entirely on the price of gold, and if the market remained at 84 shillings an ounce, large masses of gold-bearing rock would inevitably be left lying 5,000 or 6,000 or 8,000 feet underground. At that price their gold content was too low to make their mining and processing payable. At that price it looked as though gold mining in South Africa had reached its peak. From now on decline was unavoidable and the rate of decline almost calculable.

Mining men were openly pessimistic. At 84s. an ounce even gold must cease to glisten, and the gold country would be a bleak country indeed with a dwindling gold output.

True, there were also diamonds, and the names of Kimberley and De Beers still glittered more familiarly to the world than those of Johannesburg and the Rand. But diamonds never had anything like the same importance in the country's economy as gold, and their output (which went mostly to the U.S.) was worth only about a sixth of that of gold. It is proportionately even less now, though it stands at about £43,000,000 or $120,000,000. Fabulous finds like those of the Cullinan diamond (3,106 carat) in 1905, and the Jonker (726 carat) in 1934 (sold in New York uncut for $1m.) excited the world much more than the latest declared dividend of the Rand Mines, and there were times when even the South African population was excited to fever pitch by the diamond discoveries in its midst. Such a period had only just ended— the years of the last great diamond rushes, the years of the legendary "fortunes picked up out of the ground".

This had just been happening near a town called Lichtenburg in the Western Transvaal, about half-way between Johannesburg and Kimberley, where large alluvial deposits of diamond-bearing gravel had been discovered—not like at Kimberley in a Big Hole (a mile round), but in shallow ground spread over miles. To explain the deposits you had to picture some great flooding in some remote geological past. Thousands had flocked to Lichtenburg with pick and shovel and a digger's licence, and soon the country was humming with reports of marvellous finds on the new-found diamond fields.

Fortunes, it seemed, were there for the digging. Farmers were growing rich on their share of the claim licences alone. Diggers had struck pockets of stones and taken away handfuls.

In the act of fingering their gravel men had found themselves holding gem-stones worth thousands of pounds. Only a few of these stories were true, but by repetition they became legion. The rush started for Lichtenburg.

Anyone could go and dig—provided he was white. All he had to do was buy a digger's licence for a few shillings, peg a few square yards of claim, and go and dig—or get some black men to dig for him.

Old diggers, new diggers, fortune-seekers with their families flocked from all parts of the country. But the great starting point was Johannesburg, from where the road to Lichtenburg was churned up, torn up and knocked up by the hurrying traffic—the Great Road of Pot-holes.

The rushes were organised, announced and timed. For every new rush ordered by the Mining Commissioner, special trains were laid on from Johannesburg. Two 16-coach trains a night were not enough to take all the new diggers waiting on the jam-packed platforms with the look of adventure in their eyes and their bundles on their backs. As the trains steamed in, the crowds rushed at them through the windows and then sat on their bundles on seats, racks and the floors for the night journey to the diggings... and who could tell what fortunes lay ahead? If you got caught up in that crowd you might become a digger willy-nilly. When I found myself in the midst of it one night and came face to face with an old college friend whom I hadn't seen for years, it was not just he or the crowd around me who might have pushed me on to Lichtenburg, but the mere excitement and thrill of it all. I had to elbow my way out backwards and cling to my notebook.

At the other end of the journey, a few miles beyond Lichtenburg, 3,000 to 5,000 diggers lined up across the veld three, four, five and six deep. Many had got there overnight or the night before and camped in the open so as to get the front positions. Some of them were not diggers at all but athletes paid to run for men or syndicates with capital. Their employers had surveyed the ground beforehand, as anyone was entitled to do, and shown them what positions to make for. The moment the Mining Commissioner lowered his flag, usually at noon, the three thousand and more runners, pegs and mallets in their hands, surged forward with a terrific roar.

The diamond rush I attended at a place called Grasfontein at the end of 1927 was the last conducted in that way. We had to run about two miles to reach the area of the claims. You ran and you ran, tired and then slowed down, waiting for your second wind.... Nearby a man faltered, staggered and dropped. When they picked him up he was dying. The three thousand ran on, spreading and scattering over the hillside. They drove in their pegs quickly as they reached the diamondiferous ground. Digging would start almost at once. Fortune seekers were always in a hurry.

The last great diamond rush brought no great finds, no pockets of gem-stones, no tales of sudden fortunes. But by then there were 40,000 people on the Lichtenburg diamond fields, living mostly in shacks and scratching around in the heaps of gravel and "tailings" in the hope of finding enough to keep them at it and keep them hoping. Digging for diamonds never looked so drab, so hopeless and empty as among those shacks and gravel heaps.

The next diamond rush the following year was held in motor cars. You had your car standing by with engine running in a line at the Mining Commissioner's office, and as you got your licence you ran for your steering wheel.

But of course it wasn't the same. Diamond digging never was. A hundred miles away—exciting and glamorous. At close quarters—shoddy and frustrating.

And how different from the gold rush that was soon to follow, that was soon to show that gold was still King in Africa —perhaps in the world!

The Great Depression that hit America at the beginning of the 1930s had sent a cold wind down Africa. From the southern tip of the continent we watched governments in Europe totter. We watched the unemployment figures rising till in the U.S. alone the workless outnumbered our total population. We watched world prices fall and world trade shrink. America was no longer buying our diamonds, and diamond mining like diamond rushes began to look rather irrelevant.

Diamond mining was curtailed and then completely stopped early in 1932 (not to be generally resumed for several years). As employment dropped throughout the world millions of people in Britain lived on the dole. In Vienna they began singing of a Gloomy Sunday. Wealthy America was dancing to "Brother Can You Spare a Dime?" In Germany a man called Hitler was whipping up the masses and feeding the hungry with dreams of revenge.

Feeling the dismal winds from Europe and America, we in the South took warmth from the sun and the sun of gold. At 84 shillings an ounce the metal was still in demand in the world, and the proceeds percolating through our economy kept employment up and hunger down. America was no longer buying our diamonds, but London was still taking our gold, and gold was our shield. Then the incredible happened. In 1931 Britain left the gold standard ... and South Africa and its people were shaken to their roots.

Few people could really explain what "leaving the gold standard" meant. But to the average man it seemed that if the pound sterling was no longer a fixed and recognised value in gold, then gold was no longer to be used for money. And if gold was no longer money, or money could get along without it, what was it? Was gold to be merely a trinket, a toy? What was to be done with South Africa's eleven million ounces a year?

In bewilderment, the South Africans watched the movement of the money markets. It was distressing to see the pound sterling falling ... falling ... as though into space.

Said a French diplomat to me, "Oh, yes, yes—we have been through it all before with the franc. It will fall even further." It did, though never as low as he had suggested.

But something else was happening simultaneously. The price of gold was rising. And that was exciting. Gold, the deserted glamour girl, was becoming dearer. From 84 shillings, the price was soaring to a hundred and over.

It was both exciting and disquieting. The price of gold was rising in London, but not in Johannesburg. South Africa had not abandoned the gold standard, and no matter how much the price mounted overseas, within the country it remained depressed.

Now a great controversy shook South Africa. To abandon or not to abandon? The economists, experts and pundits were against it. For the country that produced half of the world's gold, now to desert it was illogical. It was more. It was like biting the breast that had lavishly fed it. Few of them stopped to think that South Africa, though it made gold, could never decide its fate.

The mining companies were all for leaving the gold standard. So at the humbler end of the producing scale, were the fruit farmers. Both were in the position of exporters who received 20 shillings for their produce in London but found that it meant only 12 shillings back in South Africa. So far had the English pound slipped off gold, while the South African pound had remained on gold and fixed.

Smuts was in England at the time, presiding at the centenary meeting of the British Association for the Advancement of Science. He immediately urged South Africa to follow sterling and sent urgent cables home counselling the country to abandon gold. To many people that looked uncommonly like madness. This was not Smuts the South African. This was Smuts having his head turned by the honours accorded him in England—not Smuts the Boer, but Smuts the Imperialist again.

It was a mad world, but those who did not go with it might be the maddest of all. Very soon people discovered the slightly disreputable but thoroughly legal art of juggling with currencies. If you sent a thousand South African pounds to England, you were there credited with 1,400 or, as sterling fell further, with 1,500. It was remarkable how many people now found it necessary to send money to England, how many found reasons for travelling to England, how many more considered it advisable to leave acquired income in England instead of bringing it home. In other words, the flight of capital had begun, and no power in the country could stop it. Facts spoke louder than professors, and they spoke more forcefully from day to day.

The struggle was over by the end of 1932. With something like a great sigh of relief the Hertzog Government accepted the inevitable, and South Africa in desperation abandoned the gold standard. Smuts was back in the country, and soon he was back in the Government.

A by-election in my old home-town of Germiston preluded the fall of the Hertzog regime. Hertzog himself went there to bring his candidate in. He stood on a platform the night before the election and ground his teeth magnificently. But Hertzog lacked human appeal. Using well-worn sentences and a voice that had no lustre, he was something like an automaton. Germiston people showed that they had lost faith in his Cabinet's financial acumen, rejected his man and sent to Parliament J. G. N. Strauss, a barrister and Smuts's former private secretary. A few months later, Hertzog acknowledged defeat and, jettisoning his Labour allies, offered Smuts the deputy-premiership in a coalition government. Smuts accepted, happy to be in the seat of power again.

Now the great gold rush started. It had been set off just after Christmas 1932 when South Africa announced its departure from the gold standard, and by the first weeks of 1933 it was in full cry.

Throughout 1931 and 1932 the world price of gold had been rising. Now at last the gold country was to get the benefit of it. By the end of 1932 the price stood at 130 shillings an ounce. Thus in less than two years it had soared from $17 to $26, and there was still no ceiling in sight. What the rising price meant was plain for all to see—higher returns on gold sales, higher dividends from the mining companies and higher prices for gold shares. To South Africa it meant even more—new life for the gold industry, new mines to be opened, old mines re-opened, vast reserves of low-grade ore declared payable.

And so the rush started—not 150 miles away in the backveld, but half-a-mile away at the Stock Exchange.

It would be wrong to say that Johannesburg has its heart in the Stock Exchange, but no city in the world has it nearer.

The pulse of the market is the pulse of the city's (and country's) well-being. When share prices are up, that is the time when men buy carpets and pictures for their homes, fur coats and diamonds for their women-folk. When shares are down, the life of the city becomes flat, and movement is slack as in an ant colony caught in the cold.

Depressed and languishing for years, the share market leaped into life at the beginning of 1933. Convinced now that the gold price was up to stay, South Africans began to buy their own gold shares, and quotations began to soar. Gold fever seized the city and the country, and if not all roads then certainly all wires led to the Stock Exchange. At home, in the office, at the movies, there was only one topic of conversation. If you called at a friend's house at night, you had to discuss the latest gains and rises. In the city a hundred brokers were at the end of a telephone eager to take your business after months in the doldrums. If the lines were jammed, you were only five minutes' walk from Hollard Street, where the brokers' offices and the finance houses clustered round the Exchange building. If you lived in a country town and caught the distant fever, there was the local lawyer, or estate agent, or the bank, or the local know-all, ready to advise and to do business.

In a week, the floor of the Stock Exchange was turned into a wrestler's ring. As the names of the shares were called, round about 10 a.m., the brokers' men fought in a wild scrum for anything that was on offer. You could call on your broker when his pokey office opened in the morning, then go up to the gallery an hour later and, in company with pot-bellied men, pinched widows, and sighing maiden ladies, watch your man in the melee fighting for your shares.

The prices rose not by pennies or points, but by shillings at a time. In their anxiety to secure a packet of shares before the price rose again, the brokers' men tore their coats from each other's backs (I saw them). In the newspaper office, young reporters telephoned brokers from their desks between assignments (I saw that too), and the order was to buy (I dare say you could see the same in any office in town). In the corridors and offices of Hollard Street, you could see young typists walking about with pencil and pad and a calculating look in their eyes. They were the "tickey-snatchers" who would buy in the morning, wait for the first rise and then sell at a quick profit. The tickey-snatchers (a tickey was threepence) were not all girls. Thousands of small buyers kept the brokers' offices lit till late at night while the staff tried to catch up with their accounts.

As gold prices rose and gold fever spread, so did the legends of shrewd deals and sudden fortunes. Walking in the street one day, a friend pointed out to me a small round-faced man walking jauntily on his heels on the other side near the City Hall. The man, he assured me, had made more than a hundred thousand (nearly half-a-million dollars) in a week. Then he had "cleared out" of the market and made sure of his gains. Judging by the relaxed smile on the little man's face, I could believe it.

I knew a man, an engineer on one of the mines, who was away holidaying in the Mediterranean when the boom started. One day in Cairo he picked up a newspaper, turned to the quotations on the Bourse and to his astonishment discovered that his gold shares had risen from 10 shillings to 45—from $2 to $9.

There is no doubt that many fortunes were amassed during those hectic months of 1933 and 1934. By the end of 1934 the gold price was £7 or $28, and all the world's wealth seemed to be gravitating to gold. Now it was that people brought out the little hoards of gold sovereigns they had been collecting over the years and months. Worth just 20 shillings when Britain was on gold, they were now worth 27, 28, 30 shillings or more and were no longer in circulation. Shopkeepers became buyers of money. You could drop into a soda fountain and sell your sovereigns to the man who jerked you a milk-shake. I crossed the road to a shop selling garden furniture and got 28 shillings a piece. The shopkeeper told me candidly that he sent the gold coins to England and made a handsome profit on them. For the time being they were more profitable than garden benches.

Boom ... boom ... When the world was still struggling out

of the Great Depression, when F. D. Roosevelt was giving Americans recovery programmes, when Mr. Baldwin was dangerously disarming Britain, and Hitler was rallying his gangs of S.S. ... South Africa found itself on the sunny side of the street and basked in the new warmth and brilliance of its gold production.

CHAPTER 8

Tambula of Vendaland

WHEN I set up house in Auckland Park in the 'thirties, the first person to establish himself in the back-yard was Jim, my mother's houseboy. On hearing that I was to have a home of my own, he had decided that this was his chance to take a step up in the world. So he announced that he was coming to work for me, accepted £5 a month cash wages without question, and actually moved in ahead of me.

Auckland Park was a middle-class suburb of half-acre plots just beyond the university campus, the gasworks and the villas of Parktown. It was bounded on the farther side by a golf course, beyond which lay Sophiatown, one of the tumble-down non-white suburbs that ringed Johannesburg. Jim was to have a little room next to the garage, later to be equipped with a stove and a shower. The announcement of the shower gave him particular satisfaction. He was certainly going up in life. And he was no longer "Jim".

He had discovered that "Jim" was a name of no status. Every black man from the country was called Jim. Every black man was addressed as "Hi, Jim!" and to be called "Jim" was as good as being nameless. So Jim now insisted that his name was "Jims", and I could see what he was getting at. That was his pronunciation of "James", and when I said it that way, he gathered confidence and added "Tambula", which was his family or clan name way back in his village in Vendaland in the Northern Transvaal. "James Tambula . . . sounds good," I said. He nodded.

On Saturday nights he'd be off to a shanty dance-hall-cum-shebeen to step it out while a drum and a saxophone drove the latest rhythms through his blood.

"I hope you don't get drunk in Sophiatown."

"I never get drunk." And he turned a sinister eye on me.

James Tambula belonged to the Venda, one of the divisions of the Southern Bantu, and he had his home 250 miles away beyond the voortrekkers' town of Louis Trichardt, which he called "Los-trich". He took charge of our five-roomed house with its broad verandah under a corrugated-iron roof as though he owned it. In his shining bronze face under a thick mat of parted woolly hair and an apron round his waist, he looked much more like the presiding genius of the place than I did. When he was in the mood for cleaning, he would turn the rooms inside out in a morning—every corner except the room where I had my books, which I called a study and he preferred to call "the office".

Back home in the tribe, all the cultivation was done by women. It had been so in the warring days of his ancestors, and though there was no more fighting for the Venda, no more raiding across the border for cattle or women, it remained beneath a man's status or dignity to do any sort of work in the fields. So any suggestion from me that he might give a hand in the arid patch among the bluegums at the foot of my half-acre garden was met with a stubborn, "No, boss, I'm general." A white man could demean himself in the garden, if he wished. But not a man of the Venda who was a "general houseboy".

To have insisted would have meant more trouble than it was worth. It would have hurt him; it would have angered me; and he might have retorted with another phrase he had acquired in the course of his haphazard education, "Not my bizimus!" He had probably picked it up in the Sophiatown dance hall, and I had heard him use it with great satisfaction when he stood at the corner gate carrying on a conversation with another "general" half way along the block across the road. They both spoke at the top of their voices and had no difficulty in making themselves heard. "Not my bizimus!" called Tambula, and he almost doubled up with laughter. So I refrained from carrying the argument to the point where he would glare and say, "Gah-den! Not my bizimus!" And I left him his unacknowledged victory.

Tambula went dancing in Sophiatown every Saturday evening. He'd spend the afternoon ironing his shirts and trimming his hair. When, with the help of a friend he had combed his hair into two little loaves, one on each side, he was satisfied.

I never found out what sort of dancing he went in for. Once when I asked him, he answered in surprise, "Fox-trot!" as though any other sort of dancing was unthinkable. He used to study the advertisements of men's clothes in the newspapers, and sometimes I caught him watching me when I dressed of an evening. I thought it was admiration; but it was more. One Saturday afternoon he emerged from his room wearing a stiff shirt and a silk-lapelled dinner jacket. His shirt gleamed much more than mine ever did, and his lapels were broader. I wondered how he'd got it, because Tambula was frugal and sent most of his money home. Perhaps from a dress-hire shop; Sophiatown had everything. He let me have one look at him as he flashed through the back-yard. A taxi was waiting for him and he was off. "Tambula's stepping out."

Next morning he was waiting for us at breakfast. He had news. Had we heard? He had won the prize.

We were slow of comprehension. "What prize?"

"For foxtrot!"

"So that's why you were all dressed up last night!"

He threw back his head and laughed as though that was enormously funny. Then he produced a long cardboard box, opened it and drew aside the tissue paper. That was his prize, a beautiful silk shawl. We admired it.

"What are you going to do with it?"

"I take it home."

"You going home?"

He nodded. That was the first we had heard of it.

Tambula was very shy about his home in the Northern Transvaal. He never liked talking about it or his people there.

I knew he had a mother; I knew that at least some of the money he sent home would go for buying cattle; but I never knew whether he already had a wife or whether the cattle were for "lobola", the bride price. Even now he said little as he put away his silk shawl. He would be away for four months, and he would leave us a friend to work in his place.

"Is your home good?"

He nodded and looked away.

I tried to picture it. That was not difficult. I had seen African villages in the Transvaal straggling in huts of mud, stone and reeds along a riverside, on the slopes of a hill or among parched fields. There was a path winding away to a main road past some low bush or baobab trees, and the main road led to a railway station miles away. That was every black man's village. That was Tambula's village. And soon he would add to the picture in my mind.

He left for home at the end of the month. He had filled his boxes and bags with all the good things of town life, and when I saw them stacked in the back-yard there was only one thing to do—take him to the station. So I put him in the front of the car with me and piled his luggage at the back. Parking outside the station, I helped him with his bags on to the platform. There were other black men and women there waiting for trains. When they saw us they shot questions at the happy Tambula who, in sports coat and grey flannels, was like a schoolboy going home for the hols. He answered them while collecting his bags, and they replied with many a "Hau! . . . Hau!" I knew what they were saying. What sort of white man was this who helped his boy with his bags?

I asked him how he would manage at the other end. He said not to worry; he would fix it.

"Hamba Kahle, James." (Go in peace.)

"Shlala Kahle, 'knos." (Stay in peace, sir.)

It was three months before we heard from Tambula. I knew that he had learned to write, because I had caught him occasionally copying advertisements from the newspaper on the kitchen table. And then I noticed that he had graduated to the headlines. The letter came in a creased envelope which carried the address in pencil, and the letter was in pencil too, written in large uneven script covering half a sheet. It went like this:

"Sir   How you   Madam   how you
I hop is good for you   is good
Here is not good   is no rain   is too hot
is no rain   is no gress   is no eat   is die
is too hot   Sun I cum back for werk
is no muny   is all my cow die   is no cow
is too hot   Sun I see you sir and madam. . . ."

That was all. We read the letter over and over again. It stayed in my memory, and with it the picture of Tambula's village was fixed in my mind.

He himself was back a month later. We saw a man walking up the garden path with a kit-bag over his shoulder. When he reached the door we realised it was Tambula. He dropped his bag and stood on the verandah.

"Sakabohna, James! Hello! You had a good holiday?"

He answered quietly. "Yes, sir." He wore the clothes he had worn when leaving, but now they hung loosely on him. His face looked smaller, and from bronze it had turned to dusty grey. I understood that. I remembered the letter. But there was something else I did not understand. He had a look of apprehension or anxiety. "Come right in, James."

There followed the usual questions to a man returning after a long absence. He answered them in monosyllables. One would hardly say this was the exuberant Tambula. He was a stranger. Then I said, "Well, James, ready for work?"

"Work?" He looked from me to my wife.

"Yes," she said. "Your holiday's over, isn't it?"

Then his face lit up with pleasure. Now I understood what had been worrying him. He wasn't sure that we would take him back. He had been away four months. You couldn't trust a white man. We might have decided we didn't need him any more; we preferred the other man. For that matter you couldn't trust a black man either. The friend who had been working in his place might have undercut him. Such things happened, and then you simply had to go tramping the streets looking for another job, another home. I think if I had told James that I now expected him to work in the garden, he would have agreed. But there was no need. We told him that he could start again at his old wage, which had risen to £7.

Now he looked at us both and at last he laughed, not the old carefree laugh, but a laugh of contentment.

"Go inside, James," said Dora. "Get yourself some tea."

"Yes, madam! Thanks you, madam!" He was off like a shot.

A few minutes later James and his deputy were facing each other over big mugs at the kitchen table, one listening with open mouth and the other holding forth on the wonders of modern travel. I had already given the friend to understand that on James's return he could stay on and work in the garden if he wished. He agreed readily, for though he knew little about gardening, he had no prejudice against the work. So they were both at their ease, and James refilled his enamel mug from the tea-pot.

Soon they were cooking extra meat and mealie meal for dinner. James had always preferred his own cooking. When he came to me later that evening, I thought that the greyness had already gone from his face. Certainly the dust had gone. He came in to show me his new pass. He had the usual documents of a man coming to town—his permit to travel, his permit to look for work in the city, and his permanent or Big Pass, which was of special interest. Back home in Vendaland, at the district office, he had had his name changed officially from "Jim" to "James".

In a day or two I would take him to the Pass Office in town, register him again, get him his Small Pass or monthly pass, and he would be James Tambula for good.

In a day or two he was sitting in the backyard combing his stubborn hair again before a broken mirror.

CHAPTER 9

Time of Decision

IN the old Government Buildings in Church Square, Pretoria, the tubby little man with the big round face was biding his time. Jan Hofmeyr had given up the principalship of the Witwatersrand University to become Administrator (chief executive) of the Transvaal Province. Smuts had put him there; Hertzog had kept him there; both were angling for him. To either, sooner or later, he must be a big catch. Whenever I thought of him, the words of the undergrads in the common room echoed at the back of my mind. "Hoffy... one day Prime Minister." And now he seemed to have taken the first step up the heights. By which way would he climb?

Five years he sat in the Provincial Offices in Church Square, a baroque pile with dim corridors inherited from the Transvaal Republican regime, learning the arts of government and giving neither side cause to claim him as its own. A man in his thirties he was still an unknown quantity, a bachelor who lived with his mother and under her domination. That was the odd thing about Hofmeyr. His widowed mother had brought him up, cherished him, watched over him, and ruled marriage out of his life. Even the gossiping students at Wits. knew all about that. The gossiping students reported that Hoffy had without doubt "fallen" for one of the women lecturers. Watch him blush in her presence! Watch her! What a catch for a hard-working girl! But she needn't waste her time. Mrs. D. C. Hofmeyr was more than a match for any young woman with hopes above her station, and that was any young woman who set her cap at Hoffy.

The two lived in a handsome old house not far from

Church Square, and it was often much easier to see him there than at his liveried office in the Provincial Building. I was passing through Pretoria once with some friends who said they knew Mrs. Hofmeyr and this was just the time to call on her. Hoffy himself opened the door to us and gave us a smiling welcome. For half an hour we sat at a big table where Mrs. Hofmeyr poured the tea, and Hoffy passed round the preserved fruits and the golden home-made cakes in the best traditions of a Boer household. The talk round that table, where there were other visitors too, flitted over the usual trivialities, from old servants to recipes, from new recipes to old fashions, and Hofmeyr joined in the small talk as though nothing else in the world was on his mind.

Looking back on that half hour while driving to Johannesburg, we discussed how a young Mrs. Hofmeyr might have fitted into that household. We decided that she never would ... not with Mrs. D. C. sitting at the head. And so it was. The old woman, a frail old woman to look at but hiding somewhere the strength of iron behind her wisps of grey hair, was to survive her bachelor son.

Jan Hofmeyr could not sit neutral at the Provincial Office for good. Soon he would have to get off the fence. And the longer he stayed outside the political bullring, the more the speculation grew about this young man's future.

Sooner or later, if "Hoffy" was to get anywhere, he would have to attach himself to a political party—and then, which way would he jump? Would he go with Hertzog's anti-British, land-owning, rural, keep-the-black-man-down Nationalists...? Or would he declare for Smuts's South African Party, also land-owning, also rural, but at the same time an urban, industrial, business man's, give-the-black-man-a-chance party? He would have to choose between the narrow conservatism of the one and the more-or-less liberal humanism of the other—and this has been the choice for the white man in South Africa ever since.

When Hofmeyr was thirty-five came his time of decision. A Member of Parliament, one of Smuts's men representing the Johannesburg North division, had died and a by-election was necessary. The logic of the time and situation pointed to this as Jan Hofmeyr's opportunity if he wished to take it. But Smuts's party had held the seat by just one vote in several thousand. Only a fighting candidate could hope to hold it.

From the newspaper office we made various "soundings" of Hofmeyr. We sent men round to see him. His answers remained evasive. We had a reporter who knew the family. He would telephone the house now and then and speak to Hofmeyr's mother. "No, no," she would tell him. "Janny has not decided. Janny will tell you when he has made up his mind. Janny will tell you himself. He himself must say."

"Janny had better make up his mind quick," was our comment in the reporters' room.

And then quite suddenly he did. He stepped down from the Administratorship, announced himself a Smuts man and was adopted as the candidate for Johannesburg North. He won popular support and admiration by his very willingness to fight this difficult seat. Moreover, he had proclaimed himself a liberal and the focus, as he was to become, of all liberal opinion.

In the contest that followed I had a personal interest. Hofmeyr's opponent was my old form-master John Duthie, the Scotsman who had taught me English and Latin for the matric. Later he had gone into law and so into politics. His Scottish background almost inevitably made him a Labour man, and as the Nationalist-Labour Pact still operated (it was 1929), he stood on Hertzog's side. In sentiment I was all for him, but not otherwise. Labour's pact with the Nationalists had made its cause nonsense in my eyes, and I was glad when the news editor, a forthright Australian called Horace Constable, pointed his nose at me and said: "You were under Hofmeyr . . . now it's up to you."

For three weeks I followed Hofmeyr to his meetings in the half-suburban, half-rural division of Johannesburg North. He addressed gatherings of smallholders, railwaymen, shopkeepers, women at tea parties. The square little man with the patch on his face spoke fluently and confidently. His personality opened up on a platform. He rarely repeated himself, and he always had something new to say.

Once or twice I also attended a meeting of John Duthie.

But my old form-master saddened me. So convincing when he talked on Shakespeare and Cicero, he now made a mistake. He talked down to his audience, and the spectacle was not edifying. Even his jokes, designed for local consumption, missed their mark. "As farming folk," he said, "you all know that the sap goes down in June." The word "sap" also stood for the South African Party, and June was mid-winter. But even the farming folk remained staring at that kind of quip, and they neither laughed nor cheered.

Hofmeyr won the election by 300 votes. As he was driving away from the polling station, I ran up to his car to congratulate him, and saw him as I never saw him again—a completely happy man. When subsequently Smuts formed his coalition with Hertzog, Hofmeyr was there too as Minister of the Interior (home affairs) and the corridors of power were opening up before him.

Bolstered by Smuts and the new prosperity, Hertzog proceeded with the furtherance of his racial plans. In Europe the National-Socialists, the Nazis, were trying to impose their racial theories on an old society; in South Africa the Nationalists were beginning to bind their race laws upon a new one. To them the non-white vote in the Cape Province had always been an eyesore in the constitution. It could not be altered except by a two-thirds majority vote in both Houses of Parliament sitting together, and so far the two-thirds majority had been beyond Hertzog's grasp.

Non-whites had enjoyed the right to vote on the same terms as whites since 1853 and the establishment of the first Cape colonial Parliament. This meant that besides the white voters, there were also Coloured voters and black or African voters. These last numbered only about 20,000 or less (for there were property and other qualifications), and Hertzog made their removal from the voters' roll his first objective.

His government had agreed in 1930 to giving women the vote only on condition that it was confined to white women. Now with Smuts at his side he proceeded with his plan to force the Africans off the roll. Smuts as his deputy was no longer in a position to resist him. He argued that the black man was getting a "quid pro quo"—a separate roll on which he could send three white men to the Assembly and four to the Senate, and this was fair recompense.

To Jan Hofmeyr the argument seemed far from valid and the black man's "quid pro quo" far from adequate. He was absent through illness from the all-important second reading of the Bill, but he was present for the third reading to say that he could see no justice in a measure which deprived people of rights they had enjoyed without abuse for eighty years. To save the coalition Smuts agreed to give Hertzog his two-thirds majority and thus he acquiesced in one of the first laws on which the Nationalists were later to build their apartheid system.

The Coloured man was still allowed to remain on the voters' roll and go to the polls with the whites. Hertzog was troubled by a sense of the white man's responsibility for the existence of the Coloured people. But their turn was to come. His successors did not inherit his qualms. The black man was now to have separate representatives in Parliament. But these, too, he would not be allowed to keep. His turn was to come again.

Depressed and crowded Europe had begun sending its tired and its poor, its "huddled masses", south to the land of the sun. This had been going on since the beginning of the century and earlier. But now the Nationalists took alarm. Immigration restrictions and quotas in America had piled up the stream trying to cross the Atlantic and diverted some of it to Africa. In 1930, therefore, the Nationalists passed the Immigration Quota Act designed to limit the number of immigrants from eastern Europe, mostly Jews. To their open satisfaction, the number of immigrants then dropped from 7,000 in 1923 to 3,000 in 1932, less than a thousand of these coming from the restricted countries of south and south-east Europe.

But the Quota Act was to fail the Nationalists just when they considered they needed it most. Germany was not one of the restricted countries. The Nationalists had a sneaking admiration for the Germans, whose Nordic race theories were something after their own heart. There was the further fact in their favour that Germans could be counted on to be anti-British.

To their dismay, the people who came streaming from Germany in the 'thirties were refugee Jews, fleeing from the Hitler terror and welcomed neither by the Afrikaners nor even by the less tolerant among the English. Hastily the Quota Act was repealed, and the Hertzog–Smuts Government passed the Aliens Act of 1937, once more closing the doors of an empty country to "the homeless, tempest-tossed" fugitives from the Old World. The spectacle of hundreds of refugees hurrying to slip into the country before the Act came into force and the door was slammed (some of them even chartering a ship) was not edifying. But the Act achieved its purpose and the number of German immigrants fell from 3,400 in 1936 to 677 in 1938.

Smuts acquiesced in the Aliens Act and, as it seemed to many people in these years of "the gathering storm", he was acquiescing too much. With Hitler rampaging in Europe, war looked more and more inevitable. The pro-German sympathies of Hertzog and his party were well known and not concealed. In 1938 Hertzog allowed his Defence Minister, Oswald Pirow (of the bush-cart commandoes) to call on Hitler. The chances were that if Britain was involved in war with Nazi Germany, Hertzog's Nationalists would be glad to stand aloof and embrace the ultimate victor whoever it might be. But what about Smuts? How far would he acquiesce in Hertzog's leadership? Was he strong enough or young enough —at sixty-nine—to challenge it?

And what about young Jan Hofmeyr, now in his middle forties? How far would he acquiesce? He was in fact already in rebellion. In 1938 Hertzog had nominated to the Senate a Minister who had been defeated at the polls, Mr. A. P. J. Fourie, giving him a seat where he was supposed to represent the interests of the non-whites. But Mr. Fourie had never shown any particular knowledge of the non-whites or any sympathy with them, and no one regarded him as qualified to hold the seat. This was where Hofmeyr showed he had gone far enough with Hertzog. He and another member of the Cabinet, Claude Sturrock, immediately resigned, and Hofmeyr's image became fixed in the country as the head and voice of liberalism.

In South-West Africa, the former German colony now governed under a League of Nations mandate by South Africa, the Germans were organising on Nazi lines. At first they worked openly under a Nazi Party and Hitler Jugend, but when these were suppressed, they organised clandestinely though no less thoroughly. Every year they sent hundreds of young Germans to the Fatherland and received them back as trained soldiers. By 1939 the Nazis had obtained almost complete control of the German population (a third of the whites in the territory) and had them under Nazi orders.

There is little doubt that Hitler's government looked upon the territory as a jumping-off ground for action in southern Africa. We knew it from the state of mind of the Germans there; we knew it from evidence that kept turning up.

Early in 1939, a sturdy, square-shouldered man of middle age called at the *Rand Daily Mail* office in Johannesburg. He walked with a strut, talked with a heavy accent, and told us he was a former officer of the German army. But he was a Jew who had recently emigrated and he had a warning for us. Because of his army record he had been treated on leaving Germany with more than the usual consideration accorded to Jewish refugees. His case was handled by officials high up in the Nazi hierarchy who were disposed to be sympathetic. They asked him where he was going.

He told them that he intended going to South Africa.

"Don't do that!" they warned him. "Don't go there! Soon we will be there too."

On April 18, 1939, General Smuts as Minister of Justice announced that he had sent a force of 300 police armed with machine-guns to South-West Africa. They were taking over the public buildings, the radio stations and all strategic points in the territory. At last Smuts had shown his hand and his will. His time of decision had also come.

In Parliament he defended his action boldly and unequivocally. "The Government received information leading them to fear serious disturbances... We are the Mandatory Power

... We are responsible for law and order ... Members must remember what happened in the case of Austria ..."

Less than five months later, General Smuts and General Hertzog faced each other in the Assembly, opponents once more on a life-and-death issue. It was September 4 and South Africa had to decide whether to remain neutral or declare for war against Germany. Hitler had already sent his armies tearing into Poland and had been at war with Britain since the previous day.

All that Monday we waited for Parliament to decide. It was known that the Cabinet was divided almost evenly. How would the Assembly vote and whom would it follow?

General Hertzog was saying that there was no reason to believe that Hitler was planning world domination. He and the German people were merely smarting under the wrongs of Versailles. Instead of making out a case for neutrality, he tried to make out a case for Hitler. "The wrongs of Versailles"—that had long been a cliché in South African Nationalist politics.

General Smuts was saying, "I am convinced in my soul that we are up against vital issues for the present and for the future of the country ..." This time the Germans had made Danzig the immediate occasion for war. Next time it might be South-West Africa. ...

The House voted in the evening, and then we heard with immense relief that Smuts had won. He had carried the Assembly with him by 80 votes to 67, a narrow margin but enough to range the country against the Hitlerian horror ... enough to prevent the use of South-West Africa as a German rallying point, which it could so easily have become had South Africa been neutral in the dangerous days of 1940 ... enough to prevent the country from being flooded, in a state of neutrality, with hateful Nazi propaganda ... enough to keep the Cape route and the Cape ports open to Allied shipping ... enough to array South Africa on the side of decency and civilisation.

The narrow majority in favour of Smuts in September 1939 meant all those unforgettable things.

CHAPTER 10

At War

For South Africa the war was, of course, only a white man's war. It had been so in 1914 and also in 1900, and a white man's war was one in which the black or Coloured people could be interested only as onlookers. Even when Japan entered the struggle at the end of 1941 and it was very plainly no longer just a white man's war, the fiction remained in South Africa that it was, and therefore it was no business of the African population.

The idea that the black folk, always regarded as a natural source of labour, could also be a source of infantry, was unthinkable. That would have meant arming them and nothing horrified the white man more than the thought of black men carrying fire-arms.

It was tacitly assumed that the black man was loyal and that his sentiments were on the side of the West. But no one stopped to think what or whom he was loyal to, or why he should be loyal at all. The white Nationalists hoped for a Nazi victory because they were at heart anti-British and they were enamoured of Nazi race theories. But the black man could have no happy expectations of the Germans, knowing of their gory record against the Hereros in South-West Africa before 1914. But what about the Japanese, who could claim some sort of kinship as a yellow-skinned race? Could he hope for a better deal from them? He could hardly fear a worse. If white South Africans gave this aspect of the matter any thought at all, they usually came to the comforting conclusion that the "Native", or the Bantu or the African, being a sensible fellow, probably felt safer with the white devil he knew than with the yellow devil he did not know.

In any case, if any non-whites wanted to serve in the armed forces, there was room for them—in the labour battalions and the transport services. And eventually as many as 125,000 (Africans 78,000, Coloured and Indian 47,000) were recruited to bolster our white enrolment of 284,000. If at any time the non-whites were allowed to carry arms, the secret was closely kept, and when a rumour did percolate down Africa from Egypt that some Coloured drivers had been issued with arms in the combat zone for their own protection, the anti-war Nationalist Party at once raised an outcry for the benefit of white civilisation. They had to be re-assured with discreetly disseminated accounts of how "raw" Africans, when taught to drive trucks, were told that the gears were an elephant, a bullock and a race-horse respectively. That seemed to put it right. It was comforting to think that the African in the army was still as primitive as all that, and also to learn later that pensions for disabled servicemen would be in the ratio of 4 (for white), 2 (for Coloureds and Indians), and 1 (for Africans). It would have been rather pointless to ask what the black man was fighting for, because it was taken for granted that he was fighting for white civilisation.

To begin with South Africa was without arms, without an army and with a divided population nearly half of which considered it was just another foreign British war that was no business of theirs. The change from a peace to a war footing was hardly perceptible. Though Poland had been ravaged, the first six or seven months were the time of the "phoney war" or "the great Bore War", a British joke which appealed especially to South Africans. It was at most a propaganda war, and when I volunteered I was given to understand that I'd be far more useful in the newspaper office than in the army. Christmas was coming and the general pre-occupation was with the holiday season—holidays at the Natal coast on the Indian Ocean, holidays in the less steamy afternoons of the Cape Peninsula on the Atlantic, holidays in the broad Bushveld. Only the overseas holiday, status symbol of the middle classes, was ruled out for the time being. But there was still America, where a neutral ship would carry one beyond all care and concern (the neutral ship became the business-man's status symbol); and to get away from it all there was still the Far East—or was there?

Even when the full storm of the war broke in the spring of 1940 with the German invasion of Denmark, Norway and the Low Countries, it was still a distant war fought over dubious issues. Over Poland? Over the Jews? Over British or Teutonic leadership? The Nationalists, mostly of Dutch ancestry and speaking a Dutch language, tried to pretend that the rape of Holland, the bombing of Rotterdam, were no affair of theirs. An ancestry of two centuries and more scarcely aroused any feelings of kinship. The English watched the German columns streaking for the Channel ports and felt the peril of the Mother Country. The Jews saw the Hitler terror spreading over a shrinking world and knew that for them there was no line of retreat.

After Dunkirk and the fall of France, the Nationalists could consider that they were "sitting pretty". If the Allies won the war, which now seemed a most unlikely event, they would have nothing to fear from the British. If the Germans won, a prospect which had suddenly come close up, it would be they who would be called upon the treat with the Nazis. Their newspapers suggested that they could hardly wait.

The night Italy declared war against a reeling Britain and a crippled France, there was a grand ceremony at the University of the Witwatersrand now settled behind Corinthian columns on its campus in Milner Park. The Great Hall behind the columns was to be formally opened, and the man to preside, at the convocation was the former Principal, Jan Hofmeyr, now Chancellor of the University, but more importantly a Minister with two portfolios in Smuts's Cabinet.

Pulling my car up the slopes of the campus, then still largely overgrown with grass and weeds, I got the news from the parking attendant, "Italy's in." The Great Hall, seating more than a thousand people, was crowded for the occasion and the ceremony went on as the news was whispered along the rows.

Jan Hofmeyr was in great form and found humour in circumstances that inclined everyone else to solemnity. As Minister of Finance he congratulated himself as Chancellor on the way in which the money had been spent on the new building. As Minister of Education he felicitated himself as Chancellor on the university's progress. And as Chancellor he thanked himself as Minister of Education for the interest he had shown in the university, and as Minister of Finance for his support and congratulations. Who could help laughing at a Cabinet Minister so happily extracting Gilbertian humour from his own situation?

But there was another role waiting for Jan Hofmeyr as senior member of the Cabinet after Smuts and as a man whose gifts lay even more conspicuously in government than in scholarship. When Smuts flew to Britain for one of his conferences with Churchill and the War Cabinet, the country was happy to learn that Hofmeyr was Acting Prime Minister, and there were those who could not help wondering how near "Hoffy" was to fulfilling his destiny.

The fall of France and the entry of Italy on the side of Germany jolted South Africa into the very midst of the war situation and its menace. Italy was in control of Abyssinia, which was only 2,000 miles to the north, separated from South Africa by the spaces of the Rhodesias and East Africa and little else. Our frontiers, until now considered remote and secure, had been swung back to the borders of Kenya and there seemed precious little to deter an enemy in the intervening distances.

South Africa in the middle of 1940 found that it had to start arming in earnest, and as it could now expect no supplies from Britain, where there was an army to be re-equipped, that meant arming from scratch. The mines' engineering shops, the railway workshops and even the Royal Mint in Pretoria, were quickly converted into munition factories. In Pretoria too, the steelworks established by Hertzog now came to the rescue of his opponents. They were turning out steel plate for use on Ford trucks being transformed into armoured cars. A man was employed all day firing point-blank into those plates as they came from the mill to make sure they were bullet-proof. They were, and yet those armoured cars stood little chance against cannon fire or tanks. Nevertheless they were good for morale. The Royal Mint was making bullets. Another steel factory at Vereeniging on the Vaal was producing mortars and shells, and an expert was flown from Scotland to show our men how to build howitzers.

The news began to circulate of troops "going North". The fact was that Smuts was sending three brigades to hold the Kenya border and link up with two British divisions in Italian East Africa. When they did link up the unbelievable happened and the Italian forces were rolled up in Abyssinia. These early successes suited the South African temperament, and "Alles sal reg kom" (Everything will come right) remained the watchword. From "up North" stories trickled down of the prowess of the wily General Dan Pienaar in command of the South Africans; of his bluffing the Italians into thinking that his forces were many times larger than they actually were; and of the ineptitude of the Italians, whose army in Abyssinia was excellently equipped, but someone had left the spare tyres behind!

The Nationalists, now led by Dr. Malan, ex-pastor of the Dutch Reformed Church and ex-editor, were listening to the German broadcasts from Zeesen and rubbing their hands over German promises and German boasts. This was when the Luftwaffe was bombing London and Manchester, and 300 children, evacuated from Britain, were on their way to South Africa. The Nationalists voiced the hope that these refugees would not be regarded as immigrants, and one of them shouted "Voting cattle!" at the sight of Allied troops in the country.

But the brilliant Wavell scuppered the Axis armies in Libya and, wonderful to behold, our frontiers were on the Mediterranean again, for the time being.

When Russia was invaded in June 1941, the Johannesburg *Sunday Times*, still printing thirty-two swollen pages plus a coloured supplement of American comics, published a special afternoon edition, and all eyes were on Moscow.

On November 23, 1941, our thin-skinned Fifth Brigade ran into German armour at Sidi Rezegh in Libya and, as an Afrikaans paper announced on the streets, that was a "black day for a South African Brigade".

Pearl Harbour, December 1941 ... and suddenly the war had spread wider and come nearer. The Japanese penetrated to the Indian Ocean, and our Civilian Protective Services (so called because Air Raid Precautions sounded too alarming) began practising with stirrup pumps in case the Japanese came a-bombing. How depressingly inadequate those stirrup pumps looked at night, especially when the instructor remarked, "If you get a direct hit—yer takes it!" but in the Civic Guard (organised as auxiliary police) we were getting revolver practice and orders to shoot at sight if anyone was found tampering with telephone lines.

And yet South Africans could not tear themselves from their easy-going ways. True, petrol was rationed; so it became a matter of prestige to "fiddle" as many petrol coupons as possible. The big question that suddenly erupted was: "Should we hold the Durban July Handicap?" Durban was the mid-year holiday resort, the July Handicap the biggest horse-race of the year, and a trip to Durban in July another status symbol. The Japanese answered at once, "We'll see to it that there's no more July." So it became a challenge to hold the race as usual ... and so we did, if rather nervously.... What's July in South Africa without the big race down there on the Banana Coast! What's holiday time without a trip to the Natal beaches, even while the biggest armies ever were grappling on the Russian steppes and the biggest fleets were shooting it out in the Pacific? So the holiday-makers flocked by road and rail to the South Coast, where there was actually a war-front, offshore, beyond the breakers.

German U-boats were prowling round the coast (one was reported to have stopped a trawler to get some herrings). They lurked in the inlets of Portuguese Mozambique and sallied forth every now and then to sink Allied shipping.

If you sat on the white sand beaches of the Indian Ocean

near Durban, you could see the British convoys going up to Egypt, twenty or thirty ships at a time. At Lourenço Marques the German consular officials could watch them too from the comfort of their easy chairs and balconies, and send their signals accordingly.

The seaside crowds were not all South African. Among them were also Rhodesians, Belgians and Frenchmen from the Congo unable to take their furlough in Europe. And the hotel-keepers were making hay while they could—perhaps with a premonition of the cry of "Sharks!" that was to empty their beaches a few years later.

The British convoys passed up or down the coast at least once a week. Lying under an umbrella on the sand you could count the ships easily. And once a week the power supply failed in the town. Just at about dinner-time, the hotels and houses on the hillside were plunged into darkness. Before the power was restored, the lights in the whole town flashed and flashed again.

"Tinkering with the lights," said someone. "Wish they'd stop it."

"It's the plant," said the hotel manager apologetically. "Can't get the right spares. The war, you know."

Here, if you like, was the perfect setting for a spy thriller. The careless holiday crowds, not too carefree to talk a little worriedly about the latest sinkings . . . thirty ships moving up the coast to the war zone in the morning . . . the town lights flashing thirty times at dusk. But no one seemed to notice any possible connection . . . Or perhaps someone did. A week or two later I heard that certain seaside types had been moved inland.

The fall of Tobruk gave South Africa another black day, a Black Sunday, June 20, 1942, when the 2nd S.A. Division was taken prisoner, and all South Africa wondered over this inexplicable surrender by the South African commander of the fortress, General Klopper.

In Johannesburg, Dr. Verwoerd, then editor of the Afrikaans daily newspaper *Die Transvaler*, sued the Johannesburg afternoon paper, *The Star*, in the Supreme Court, for accusing his newspaper of "speaking up for Hitler" and using the news in support of Nazi propaganda. He lost the action, and the judge found that Dr. Verwoerd "did make his newspaper a tool of the Nazis in South Africa, and he knew it".

On June 21, 1957, in Parliament, when Verwoerd was Minister of Native Affairs, he was reminded of this judgment by a Member of the Opposition.

He retorted, "Who was the Judge?"

"Why do you ask that?" demanded another Member, but got no answer.

(Everyone knew, of course, that the judge was Mr. Justice Philip Millin, a Jew.)

One night early in 1945 during a midnight patrol in the north-western suburbs of Johannesburg, my half-section in the Civic Guard confided in me, "Hitler is speaking tonight, broadcasting to the German people. Care to hear?"

I remembered Hitler's broadcasts in the 'thirties, his frenzied oratory and his ferocious outbursts against Austria and Czechoslovakia . . . Hitler shrieking defiance at the world, and his followers answering with massed roars of triumph.

We went to a house on a ridge and switched on the radio. Presently, clearly, incredibly, the voice of Hitler came over the distances. It was a weary, low, growling voice, coming from somewhere deep in his throat, heavy with gloom, dragging with despair. It was the voice of a man staring at his ruin and receiving no answering roar . . . Hitler in his bunker. Hitler in defeat.

Whilst all this was happening on the stages of the world, something else was developing in South Africa that few noticed, or if any noticed few read its significance. The new industries that had grown up to supply war needs had been drawing workers from the African country districts. The "Bantu homelands" were either semi-desert, or they were eroded and impoverished. The black people looked for work in town. They streamed in from the Northern Transvaal, the Transkei, Zululand, Basutoland, Swaziland. Johannesburg had received 140,000 in ten years. They came hungry and bedraggled, by road or rail if they could hitch a hike or raise the fare. Or they came on foot.

The new labourers crowded into the back-yards, the townships and the "housing schemes". In the posh suburbs of Killarney, Parktown, Rosebank and Westcliff, the lodgers flitted in like bats at night and slipped away unseen before morning. And if they were seen, how could you scold your servant for giving a night's hospitality to a visitor? In Sophiatown, the sheds, lean-to's and shacks proliferated with the sub-tenants, and the rack-renting owners drew good money for a corner, a bed or a heap of sacking. In Orlando, south of the city, the shanty-towns erupted over the veld.

The police went on their back-yard raids. Two o'clock in the morning was the usual time to rout the lodgers out of the shacks and march them off to the nearest jail. As a Civic Guardsman I once accompanied the police on one such raid and helped to pull twelve sleepy men out of a room that normally held no more than two. I subsequently managed to avoid duty when more raids were planned.

Sophiatown was a different problem. The knife gangs were daring and ruthless. The "shebeen queens" were defiant. Rounded up by the police, they paid their fines and carried on their liquor dens as before.

The shanty-towns that at the beginning of 1945 sprawled ten miles south of Johannesburg were a law to themselves. Police headquarters issued orders; the City Council prohibited further settlements; yet they continued to grow both inwardly and outwards. When the shacks were bulging with breeding families and half-naked children, there would be another eruption and overnight another "Sofasonke" as it was called when the squatters found a slogan—"Sofasonke" . . . "We die together."

Ten miles north of Johannesburg there was another black township called Alexandra, almost within sight of the elite white suburbs and alongside the main road to Pretoria. Alexandra was another agglomeration of tumble-down houses that held 60,000 people, another dark township where a man would not willingly be out at night and a white man was not safe at any hour. Thousands of the Alexandra folk travelled in and out of town six days a week—a journey which at fourpence was probably the cheapest bus ride in the world. But it was still a lump out of the black man's wages or the washerwoman's sporadic pocket. When the bus company raised its fares by a penny, the people of Alexandra refused to pay. They boycotted the buses and they walked the miles instead.

Some of them bought bicycles; some of them got lifts from white motorists; but thousands tramped for weeks along Louis Botha Avenue, up Orange Grove Hill and past the lordly dwellings of Houghton Ridge. This daily affront to the conscience of white Johannesburg could not go on. The bus services were re-organised; the fares remained as before; the black folk had demonstrated their power to resist and endure.

Here was matter in plenty to feed the inherited fears of the Afrikaner-Boer population. Now was the time for the Nationalists to raise their banner of apartheid and cry the warning that the black man had to be kept down, and the way to keep him down was to keep him apart. If they had not been able to win the war for the Germans, they would at least forge a weapon out of it for themselves.

During the war years General Smuts—now a Field-Marshal of the British Army, but still known in South Africa as "the General"—was at the height of his influence and prestige. He was now in his seventies, known and respected throughout the world for his vision, courage and statesmanship, and in his own country loved by all except the "purified Nationalists" among his own people.

He was referred to throughout the country, even on formal occasions, as the "Oubass"—the "Old Boss", "Old Man", "Old Master"—and he was more approachable than he had ever been before, seeming to the common man closer and more understandably human. For this his wife was much responsible. She was known as "Ouma"—Granny—and it was she who made him accessible. She could talk ordinarily and intimately with people on their own level, and she became the link between him and the people, even the soldiers, whom she used to address as "my boys". (The little wife of the Boer general had come a long way since the days when she used to have a Boer flag unfurled over her bed when a child was to be born.) She patted them on the khaki shoulder, at a public reception or in a crowd. "Look after yourself, my boy." It was a little embarrassing, but she meant well.

This was when I met Smuts again. At last the war was moving to its great conclusion. There was no doubt now of the outcome. I had written a book on South Africa to explain the country to the people of Britain and America, and it had been published in New York and London. Anyone who could do that in South Africa was then regarded as having performed a notable service for his country (today it is different; he is regarded with suspicion), and I sent a copy to General Smuts. In due course I was summoned to see him and went to Union Buildings—his Union Buildings, which were strung like a great jewel in a floral setting across the hills outside Pretoria.

So I spent about fifteen minutes with him at his desk in the Prime Minister's office, surrounded by busts and other reminders of the past. He had the book before him. I doubt whether he had properly looked at it till then.

His glance fell on the blurb on the wrapper of the handsome American edition, and he broke into laughter. "Ivory, apes and peacocks—and Jan Smuts"—it began. I had to laugh with him.

He was serene, fulfilled and resting on his achievements, far from the resentful man to whom years before I had spoken on Johannesburg railway station. I recalled that meeting. "I met you once before," I said.

That startled him. "Where? When?" It troubled him that he could not remember.

I described the occasion. "And all you said was no."

He laughed again. "You shouldn't have taken no for an answer."

"You were not in a talking mood," I said.

"Perhaps I wasn't."

He turned the pages of the book and saw his own photograph as the frontispiece.

"That's right," he said. "In America, when they think of South Africa, they think of me. That is all they know. They have not heard of anything else." His voice as ever was clipped and high-pitched. "All they know about South Africa, is me, Smuts, nothing else. That's all they hear . . . just Smuts. It is so."

I had time to reflect that vanity is an almost inseparable part of greatness. Then he went on to talk about America.

"They have the same problem there with their Negroes as we have here with our natives, just the same. During the war, there has been a great movement of Coloured workers to the west coast, to the new war industries in California—and what happens? They have troubles, difficulties. Problems arise just like ours. On the west coast, the Negro worker was not known before. So when he arrives there in numbers, he is not wanted, not socially . . . problems . . . colour bar . . . just the same as we have . . . you see, it is not unique. It is the same all over when colour comes among us . . . the Americans are finding that too . . . We have to face it . . . We shall have to work it out. . . ."

General Smuts was not offering me an argument; he was merely stating a fact. There was no time to ask him how he hoped "to work it out", and I doubt whether he would have been disposed to tell me. It seemed to me that he was merely drawing comfort from the contemplation of his country's difficulties repeated elsewhere and causing similar complications.

So I came away from Smuts with two impressions that have deepened with the years—vanity, vanity! which is a pardonable sin—and his habit of thinking of Coloured folk not as people, but as problems, problems, a habit that came out of his Boer past and background. For both sins he was to pay —and soon.

Yet Smuts could see the world clearly enough, if he could only half-see what was happening around him. When he visited Britain in November 1943 and addressed a meeting of Members of Parliament he pointed prophetically to the two colossi that were soon to bestride the world—the U.S.A. and the U.S.S.R.

And he saw too, as he confided to a colleague of mine, A. B. Hughes, then editor of the Johannesburg *Sunday Express*, "It is a Coloured world, Hughes; it is a Coloured world."

That quarter-hour in the Prime Minister's office at Pretoria was the last time I saw Smuts.

The last time I saw Hofmeyr was in his office at Cape Town when Parliament was in session and my wife and I called on him to enlist his interest in an exhibition of South African books we were arranging for the P.E.N. Club in London. At his ministerial desk he was large, square and friendly, and he gave us all the help we wanted.

He was then, because of absences and illness in the Cabinet, in charge of four portfolios, and when he answered questions in the front bench of the Assembly, he had them all at his finger-tips.

From the Opposition benches I remember Eric Louw in his rasping voice, "Onse mense . . . Onse mense!" ("Our people. Our people!")

The matter under reference was immigration and all Louw could think of were the jobs that might be taken away from "onse mense", by whom he meant of course not all the people of the country, but only his own "Afrikaner volk" . . . That was what the Nationalists always meant when they talked of "onse mense". . . their people.

CHAPTER 11

The Crucial Year

On a grey Saturday, February 1, 1947, the battleship *Vanguard*, 42,000 tons, sailed south from Portsmouth carrying King George VI, Queen Elizabeth, Princess Elizabeth and Princess Margaret, on a holiday tour of South Africa. On a hot sunny Monday, six thousand miles away, on February 17, H.M.S. *Vanguard* docked in Table Bay, Cape Town, below the line of Devil's Peak, Table Mountain and Lion's Head that there festoon the sky, and the Royal Family stepping ashore in one of their distant dominions, received a tumultuous welcome.

On the same afternoon, when wisps of sunlight were stealing through the London sky, the Queen Mother, Queen Mary, called at South Africa House, in Trafalgar Square, to visit the first exhibition of South African books assembled for the South African P.E.N. Club. At the request of the South African High Commissioner, Mr. G. Heaton Nicholls, she had agreed to open the exhibition two weeks earlier; but she had overstrained herself seeing the King and Queen and the Princesses off at Portsmouth, and she had been unable to attend the opening. Her place was taken by H.R.H. Princess Alice, Countess of Athlone (wife of a former Governor-General of South Africa) and Queen Mary came this day instead. She was a great lady who radiated majesty in a crowd; but she was also a woman of true simplicity of outlook, which made it easy to talk to her face to face. Now in her eightieth year she was erect and tall, or seeming tall because of her head-dress, and her movements were slow but alert.

My wife and I were presented to her in the oblong Reading Room and I was asked to show her round the display of a thousand English and Afrikaans books which lined the walls and heaped the tables. As we stepped up to the shelves, she took no more than a glance at the volumes and turning to me began talking of "the children". For a moment I was nonplussed, wondering who "the children" might be. But I realised in time that she was referring to the two Princesses, Elizabeth and Margaret, for at that moment she was a grandmother thinking of the two girls on a distant shore, and though Elizabeth (later to be Queen Elizabeth II) was approaching her twenty-first birthday, to her they were "the children" and she was anxious on their behalf.

She wanted to know what the news was from Cape Town and whether the royal party had had a good landing. She had heard, she said, that certain tidal difficulties had been experienced at the new harbour (built during the war) and she wanted to know whether the great battleship had docked safely.

Her Majesty seemed to take it for granted that I would have the latest news, and I, remembering what was due to a mother and a grandmother, had the presence of mind to give the right answer. I assured her that there was no difficulty at all in Table Bay; I had seen the new foreshore works quite recently; I felt certain that the *Vanguard* was in dock by now and Their Majesties and the children were ashore. She was pleased to hear it, so I repeated, "By now they are all ashore and they have had a wonderful welcome."

That satisfied her and she turned to the books. Before her arrival I had been instructed to address her first as "Your Majesty" and then simply as "Ma'am", but I could not bring myself to use "Ma'am" to that presence and dignity, and as I noticed that the Lady-in-Waiting kept addressing her as "Your Majesty" without sounding a bit pompous, I did so too and all went well.

She opened a book at a full-face portrait of General Smuts. "Ah, my dear old friend!" she said. "You know he always comes to see me when he is in London. So nice of him!"

Presently she was talking of the children again. I think she loved talking of those two girls more than of anyone. She talked with a distinctly German accent (for, though London-born, she was the daughter of a Prince of Württemberg) and she told me with some pride that "the children" had been eagerly looking forward to this tour of South Africa and they had both been learning Afrikaans. She thought Elizabeth was better at it than Margaret.

Queen Mary spent nearly half an hour looking at the books and pictures, and showed a connoisseur's eye for a good drawing. I remembered the stories antique dealers used to tell of her. When she came to a platform at the end of the room, she asked me for my arm up the two steps and took it as simply as that.

When she left South Africa House there was a crowd in the cold February mist outside in Trafalgar Square waiting to catch a glimpse of her, and I could understand why. She was a person on whom greatness sat as though belonging there.

During the period of that exhibition we became a temporary information office for South Africa. People preferred coming to us to going upstairs to see officials who had little time to talk and gave stock replies. But of all the people who asked questions, silly, serious or wise, one elderly lady has remained in my memory. She did not say so, but I guessed she must have had some early association with South Africa. She wanted to know whether the visit of the Royal Family would possibly have any influence on the general elections to be held in the ensuing year, 1948.

I told her that the visit was not supposed to have any political significance whatever and it was precisely because the elections were due only next year, not this year, that it had been possible to invite the Royal Family to tour South Africa. But she was not content with that answer.

"No, no! That is what they say upstairs. But you who have just come from the country, what do you yourself think?"

I had to admit that the warmth with which the Royal Family had been received throughout the country spoke plainly of a strengthening of pro-British sentiment, and this must help Smuts in the elections next year. In any case, 1953 was regarded as the crucial year, not 1948. "Be back by 1953," my M.P. Sarel Tighy, had warned me.

She was still doubtful, but thanked me and left. Since then I have had a lurking respect for the pre-vision of old ladies. But what I told her I sincerely thought, and I don't think anyone would have told her otherwise. That's what things looked like in 1947.

The last Royal Tour of South Africa had all the appearance of homage and triumph to be expected in a well-established monarchy, in spite of the muted hostility of the Afrikaner Nationalists. When the King and Queen went ashore they received loyal addresses of welcome at Government House from members of the Assembly and the Senate, though most of the Nationalists absented themselves. When the King opened Parliament he used both Afrikaans and English. When the family toured the country they were feted by whites and non-whites—by an African choir of 8,000 at Lovedale, the African college in the Eastern Cape; by a great assembly of African tribes in the Transkei; and 70,000 Basuto in the greatest pitso—tribal meeting—ever held in Basutoland.

When the royal train reached Bloemfontein, capital of the largely Nationalist province of the Orange Free State, it was greeted with a salute of twenty-one guns. The King was met by the Minister of Labour, who was Dr. Colin Steyn, son of the last President of the Orange Free State republic before the Boer War. The King also, at his own request, paid a private visit to the old President's widow, who was eighty-two.

At Eshowe, the nominal capital of Zululand, the Royal Family were welcomed by 100,000 Zulus and were entertained to an exciting display of tribal and warrior dances. This was believed to be the first time the Zulus had danced as a nation since the overthrow of their King Cetewayo by Lord Chelmsford's forces at Ulundi in 1879.

In Durban half-a-million people lined the streets to see the arrival of the royal guests; 20,000 ex-servicemen and women marched past the King; the Indian community paid their homage. In Swaziland 8,000 warriors performed ceremonial

THE CRUCIAL YEAR

dances, and the Swazi Paramount Chief Sobhuza Dlamini II welcomed their "great Lord, Protector and King".

The climax of the tour came in the Transvaal. The Nationalist newspaper, *Die Transvaler*, then edited by Dr. Verwoerd, ignored the royal tour; but that did not impair the enthusiasm of the Transvaal population. In Pretoria, a thousand Boer veterans of the Anglo-Boer War paraded at the statue of General Louis Botha before Union Buildings to greet the great-grandson of Queen Victoria and her great-great-granddaughters.

When the Royal Family came to Johannesburg over a million people crowded the decorated streets and greeted them with cheering unequalled elsewhere during the tour. On the outskirts of the northern Transvaal town of Pietersburg, 40,000 Zulu, Xhosa and Venda tribesmen greeted the King as "great chief of all the chiefs".

In two months the Royal Family travelled more than six thousand miles through Southern Africa, and before the tour ended on April 24, Princess Elizabeth turned twenty-one. Her birthday (April 21) was marked by a public holiday and a parade at Cape Town where she took the salute. Later that day she broadcast to the peoples of the Commonwealth, and in a girlish voice the future Queen dedicated her life "to your service and the service of our great Imperial family".

We watched the election campaign of 1948 from various points in Europe—from rationed and grousing post-war Britain; from restless, soul-searching France trying to be cordial to tourists once again; and from friendly, good-tempered Denmark. In the train across Zealand I turned to a man with a Danish paper to see if I could get any news of the election results. He seemed anxious to communicate, but when I asked him how many seats Smuts had won, he consulted his paper and told me seventy-eight. That seemed to me likely and we travelled on re-assured. It was actually quite wrong. The man had given me Smuts's age.

The shock of the election results came to us next morning in our hotel in Copenhagen. Buying a copy of the London

Daily Telegraph the first thing I read was that Dr. Malan was to form a government. The unbelievable had happened. Smuts had been defeated. It was stunning news, inexplicable, fantastic. To me and my wife it was all the more shattering because we were strangers in a foreign city and suddenly we felt cut off from our own country—with no one even to tell of our distress. My wife wanted to leave Denmark at once and return to South Africa.

Half an hour later we met a member of a famous British publishing firm. At last someone to talk to, I thought.

"This is a Hitler victory," I told him. "Three years after the war Hitler has had a victory in South Africa."

He looked at me indulgently and smiled. Suddenly I knew what he was thinking. "These colonials. How excitable they do get . . . How they exaggerate!"

I swallowed my agitation and shut up. But later that morning we ran into Joseph Leftwich (biographer of Zangwill) who had recently won repute as compiler of a Jewish anthology, *The Golden Peacock*. To him we could talk. The man of the Golden Peacock knew what it meant to feel cut off from one's home. He listened and understood.

To do the publisher justice, when I met him again two or three years later he recalled that agitated morning in Copenhagen and admitted that I was right.

Even the Nationalists were surprised by their success. Dr. Malan spoke of "this amazing result". The ex-pastor and ex-editor, Dr. Daniel Francois Malan, was round, small-eyed and chubby. He could easily have sat for a rather portly Mr. Pickwick. He could even make a heavy-footed pun. When travelling by train from the Cape once, he chuckled as he told his audience at a backveld stop that wherever he came the country was "pap nat". That meant both that it was "wet as porridge" (nat-wet) from recent rains, and that it was thoroughly Nat. (or Nationalist). But that kind of benignity was no indication of the political forces which animated him and made him now the spear-point of Boer nationalism.

On June 2, 1948, when he formed his Cabinet, he said, "In the past we felt like strangers in our own country, but today South Africa belongs to us once more. For the first time since Union, South Africa is ours." In other words, he had not just won an election. The ex-pastor had fought the Boer War all over again, and he had snatched the country from those others who were English, Dutch, French... but mainly English of course, and all of them uitlanders. The old anti-uitlander mentality had won, and Afrikaner children could ride in the street in Johannesburg (as they did) and shout at passers-by, "The country is ours now!" Forty years of union had not made South Africa a nation.

The Nationalist victory was inexplicable at the time even to the Nationalists, but the reasons for it became gradually clear.

The Nationalists won because of the discontent with the ruling party that so often follows a war.

The Nationalists won because the Afrikaner soul took fright at the wave of immigrants, uitlanders, that had been coming to the country since the war. Other countries like Canada and Australia had opened their arms to the restless masses from Europe. Malan's Nationalists saw immigrants not as reinforcements to the white settlement in South Africa, but as a threat to the existence of the "Afrikaner volk"—"onse mense". While protesting that their apartheid policy was designed to save white civilisation, they were concerned only with saving the one-and-a-half million Afrikaner people as a people, and otherwise—to hell with white civilisation!

It had been so all along. For years I had known why in my youth the crowded emigrant ships kept passing South Africa's doorstep. The Nationalists had always opposed immigration: they had always used it to alarm the electorate. They had always been able to flaunt some threat to the country in any move to encourage immigration—Unemployment ("They'll take your jobs!")—Communism from eastern Europe—Jews from anywhere.

They had always been able to menace a government with loss of votes and support in the country if it actively promoted immigration, and now when Smuts opened the doors after the Second World War they showed that that had been no empty threat. They turned him out.

There was a Member of Parliament, Morris Kentridge, who represented a largely Jewish district of Johannesburg and who made immigration his especial study. With spectacles pinched on the point of his nose he used to tell the Nationalists, "Every immigrant brings his own absorptive capacity." His words fell on deaf ears. The Nationalists on the opposite benches in Parliament used to turn away when he spoke. How hollow his words sounded now.

The Nationalists won because of the influx of Africans into the towns—and into the agglomerations of slum townships with which the Smuts Government had as yet been unable to cope.

And finally the Nationalists won because Hertzog's generation had come of age and had gone to the polls.

During the 1920s Hertzog had begun to enforce his two-stream policy in education, building separate schools for the English-speaking and the Afrikaans-speaking children. It was common knowledge that the Afrikaans schools were used for the indoctrination of Nationalist principles, and now these youngsters were old enough to vote. And they voted as they had been taught. So it was really a Hertzog victory as well. General Hertzog, dead six years, had beaten Smuts again.

Even so, Smuts might still have won the 1948 election had he taken advice—so narrow was his defeat.

His United Party had won 65 seats in Parliament, and together with the Labour Party's 6 and the 3 Africans' Representatives, he could have mustered 74 in the House of Assembly. The Nationalists had 70 and together with what was left of Hertzog's followers who had made a pact with them, 79—only five more than the Opposition.

Smuts might have won if he had listened to the men who urged that now was the time to restore the non-whites of the Cape Province to the common roll, from which they had been removed with his acquiescence in 1936. Now was the time to undo that injustice. In 1936 he had had excuses for it. But now he could face it for the shabby manoeuvre it was, and by reversing it he could have secured several Cape seats. But Smuts was too much enclosed within his Boer (or party) mentality to do it, and so he forfeited the extra seats and the respect that such a measure might have won him.

He might have made it practically impossible for the Nationalists to govern had he done what the Indian community wanted. He had offered them three white representatives in the Assembly (just what the Africans had), but Indian pride would not allow them to accept white men as their spokesmen in Parliament, and the United Party could not bring themselves to allowing Indians into the Assembly. So the Indians turned down his offer—to their loss and his.

Smuts would certainly have won had he done what members of his own Cabinet had begged him more than once. They wanted him to adjust the lop-sided electoral system that had governed parliamentary representation since 1910, and it was the logical thing to do.

In 1948 the Nationalists won a majority of seats in the House, but a minority of votes in the country. They polled 442,000 votes against 524,000 for Smuts and 27,000 for the Labour Party, and yet they were able to control the Assembly. The reason for this went back to the Act of Union.

In a mood of conciliation the British in South Africa had then agreed that the rural voters, "the poor farmers" again, should be given an advantage against the towns. To make the farmers feel they were not to be dominated by the urban population, it was agreed that at the delimitation of constituencies, the rural seats could be "unloaded" to 15 per cent below average, and the urban seats "loaded" to 15 per cent above average. In practice this meant that the rural divisions where the Nationalists have always had their main strength, need have fewer voters than the town divisions. In time it meant that a rural division had to have only about 7,000 voters, and a town division could be loaded with as many as 11,000. A vote in the country was thus worth one-and-a-half votes in the towns, and this always worked in favour of the Nationalists.

Men in the Cabinet advised Smuts that now was the time to end this unequal system. Claude Sturrock, his able Minister of Transport (the man who had resigned with Hofmeyr in 1938), went to Smuts and urged him to reform the electoral system before 1948. But Smuts refused, saying (as Sturrock himself told me later) that he needed the conservative vote of the country districts as a protection against the socialism of the towns. There was Smuts the Boer general again—Smuts of the 1922 revolt.

So the lop-sided vote remained and undoubtedly brought about the defeat of Smuts's party in 1948—since when the Nationalists have increasingly battened on it.

The paradox of the situation was that Smuts might have won had he been less liberal and not frightened away the Boer conservatives who would have been glad to follow him. And he could have won had he been more liberal—had he been willing to accept the Indians on their own terms; had he been willing to re-admit the Coloured voters; had he been willing to throw off the heavy hand of the country electorate. But then Smuts had a blind spot. He knew it was a Coloured world, yet he would not see it. He was a liberal only in the light of his time and enclosed in his time like a fly in amber. For that matter, how much of a liberal was Jan Hofmeyr, who was afterwards blamed for Smuts's defeat? During the war years, when he was Minister of Finance, the Nationalists had pinned on him the nickname of "Jan Tax"; and after the war they had made play with a growing fear that Hofmeyr was a "kaffir-boetjie", a kaffir-buddy. When Smuts went, was such a man to lead the country? Yet Hofmeyr too was afraid of fancied socialism. And he too rejected the electoral reforms that would have shifted the power from platteland to town and kept Smuts's party in power.

But if Hofmeyr had really become a drag on his chief, he did not remain so for long. Early in 1948 he gave up the Department of Finance, pleading the strain of overwork, retaining Education and his position as Leader of the House. No one quite understood how much the burden of work had told on him until eleven months later. At the end of November 1948, Jan Hofmeyr became ill with a coronary thrombosis and on December 3 he was dead at the age of fifty-four.

So ended the high hopes which the country had had of the brilliant man from the universities. So were frustrated the students' prophecies—"Hoffy, one day Prime Minister"—which had come so near to fulfilment.

But much more than that died with Hofmeyr. Since 1948 the liberal cause in South Africa has had no spokesman or leader of political stature—and certainly no brain to match with his. He could have rallied liberal opinion and united liberal forces that have since wasted themselves in dissension and aimlessness.

Moreover, his death meant that when Smuts himself died eighteen months later, at his farm near Pretoria aged eighty, he was to have no successor. Smuts was a man beneath whose shade others found it difficult to grow. Only Hofmeyr had been able to flourish next to him, and now that he was gone there was none to take his place. The party would have other leaders, but Smuts would have no successor—a result that was tragic for the party and the country.

CHAPTER 12

Enter Apartheid

HAVING soaked up as much as we could take of the mists and fogs of Europe, my wife and I returned to South Africa at the end of 1950 in the *Bloemfontein Castle*. That was the ship the Union-Castle Line had built for the emigrant traffic to South Africa, and she was on her maiden voyage.

The sleek 18,000-ton motor vessel carried a full complement of passengers, who travelled more in the style of holidaymakers than emigrants. They included a considerable number of Germans going to South-West Africa, some settlers who announced themselves in the strange questions they asked at breakfast, and many more who were merely in search of the sun. But already the career of the beautiful ship was a matter of doubt. The attitude of the new government towards settlers was well known, and it was clear that as a carrier of immigrants the ship was to have a restricted career.

We returned to a South Africa that was still a country of cheap and plentiful food, low rents, good living and easygoing ways. The portions heaped on our plates in the dining cars of the South African Railways were unlike anything we'd seen in Europe; the white waiter or the Coloured bedsteward was delighted with his tip; the sunshine, the light clothes, the informality made one feel that this was a land of the rest-cure.

Johannesburg was booming again. New gold deposits had been uncovered west and south of the Rand in the Orange Free State; new towns with new names were claiming to be new El Dorados—Odendaalsrus, Virginia, Welkom; the nerve centre of the city, the Stock Exchange, was charged and bristling. The atmosphere in the drawing-rooms of Parktown and Houghton was much like what it had been in 1932 : if you couldn't talk share prices you had no one to talk to—unless of course you could talk about the gold price.

America was now paying 35 dollars (or £12 10s.) an ounce, and there was a widespread belief that she would be forced to pay more. Anyone returning from overseas like me was eagerly questioned on the possibility of the gold-price rise. When I showed complete ignorance on the subject I was regarded as a slightly unsatisfactory traveller.

We returned to a political scene where the Nationalists were still enjoying their "witbroodsdae", their honeymoon days, in government; where Jacobus Strauss (fifty, but looking little older than when he had frustrated the Nationalists at Germiston in 1932) was trying to strengthen his leadership of the Opposition which had descended to him from Smuts; and where an ex-servicemen's organisation called "The Torch Commando" was holding street demonstrations and making ineffectual protests against the Government's Nazi-like methods.

Back on the *Rand Daily Mail* I was soon writing editorials for Rayner Ellis, who had become editor during the war. A Cambridge man, he had arrived in Johannesburg in the 1920s, shy and spare-looking. Now he was in his rotund but vigorous middle-age and he had made the *Rand Daily Mail* the most outspoken critic of Dr. Malan's government. He wielded a pen like a lash and he used me often in helping to crack the whip. He incurred the increasing anger of the Nationalists, sometimes to an extent that embarrassed the newspaper owners, but he kept on doing it till his untimely death three years later. In his day the *Rand Daily Mail* became known as a bold defender of freedom of speech and the freedom of the individual, and so, I am happy to say, it has remained.

As soon as the Nationalists came into power in 1948 they began to fasten upon the country the clamps of apartheid—a way of life which, next to slavery, is the most arrogant ever devised in the name of civilised government. Their objectives were the subjection of the non-white population and the dominance of the Boer-Afrikaner section of the whites. They pursued the first purpose openly, and they never lost sight of the second. Their victory would in fact be meaningless for them if it did not promise the ultimate subjugation of the English—"ploughing under" was the term soon to be whispered—as well as the bondage of the Africans.

Right from the beginning the Nationalists were well placed for the furtherance of their ambitions. The morning after the elections they were not merely in control but in possession of almost all the departments of government—the police, the civil service, the state-owned South African Railways, and the education system. They had achieved this during the preceding two years in two ways, one open and the other clandestine.

By insisting on the bilingualism of people in government employ, by holding tests of proficiency in Afrikaans, by ensuring that promotion was withheld from anyone unable to use Afrikaans freely, they had gradually secured a majority of Afrikaners and Nationalists in the public services. The British had been reluctant to learn Afrikaans either because they disliked the language or, like English-speakers everywhere, they were slow at learning other tongues. They became stubborn and protested that they objected to having a language rammed down their throats. Or they found that with or without Afrikaans they could get better jobs in industry, better pay, better careers and a better life. In short, the Nationalists used the indifference of English-speakers towards minor languages to elbow them out of government, and the English had only themselves to blame for the result.

Perhaps they did not grudge the Afrikaners their success. Temperamentally the arrangement suited both sections. The Afrikaners, coming largely from the country, and accustomed to looking to the Government for assistance, were glad to have sheltered jobs in the public services; the English were happy to snatch the plums that were going in the more cosmopolitan world of industry, commerce and finance.

The Nationalists also had other ways of climbing into the seats of power. They had a secret society known as the

"Broederbond" (Band of Brothers), which was dedicated to the promotion of Afrikaner Nationalist interests in all walks of life. The Broeders worked through an underground chain organisation, and they had men in high places where they were able to advance other Broeders into similar positions. Under the Smuts regime the Broederbond's activities were checked, and men in high posts known to be of the secret fraternity were ordered to resign. But with the Nationalists in power again came the hey-day of the Broeders. It was common knowledge that no one could hope for preferment in the upper layers of the public services unless he was one of them or in good standing with them—which meant that he was a "boetie" (a buddy) of theirs, a brother of the Brothers.

If an appointment to any public office, from technician to Cabinet Minister, seemed odd or unexpected, the explanation was that it had been contrived by the Broeders. If any man's rise in the public service, whether in the judicial system, the education department, the armed forces or the railway and air services, was unusually sudden, rapid or short-cut, it was for similar reasons. The helping hand of a Broeder was suspected even if it was not there—but mostly it was.

In these ways the railways, civil service, post office, police and educational administration had become Afrikanerised, and when the Nationalists took over they were in immediate command of the "right-minded" or "national-minded" personnel. Only in one department did the Nationalists find themselves at a disadvantage. During the war the Department of Defence had inevitably grown in importance and was naturally Smuts-oriented. The Nationalists were to lose little time adjusting the situation and showing their sentiments towards the men who had fought in the war against Hitler.

A week after Dr. Malan's Government took office in June 1948, the Minister of Justice Mr. C. R. Swart, announced the release from prison of several men who had been sentenced to long terms of imprisonment during the war for sabotage or treasonable activities. One of them was a former heavyweight boxer, Robey Leibbrandt, who had landed from a German submarine on the west coast of Africa and had been sentenced to death. The penalty was commuted to life imprisonment, but he served only five years. Mr. Swart (to become the first State President of the Republic of South Africa in 1961) said on releasing him: "This decision was taken as a result of the deep desire of the new Government to relieve the people of the Union from the strain of the war years and to endeavour to end all the unpleasantness and rancour which followed from it." The announcement of the release of these men immediately gave rise to protest meetings, largely attended by ex-servicemen, in Johannesburg, Pretoria and other places. But the Government turned the deaf ear that was soon to become habitual towards any protests from the non-Nationalist or non-Afrikaner section of the population.

A month later the Minister of Defence bowler-hatted Major-General W. H. Evered Poole who had commanded the South African Sixth Armoured Division in Italy with distinction, and sent him to Berlin to be head of the South African military mission, a position of minimal importance. A year later, similar treatment was meted out to the General Manager of Railways, Marshall Clark, another wartime appointment made by Smuts with brilliant results. Clark was shunted to the Central African Transport Conference as interim secretary. At about the same time the Chief of the General Staff, General Beyers, resigned after accusing the Minister, Mr. Erasmus, of undermining discipline and creating jobs for political friends.

This was when Mr. Erasmus began designing uniforms for various units, removing British style wherever he could on the principle apparently that if he could not change the composition of the army at once, he could change its appearance. Showing a distinct predilection for headgear of a Central European or even Ruritanian cut, he was a delight to the cartoonists, especially to Bob Connolly of the *Rand Daily Mail*, an American from Paterson, New Jersey. Connolly made great play with caricatures of the Minister dressed in all the uniforms he was designing for others.

With immigrants still entering the country at the rate of two or three thousand a month, the Nationalist Press raised the cry, "What we have won by the cradle, we must not lose to the steamship", and the Government at once took steps to check the flow of "voting cattle". It passed the Citizenship Act of 1949 depriving British subjects of the right to acquire South African nationality after two years' residence and laying down a naturalisation procedure after five years usually demanded of non-British aliens.

It also discouraged and reduced the flow of immigrants by administrative methods. In 1948 the number of settlers had risen to 35,000. But it was down to 14,000 the following year, and in 1950 the 12,000 newcomers were actually outnumbered by those who emigrated.

Humbling the British, whether in the army, the civil service or the citizenship laws, was only a petty process, however, by comparison with the Government's full programme. But before the Nationalists could mount the steps of their racialist projects, they had to strengthen their position in Parliament. Their majority of four or five votes in the Assembly was too tenuous to be relied on for long, and they had to find a way of augmenting it. They had a simple expedient at hand.

South-West Africa had been administered by South Africa under a mandate of the League of Nations since the First World War. It was not and is not part of South Africa, but South Africans have always liked to think of it as a fifth province. The Nationalists decided to give the territory representation in Parliament by way of seats in the Assembly and the Senate. They were expected to allot them three Assembly members, but the Nationalists decided that this was an occasion for generosity and gave them six in the Assembly and four in the Senate—all this for about 26,000 white voters. It made a vote in the territory worth nearly three times a vote in Johannesburg or Pretoria.

The Nationalists felt sure that their generosity would pay. They expected the Germans of South-West Africa to vote for them solidly, and so they did. The Nationalists won all the seats in the territory and so they were able to increase their Assembly majority to a comfortable ten. Now they were ready for the apartheid legislation for which until now they had been getting into position and sharpening their weapons.

They already had on the Statute Book the rough foundations for the structure they were preparing to build. They had the Native Land Acts which went back to 1913 and 1936 and limited the African population to the possession of not more than about 13 per cent of the land of the country. They had the Colour Bar laws which excluded Africans from skilled work in industry. They had the Native Urban Areas Act of 1923 and 1945 controlling the residence of Africans in and about the towns. And they had the Pass Laws, under which arrests and convictions were now running at more than 200,000 a year.

Hertzog's two-stream policy had long ago determined that there were to be two nations in South Africa, the English-speaking and the Afrikaans-speaking. The apartheid laws to be passed from 1949 onwards were designed to separate off a third, a black or African nation; and a fourth, the Coloureds; and if the Nationalist philosophy was to be carried to its logical conclusion, a fifth, an Indian nation. And all were to be apart—separated by legal, social and physical barriers that were henceforth to be the distinguishing mark of white civilisation in South Africa, Land of Apartheid, Land of Barriers.

First came the prohibition of the Mixed Marriages Act of 1949, prohibiting marriages between whites and non-whites. Designed of course to prevent miscegenation, it could itself achieve little, because miscegenation is no respecter of wedlock. The following year, therefore, came the Immorality Amendment Act which made sexual intercourse between white and non-white illegal whether in or out of wedlock. But here the Nationalists struck a snag. They knew it and they were ready for it.

In South Africa, a country habitually aware of white and non-white status, it is not always easy to tell whether a person is white or Coloured. There are many Coloured people who could pass as white in most parts of the world. On the other hand, many people are accepted white though they display clear characteristics of colour. When I returned to South Africa at the end of 1950, I could not help noticing people in white coaches on the train from Cape Town who by all South African rules were Coloured. Yet they were travelling as whites among whites.

Something had to be done about this. So the Nationalists established the Population Register or South African Stud Book (as it is often called), designed to give every adult documentary proof of his or her ancestry at birth, death and marriage—especially marriage. The document was called an Identity Card, and as Africans already carried passes in and out of jail, Government spokesmen argued that it was reasonable to expect whites to have identity cards. But the real purpose of the Population Registration Act was to sift out the Coloured folk from the whites and to reduce all who had one-sixth black blood to the level of non-Europeans.

Having thus legislated for sex apartheid, the Nationalists turned their attention to producing even more tangible manifestations of their new racial order. Contemplating the country that had grown up in three centuries since the first landing of the Dutch in Table Bay in 1652, they saw it as a great and untidy mingling of peoples. There were whites; there were blacks (Africans) of many tribes; there were Coloureds (half-castes) of Malay, European and African descent; there were Indians living in close Hindu and Moslem communities; there were even some small groups of Chinese traders.

This mingling had been going on from the days of the first Dutch governor, Commander Jan van Riebeeck, the Founder of South Africa, who had imported slaves from Java and Madagascar and had encouraged his men in the Dutch East India Company to marry native Hottentot women. In those days there was no colour pride at the Cape settlement. One of the most brilliant of the early governors, Simon van der Stel, who arrived in 1679 and whose ability earned him the title in history of the "Second Founder", was the dark-complexioned son of a Dutch governor of Mauritius and his Indian wife known as Monica of the Coast, a fact carefully withheld from all schoolbooks.

The Nationalists surveyed this social, geographic and historic mixture of many races and they conceived the wild desire to unscramble the egg. The instrument they created for the purpose was the Group Areas Act, the most complicated, jerry-built and patched-up piece of legislation on the Statute Book, or perhaps on any statute book. Dr. Malan described it during the second reading in Parliament as "the essence of the apartheid policy". It was first passed in 1950 and has since been amended, re-amended and further amended at least ten times. What else could be expected of a law designed to unravel the strands of the South African population, evict people from their homes or places of work or both, and confine them to their own delimited and restricted areas?

There was not, it should be noted, to be complete territorial segregation of the races. Even the most ardent of the Nationalists have given this idea up as impossible, though the wisps of the dream linger on and occasionally flicker up in their talk and speculations. They have accepted that there will always be large numbers of non-whites in the white parts of South Africa, and that the whites in their own parts of the country (which comprise more than four-fifths of it) will always be outnumbered by the non-whites. When in 1956 I interviewed Professor F. R. Tomlinson, chairman of a commission which had just drawn up a voluminous report on the African areas, he spoke of this as a "terrific dilemma" of the white man and observed resignedly, "Perhaps South Africa will always be in that dilemma".

The main purpose of the Group Areas Act was to "cleanse" the white towns of non-white enclaves—to filter out, so to speak, the Africans, the Coloureds, the Indians, the Malays and even the few Chinese, and confine them in their own townships beyond the city borders (twenty miles beyond if necessary), keep them isolated from the whites and from each other, and allow them into the white towns only as servants or commuting labourers. So while in other countries the commuting classes are the well-to-do or the middle-classes, who live away from the city's congested streets and smoky air, in South Africa the poorest working masses are the great commuters between town and suburb.

One of the most aggressive measures passed by the Nationalists early in their regime was the Law for the Suppression of Communism, which has caused many a stormy debate in Parliament and out since 1950. Not that Communism has ever had a powerful hold in South Africa; on the contrary, it has made little progress. Under this law the Government gave the Minister of Justice power to act without reference to the courts, making him policeman, prosecutor and judge in his own cause, and leaving the victim without right of appeal to any judicial body. The Opposition protested vigorously that the Minister would be able to use this law not merely against Communists, but against any opponents of the Government; and so it has proved. As that cool-headed historian Professor Eric A. Walker has put it in his standard *History of Southern Africa*—"The Minister of Justice asked for almost dictatorial powers to deal decisively with anyone who was even faintly tinctured Red."

Strictly speaking, the law for the Suppression of Communism is not an apartheid law; but it was to be used to smear the Government's opponents and label as Communists those who merely opposed its apartheid policies and laws.

In 1953 came the Separate Amenities Act compelling local authorities to exclude non-whites from public premises and vehicles and provide separate facilities. In the same year the Bantu Education Act transferred African education from the Provinces into the hands of the central Government for its better control. In 1956 job reservation was made possible under the innocently named Industrial Conciliation Act and under the pious pretence of safeguarding "against inter-racial competition". It was not enough that non-whites were excluded from skilled jobs; they also had to be excluded from certain unskilled jobs which had to be reserved for whites.

It became a habit of the Nationalists to invent innocent titles for their apartheid laws. When they planned the removal of non-whites from the white universities, they called the measure "The Extension of University Education Act", though as far as the non-whites were concerned it meant exactly the opposite. And when in 1951, they began to manoeuvre for the fulfilment of their old dream to remove the Coloureds from the common voters' roll, they called the legislation they devised "The Separate Representation of Voters Act". This was the measure that was to lead to a long legal battle over the inert body of the South African constitution and was to remain in doubt for five years.

CHAPTER 13

The £20 Senate

My beat on the *Rand Daily Mail* was an eccentric one. I was not regarded as a political man (for which I thanked my stars); but I could apparently write editorials with a bite, and I could write theatre notices that were interesting even when the shows were not. Soon therefore my daily work went into a kind of oscillation between editorials and correspondence by day and book reviewing and first nights in the evening. But I had retained some facility at shorthand from the days when we used to report Smuts or Hertzog in two columns of solid 7 point type. I had retained it by having acquired the habit of taking shorthand notes whenever I spoke on the telephone (sometimes to the astonishment of the person at the other end), and this made me useful for certain outside jobs that now and then released me from office routine.

That was how in the third week of October 1956 I found myself in an old brick building in Bloemfontein, the slumbering little Orange Free State capital that calls itself "the Centre City". I was here with other reporters to watch eleven judges at work, considering the validity of a law by which the Nationalists hoped to gain a purpose they had sought for thirty years.

The building in which they sat from Monday to Friday on a Bench which stretched the whole width of the gloomy hall, was the old Raadsaal or Parliament House of the former Orange Free State Republic, now used as a Court of Appeal, the highest in the land. This was the place where in 1909 the leading South African statesmen (Botha, Smuts, Hertzog, Starr Jameson and John X. Merriman among them) had met in convention to lay down the basic tenets of the South African constitution to be embodied in the Act of Union. There were two plaques in the wall behind the judges' Bench recording the final sitting for the benefit of future generations. Now, by one of the ironies of history, the judges were met here to decide whether the law-making of 1909 was proof against the contrivancies of 1956—whether, in effect, an honourable undertaking in one generation could be circumvented by a legal process in another.

The Act of Union, which came into force in 1910, contained provisions laying down that the voting rights of the non-white people of the Cape Province could not be changed except by a majority of two-thirds of both Houses of Parliament (Assembly and Senate sitting together). To the Nationalist Party these entrenched clauses, as they were called, became a provocation and a challenge. Every Nationalist leader had his mind fixed on overcoming them in one way or another, so that the non-white voters (relic of British liberalism) could be separated out from the whites.

Hertzog had removed the Africans when Smuts had agreed to his Representation of Natives Act of 1936. Now it was the turn of the 24,000 half-caste voters of the Cape, to whom Dr. Malan's Nationalists turned their attentions almost as soon as they had warmed their seats in Parliament. But now the Opposition (both before and after Smuts's death) was not going to agree. It was strong enough to deny Malan the two-thirds majority that Hertzog had obtained in 1936, and the fight was on.

The Separate Representation of Voters Act, which provided for the removal of the Coloureds from the roll and their separate representation in Parliament by four white members, was first passed in 1951 by a simple majority. The United Party took the matter to Bloemfontein, and in the following year the Act was declared void by the Appeal Court.

For the time being the Government was thwarted, but not defeated. In 1952 they turned Parliament into a "High Court of Parliament" and at once gave it the task of adjudicating on its own law and validating the Separate Representation of Voters Act.

This was the clumsiest and most transparent manoeuvre ever devised by a legislative body. It soon had the newspaper cartoonists busy on heaven-sent material, and it had the country in laughter. My stable-companion, Bob Connolly, made great sport depicting the Parliamentarians sitting about in full-bottomed wigs, and ribald stories went round the country of Nationalist Members addressing each other as "yer honour" and "milord".

Indifferent to lampoons, the "High Court of Parliament" adjudicated on the Separate Representation of Voters Act (without full-bottomed wigs) and dutifully declared it to be valid. The United Party at once took the High Court of Parliament Act to law, and the answer came quickly in terms which hardly concealed the judges' scorn. The Appeal Court ruled in November 1952 that the "High Court of Parliament" was not a court of law; it was simply Parliament functioning under another name and what it could not do as a Parliament it could not do by calling itself something else.

Thwarted again, the Nationalists had to think of another manoeuvre, and this time they thought of a "packing" device. They could not pack the House of Assembly, which was elected by the registered voters; but they could pack the Senate, which was partly elected by electoral colleges of Members of Parliament and Provincial Councils, and partly appointed.

They therefore produced and forced through Parliament the 1955 Senate Act, which enlarged the Senate from 48 to 89 members, and enlarged it in such a way that 77 of the 89 would be Nationalists. These, together with the Nationalists in the Assembly (now 91), would give the Government a two-thirds majority to carry through the anti-Coloured legislation on which it had set its heart. But this Senate Act was also to be tested in the courts, and that was why eleven judges, the Chief Justice and ten other Judges of Appeal, met in Bloemfontein in October 1956, and wrangled with counsel for a week.

The new Senate was usually referred to as "the inflated Senate" or even "the £20 Senate", the name by which it will probably go down in history. It acquired this title because when the Government had to fill the additional seats, there was a great rush of party men eager to serve and fill the well-upholstered benches of the Upper House. The little Senate building was going to be crowded, but still tolerably comfortable, and its occupants well rewarded. The Nationalist Party therefore ruled that nominations were to be restricted to paid-up members who were willing to make a non-returnable deposit of £20, which went into party funds. This had the desired effect of limiting the number of aspirants and obtaining contributions to branch treasuries.

To a public with little knowledge of legal principle or hair-splitting the artifice of the Senate Act was only too apparent. But the Nationalists protested that the thought of going to the polls side by side with Coloured people was intolerable.

The Leader of the Opposition, Jacobus Strauss, speaking in the Johannesburg City Hall, condemned the Bill as one of "evil intent", a "horrible political fraud conceived for the sake of power politics". Amid protests, counter-protests and "Black Sash" parades, it was forced through Parliament, and then the lawyers got ready for the legal battle.

The Act came unscathed through the High Court, and then it was the turn of the eleven judges at Bloemfontein. This was the first time that so many judges had sat on one Bench in any court, for the Government in an ostentatious demonstration of righteousness, had enlarged the Appeal Court from the original six specially for the consideration of constitutional cases. In Parliament, however, Strauss criticised the manner in which they had been appointed. The Opposition newspapers recalled a statement made by Mr. Donges, the Minister of the Interior, in 1953 that "unless Parliament can be assured that its Acts will not be declared invalid, it will be compelled to use the American expedient of appointing judges who share its views". And a majority group of members of the Johannesburg Bar pointed out "that there are several judges whose eminence, ability, and experience are such that it is incredible that all of them should be passed over in any genuine attempt to strengthen the Appeal Court".

But they *were* passed over. Judges were appointed who might never have reached such eminence in any other circumstances and whose sole claim to distinction was henceforth to be that they had sat for a crucial five days at Bloemfontein. As matters turned out, however, the Government could have dispensed with their aid. The issue at Bloemfontein was to be decided not as a matter of morality but law, and what the simplest person in the land could recognise for trickery, the greatest lawyers in the land (but one) could still regard as good in law.

Head of the court was Chief Justice Centlivres, a weather-worn rock of a man looking something like the great pile of "hundred books" which his name signified. When I arrived in Bloemfontein for the case, I found that he and I were staying ing the same hotel. One evening when I stopped him in the lobby as he was going in to dinner, and asked him a question to clarify some formal point, the mountain shuddered ever so slightly and muttered agreeably from a great height.

With him on the Bench was Justice H. A. Fagan, a volatile man snapping questions, a former Minister of Native Affairs and soon to follow Centlivres to the head of the court. There, too, was Justice Oliver Schreiner, solid, grave, whom I remembered from my student days when he used to take law classes in the late afternoons in the building with the atlantids. He was a nephew of Olive Schreiner, author of *The Story of an African Farm*, the first South African novel to win fame, and though he had been a dull lecturer he had won great prestige as a barrister and even more as a judge.

Six advocates faced the Judges of Appeal. The attack on the Senate Act was led by Graeme Duncan, Q.C., a barrister of the hatchet-faced unemotional school; and the defence was headed by D. P. de Villiers, Q.C., a man of thirty-seven with eloquence but temperamentally not altogether proof against the ordeal he was to face in that court. For the outstanding impression with which I came away from that five days' hearing was of the old judges seizing on his arguments, tearing and worrying them, and the young barrister, bruised and shaken in the encounter, but stubbornly holding his ground.

Every man there knew well enough the rights and wrongs of the issue. The argument, however, was eventually to be not about right and wrong, but about the validity of a legal framework which made ordinary moral considerations irrelevant.

Mr. Duncan argued that the Senate created by the Senate Act of 1955 was not a House of Parliament within the meaning of the entrenched clauses protecting the rights of Coloured voters. It was a "packed" Senate, packed in order "to get a majority for a particular measure".

He kept hammering at that word "packed", which of course carried the essence of the case.

Judge Schreiner, a man of taste, disliked the word "packed", which was capable of emotional meaning. He suggested an objective expression like "ad hoc". He preferred to speak of an "ad hoc Senate".

Once during the second day's hearing the ghosts of history stalked into the hall. One of the judges, Justice de Beer, inquired whether the entrenching proviso safeguarding the Coloureds was not just a subterfuge. "The Cape would never have come into the Union if the Cape vote had been abolished."

Mr. Duncan: "Then the Cape voters were bluffed."

Judge de Beer: "Their consciences must have been very elastic. They must have understood that the Coloured vote was transitionary and it would pass away."

Mr. Duncan squarely faced the two plaques behind the judges commemorating the final sittings of the 1909 convention. "Milord," he said, "this discussion should have taken place in 1909 after the convention had dispersed. One can imagine the delegates sitting down to tea and asking each other—'Now what exactly does this entrenching proviso mean?' ... I maintain it was meant to be a solemn guarantee, not a subterfuge..."

In spite of Judge Schreiner's suggestion that "ad hoc" was the more proper term, that word "packed" kept coming up like a chorus throughout the argument. Often it was implied rather than expressed, as when the Government's counsel, De Villiers, wrestling with the judges, was held in a vice of questions.

He argued that "only the legal effect of the Act" was relevant.

Judge Fagan snapped at him: "Was there any other purpose in passing the Senate Act except to get a two-thirds majority? It was passed for that purpose only. Is that relevant?"

De Villiers: "We have the Prime Minister's statement that there was a constitutional deadlock. He said he had to act in the interests of the country and end the deadlock."

Chief Justice: "His hope was that the increased Senate would provide the two-thirds majority?"

De Villiers: "An increased Parliament."

Judge Hoexter: "I suggest to you all these steps were part of a scheme to change the constitution by a two-thirds majority."

De Villiers: "Whose scheme?"

Judge Hoexter: "I speak of the Prime Minister's intention."

De Villiers: "He says that as far as the Government was concerned, there was no scheme envisaged which would invade any rights."

Judges Hoexter and Schreiner together: "That is a matter of law!"

Judge Fagan: "The appellant says that they would never have increased the Senate to 89 for any other purpose? Is that relevant?... If you put history before you, are you attacking it or saying it is irrelevant?"

De Villiers: "... As for the Members of Parliament, who can say what motivated them?"

But the snappy judge would not let the advocate go. He kept demanding: "Is the question of motive relevant or not? If it is relevant can we go into the facts?"

At last the advocate answered: "I am prepared to admit that the purpose was to end the constitutional deadlock, but that is irrelevant."

And so the hair-splitting went on till late on Friday afternoon, and in the last half hour they were still arguing about "packed Houses", "ad hoc Houses" and "other mad ideas about Houses". This last expression was used by the Government counsel, De Villiers, and Opposition counsel, Duncan, seized on it.

"It might have been better," he said, "to have had a mad Senate than a packed Senate. Mad people might leave me on the roll. A packed Senate won't."

And he had the last word.

But the battle for the Coloured vote was a lost one.

When judgment was delivered on November 9, ten judges found in favour of the Government, saying that its legislative scheme could not be attacked in law. Only one, Judge Schreiner, found that law must go together with morality. He declared that a "Senate constituted ad hoc" was not a House of Parliament within the meaning of the constitution, and he found against the Senate Act.

So the verdict was ten to one in favour of the Government. But it would have made little difference to the Nationalists had it gone the other way. They were determined to remove the Coloured people from the common roll, and it is quite certain that had they been thwarted by the courts again, they would not have shrunk from destroying the whole constitution for the sake of uprooting one proviso of it.

The 24,000 Coloured voters of the Cape Province were accordingly placed on a separate roll so that they would not jostle the white voters when going to the polls, and they were given the right to send four white representatives to the Assembly.

Three or four years later, the "£20 Senate" was dissolved and replaced by a normal Senate of 54 members. It had served its purpose.

CHAPTER 14

The Treason Trial

BEFORE the end of 1956 the next chapter opened in the story of the Nationalist Government's accumulation of power. It was the Treason Trial and was a build-up of power not by legislation but by intimidation—by a display of force against the opponents of the Government. And though the trial failed as a prosecution, it fulfilled that ulterior purpose.

On the morning of December 5, 1956, the people of South Africa awoke to hear of police raids in various parts of the country and arrests of scores of people on allegations of high treason. "Awoke" is the right word, for this was the first great swoop that set the pattern for the "pre-dawn raid" later to become a routine operation of the South African police. Men had been standing by at headquarters since 2 a.m. and by morning 140 persons had been arrested in Johannesburg, Cape Town, Durban, Port Elizabeth and other towns. Three military transport planes were used to concentrate them in Johannesburg.

Detectives of the Special Branch had raided not only homes, but also offices of political organisations like the African National Congress, the Transvaal Indian Congress and the Congress of Democrats, from which they removed loads of books and documents. Among the papers seized were a copy of Father Trevor Huddleston's book, *Naught for your Comfort,* a life of Dr. Johnson, and an anthology of English poetry, which one may presume the detectives did not pause to read.

The people arrested were men and women of all races, and they included one of the Africans' white representatives in

Parliament (L. B. Lee-Warden), a Methodist clergyman, two Anglican clergymen, the acting principal of Fort Hare (Professor Z. K. Matthews), the non-white university college, Albert Lutuli (president of the African National Congress and former chief of a Zulu tribe), two barristers, attorneys, trade union officials, housewives, doctors, shopkeepers—all of them associated with liberal political movements.

Newspapermen knew what there was to be known of the work of the African National Congress which had continued for thirty years or more ineffectually but lately with growing influence. We knew of the internal struggles between the moderates under Lutuli and the extremists, but even in the agitations of the extreme wing which afterwards formed the Pan-African Congress under Sobukwe, there was nothing to suggest anything so well planned or far-reaching as treason would have to be. There was no one who knew how to plot or organise to such purpose. If the police had any information in advance of what had come our way on the newspapers, it would be very startling indeed.

By the time the court proceedings opened two weeks later, the number of prisoners totalled 151. There was no court large enough to hold them, and a court room was therefore arranged in the Johannesburg Drill Hall, which was at the Witwatersrand Defence Headquarters in Twist Street. There could have been no more unsuitable venue for a trial. A Bench had to be set up for the magistrate (for this was to be only the preparatory examination), a dock improvised for the prisoners, accommodation somehow set aside for the public and tables for the Press . . . and all in a hall of about 90 ft. by 120 ft.

The opening of the examination was in keeping with the clumsiness with which the entire proceedings were conceived, the kind of affair (sometimes called "The Twist Street Affair") which has prompted someone to describe the Nationalist regime as "a tyranny tempered by inefficiency". It was a hot midsummer, six days before Christmas, with the sun burning from a brilliant sky. The streets around the Drill Hall were cordoned off by squads of police—I had to show my Press pass to get by—but that did not prevent a crowd that reached about 5,000 from collecting around the building.

I was one of forty reporters present (seven or eight from overseas) all for a first day's hearing that lasted only twenty minutes. When proceedings began, it was found that there were no interpreters in court for the Africans, and there was no loudspeaker system amid the foggy acoustics. So the court adjourned till the afternoon.

The 151—the twenty-three whites separate from the non-whites—sat on ten rows of chairs, and when they had their lunch—prison fare on trays, or food brought by friends—the hall looked like a picnic ground.

After lunch the courtroom was still without loudspeakers, but in the street outside there was a great mass of people pressing up against the court-yard gates and railings. They were mostly Africans, shouting, singing and giving the "thumbs-up Africa!" sign whenever they thought they had a glimpse of the prisoners in the yard behind.

To get into the courtroom now was not easy. When, after pushing my way through the crowd, I came up against the closed iron gate and tried to open it, I was at once prevented by three harassed constables in khaki. They were afraid to open the gates lest the crowd broke through.

"You'll have to climb over if you want to get in," they said.

So with their assistance I clambered over the railings set in a low brick wall, about 5 ft. high in all, and presently I was astonished to see the somewhat rotund barristers doing the same.

When the court resumed, it was clear that no public-address system would be ready till the following day, and the court was adjourned till next morning.

Next day was the day of the shooting—also the day of the cage.

Overnight the court officials had worked to some purpose. They had installed loudspeakers over the prisoners' dock and, the better to control the prisoners, they had enclosed the dock area in a six-foot high fence made of stout diamond-mesh wire and iron poles—the kind builders use for scaffolding. When the magistrate took his seat on the bench, the 151 prisoners faced him from inside a wire cage.

At once defending counsel, Maurice Franks, Q.C., rose to protest. He was a man of grave deliberate speech, but this time he could scarcely conceal his emotions. "The scene is unprecedented. The accused are caged. I am most anxious not to allow my indignation to get the better of me . . . I mean caged like wild beasts . . . it is a shame on everybody who is responsible . . ."

He added that he and other counsel had agreed that unless the cage was removed they would withdraw from the proceedings. The white-haired magistrate, Mr. F. C. A. Wessel, mild-voiced but visibly distressed, ordered an adjournment for consultation.

While he and the barristers conferred in a back room, the prisoners sat or strolled about the cage. I went up to talk to some of them and presently found myself facing Albert Lutuli on the other side of the wire. The ex-Chief, who had been deposed from his chieftainship by the Government in 1951 because he preferred to remain president of the African National Congress, was now in his sixties. He was well-built, broad-shouldered and calm. Talking through the wire he was friendly and told me that the police treated him courteously. He had no complaints against the food or the accommodation. He smiled when I turned the conversation to the court proceedings and to the allegations soon to be made in open court; but there was little time to discuss them before the court re-assembled.

The barristers returned from the magistrate's office. It had been agreed that the cage would be modified (lowered and opened in front), and the hearing was resumed, but not for long. The prosecutor was outlining his case, reading from pages of foolscap in a dull monotone that contrasted with the sensational allegations he was supposed to be making. He quoted from documents going back to 1953 and dealing with the activities of a so-called National Liberation Movement.

He quoted from a "Freedom Charter" (which had been in circulation for two years) and from speeches made on various occasions against "reactionaries at work in this country", urging a "programme of political education", the "need for a strong democratic front" and for "organising the people against the Fascist reactionaries". The prisoners looked on from the cage scarcely following the arid recital, but some of them burst into laughter when the prosecutor read out that "Congress wants money to buy machine guns".

When the prosecutor seemed to be approaching his main accusations uproar broke out in the street. In a few moments the court became half-empty. The pressmen left their tables. The din from the rioting filled the hall and the prosecutor's voice faded in the noise.

With other reporters I had left the courtroom, going to the assistance of one of our photographers who had been taken into temporary custody by the police. I found him in a small room at the back of the yard arguing with officials about his camera. The police resented the activities of photographers and needed little pretext for intervention when they saw them close at hand. The discussion was suddenly cut short when the sound of firing broke from the street thirty or forty yards away—first sporadic shots, then a burst which might have come from ten or more guns. The young policemen, some of them under twenty, were armed with sten guns and I had seen them that day swinging them jauntily.

The shooting was followed by running in all directions. Before I followed into the street I made sure that the firing had stopped. In front of the building I came up against Dr. Ambrose Reeves, the wiry little Bishop of Johannesburg. "They've lost control!" he exclaimed. "They've lost control!" Then he ran past me holding a hand up and appealing to the crowd to keep calm.

The shooting was the culmination to a morning of anger. The crowd was resentful of the small numbers allowed in the public enclosure in the hall. They pressed against the gates and railings. The police decided to clear them and made a baton charge. This was answered by stone-throwing from a vacant lot across the street. And the reply came from the guns. The police claimed that they had shot above the heads of the crowd, and the injuries were fortunately few. That was the high-point in the excitement of the treason trial—a midsummer noon with the sunshine brilliant in the street and women wailing from the cage in the gloomy courtroom as they heard the firing outside.

The rest was a long and slow anti-climax that dragged on for more than four years—dreary for the people involved (out on bail but unable to earn a living) and gradually drained of interest for the public. The preparatory examination lasted a year and ended with ninety-two people being formally charged with high treason, the others (including Lutuli) being discharged.

The trial proper was held before a Special Court in Pretoria in a building known as the Old Synagogue because that's what it was. In November 1958, the charges against sixty-one more were suspended, leaving only thirty-one to face the three judges.

The evidence against the accused never looked more impressive than on the opening days when I sat there listening to the droning voice of the prosecutor and to police witnesses stumbling through their barely coherent evidence and reading from documents which it sometimes seemed doubtful that they themselves understood.

On March 29, 1961, Mr. Justice Rumpff, the presiding judge, took thirty-eight minutes to read the unanimous verdict of the court declaring all the accused to be "not guilty". The court had been unable to find any policy or conspiracy among the accused or their organisations to overthrow the state, or that the state pictured in the Freedom Charter was a Communist state, or that the African National Congress had been taken over by Communists. The court was also unable to find any proof that the accused had knowledge of or propagated the doctrine of violent revolution.

So ended the most extraordinary trial in South African history, an extraordinary trial by any standards. It was claimed as a vindication of the integrity of the courts of law, but it also demonstrated the clumsiness, even the naivete, of Nationalist Government methods.

The night the verdict was pronounced there was singing and dancing in Orlando as the acquitted men were feted from house to house, and "Nkosi Sikele Africa" sounded in massed voices down the long narrow streets.

CHAPTER 15

In Parliament

EVERY January the Government of South Africa extricates itself from its offices and filing cabinets in the Union Buildings at Pretoria, and moves a thousand miles south-west to the coast at Cape Town for the parliamentary session. This annual journey, which used to be done entirely by rail in what was popularly known as "the Zoo Train", is necessitated by the system of dual capitals which South Africa has observed since 1910.

That was another of the extraordinary conditions on which the union of the four provinces was brought about. Pretoria claimed the seat of government as the old Boer capital of the Transvaal Republic. Cape Town claimed it as the Mother City, the oldest city in South Africa. The compromise reached was to make Cape Town the legislative capital, where Parliament would sit for four or five months each summer making laws, and Pretoria the administrative capital, or seat of the executive, for the rest of the year.

The arrangement has often been criticised and even ridiculed, but all suggestions for change have had to contend with the jealousies between the Cape and the Transvaal. They have also foundered on the still more compelling consideration that the annual change of climate from the Transvaal highlands to the Cape Peninsula is good for the government and its officers, and the relaxed atmosphere of Cape Town in summer (a favourite holiday resort) is good for Members of Parliament.

In 1957 I joined one of the Zoo Trains to go and do some reporting from the Press Gallery. The editor of the *Rand*

Daily Mail was now A. P. ("Paddy") Cartwright, a man with a dome of a head who had a cramped handwriting but a lucid style. He also had the habit of addressing everyone around him, even his fair secretary, as "Colonel". No one could explain this. He had been a naval officer during the war, and being the most senior South African available in the Pacific at the time was among those who accompanied Admiral Fraser at the formal surrender of the Japanese on the U.S. battleship *Missouri*.

He asked me (Paddy Cartwright never instructed) to go to Parliament and send the *Rand Daily Mail* more readable reports than we were getting from the agency. All the newspapers were served from Parliament by the jointly-owned South African Press Association which, having to please both Afrikaans (pro-government) and English (anti-government) newspapers, reduced its reports to a non-committal greyness.

I accepted the assignment readily, glad to get down to the sea for a term, and glad to break away once more from my desk and first-night beat and do some straightforward reporting. Moreover, a measure already known as the "Church Clause" was due to come before Parliament and without doubt there would be wrangling (and copy) over this niggardly piece of Verwoerdian legislation.

So for a number of weeks in the late summer I sat in the Press Gallery of the House of Assembly or haunted its lobbies, conscious most of the time of that feeling of quarantine which the South African Parliament likes to impose on newspaper correspondents. A pressman in Parliament, especially if he is from "die Engelse Pers" (the English-language Press) is very soon made to feel as though he is suffering from a highly contagious disease. Although he is permitted to appear in certain of the lobbies, he has to observe the utmost circumspection in approaching a Member, lest in some subtle way he should compromise him or subtract from his dignity. Moreover, certain lobbies are sealed to him, and one afternoon when I unwittingly took a step—and by a step I mean no more than a step—into this forbidden territory, I was brought to a halt by a liveried attendant who made me feel—one step more and I would have been thrown into chains.

The Members are aware of the asperity with which Parliament officially regards pressmen, and to soften it they occasionally invite you to lunch in the Members' dining-room—if they like your newspaper. Otherwise the pressmen (unless they leave the House) lunch at a long table in a roped-off corner.

Six weeks of tip-toeing about the lobbies and sitting in the Press Gallery listening to the debates droning up from below through a blur of acoustics, was going to be quite enough for me.

By now Dr. Malan, the Father of Apartheid, was in retirement. He had led his Nationalist Party to another successful election in 1953, assisted by a new delimitation of constituencies and the growing fears of black nationalism now bearing the face of the Mau Mau of Kenya. Throughout the 'fifties, as the tide of black nationalism rose in Africa, the fort of white nationalism was to gather more and more adherents at the southern tip of the continent. So Malan saw his party strengthened and entrenched in the seats of power and at the end of 1954 decided to retire.

He was then eighty, to his people a benignant father figure, but to the younger men in the party a man in the way. They were impatient to forge ahead with their apartheid plans. So they decently helped out of office the weary old Prime Minister, honourably farewelled him, and elbowed his nominated successor into the wings. They chose J. C. Strydom, a Transvaaler who had made his name in politics as "the Lion of the North", but who was to achieve little else. Illness and death were to make Strydom's tenure of office as Prime Minister brief and undistinguished.

His successor was already waiting behind him in the person of Dr. Verwoerd, who had been taken from his editor's chair in Johannesburg and given a seat in the Senate and a portfolio in the Cabinet. (In the Afrikaans press there has always been a tendency to think of editors as good politicians rather than good journalists.) As Minister of Native Affairs he had the most onerous post in the government and the most powerful. His devotion to the cause of Afrikanerdom (though he was born in Holland) and his confidence in his own righteousness made him equal to his task. I remember Strydom sitting back in his front bench with an air of detachment while the wrangling went on around him. Sallow-faced and puffy, Verwoerd was the grey eminence in the background, his mind fixed on the apartheid legislation which he had made his objective that session.

The so-called Church Clause, which was to be the main bone of contention, was a provision in a measure that went by the innocent name of the Native Laws Amendment Bill. This was a Bill to control the conduct of Africans in the towns by giving the Minister power to evict Africans and to ban their schools, hospitals and clubs, where he considered they were undesirable. It also empowered him to ban the attendance of Africans at church in white districts, and this was principally the thing that Verwoerd now gritted his teeth to obtain.

He had to fight hard, for few measures hit the conscience of the churches as much as this one. Its moral implications were clear enough in a country that was struggling over apartheid and the soul of the black man at the same time. Protests in the country were widespread, and even the Nationalists' own Dutch Reformed Church was uneasy about this erection of barriers to worship in a Christian country.

Moreover, the Dutch Reformed Church had to reckon with the Catholics, the Anglicans and the other Protestant churches, all more liberal than themselves and not identified with a political party as they were. The Catholics had a strong appeal for non-whites because of their more sincere welcome of them. And by reason of the excellence of their schools, run by their teaching orders, they also had a strong influence on many non-Catholic whites, even Afrikaners. Recognising the threat to the Afrikaner conscience and exaggerating it, the Nationalists accused the Catholics of enticing members away from the Dutch Reformed Churches and alerted their people to the growth of "die Roomse gevaar"—the Roman peril.

The Anglican leaders, though their flocks were in two minds about it, at once pronounced their abhorrence of the Church

Clause. (The Anglican Church in South Africa has always had better leaders than followers.) Their St. George's Cathedral in Cape Town displayed a notice at street level declaring that the church was open to worshippers of all races. As the entrance to the Cathedral was little more than a stone's throw from the Houses of Parliament and in the eye of many a Member going to the Assembly, it annoyed the Nationalists intensely. Bishops, both Anglican and Catholic, announced that they would defy the law if it came to the point that their congregations were subject to a racial ban. Though few Africans did in fact attend white churches, they maintained that it was contrary to Christian ethics to deny them access by law.

Dr. Verwoerd had therefore to do battle both with the Opposition (in and out of Parliament) and with the misgivings of his own churchmen. When he rose in the House of Assembly to defend this petty religio-political device, he presented a study of a man struggling with his reason, his inhibitions and the enemy in the seats opposite. He stood at his bench slightly in front of the Press Gallery, and as I had taken a desk in the first row I was nearly in line with him and facing him from above.

I used to wire to Johannesburg, often for the front page, about two columns every evening, after writing hard from 3 to 6 p.m. One morning a Member stopped me and said, "You report the debates as though they were a dog-fight. And you're right. They are!"

Defending his clause designed to prevent non-white worshippers from walking through white suburban districts on their way to church on Sunday, Dr. Verwoerd declared that the object of the clause was the "avoidance of a nuisance" caused by church-going Africans. "Nuisance" was the word he used more than once, and he did not improve matters by adding that some Africans insisted on going to white churches as a provocative demonstration. Trying to justify his attitude, Dr. Verwoerd soon lost himself in a fog of hair-splitting, argumentative, half-finished and unending sentences.

At his best, Dr. Verwoerd had a heavy, Teutonic way of expressing himself. (*Die Transvaler* was never more ponderous than under his editorship.) He tried to force his meaning through a maze of conditional, dependent and qualifying phrases. When he had to fight for the Church Clause he was soon out of sight, so to speak, in a cloud of his own making. I watched him as he struggled to extricate himself from the tangle of his own unmanageable, tormented sentences ... as the enthusiasm of his own Nationalists around him turned to perplexed weariness, and the members of the Opposition facing him began to yawn and stretch themselves.

He was quite unable to make himself clear. He was unable to finish or shorten his argument. He was unable to free himself of its mesh. It was forty minutes before he could persuade himself to sit down, to the great relief of both sides of the House, having added practically nothing to what he had said in the first five.

When the Assembly rose gratefully a few minutes later for the evening adjournment, a front bench member of the United Party Opposition, H. G. Lawrence, a former Minister of Justice noted for his thrusting style of debate, looked at the Clerk of the House as the Members were dispersing and observed sotto voce (but audible in the Press Gallery directly above), "The Minister of Native Affairs will now address the House for another hour-r-r-r . . ."

While the wrangle was going on in Parliament, the Dutch Reformed Church showed every sign of distress. It is the largest Church in the country, strongly Calvinist in outlook, claiming about two million adherents (over two-thirds of them white). Now its elders were in a quandary. Openly to condemn the Church Clause would place them in the position of critics of the Government together with the United Party, the Labour Party, the Catholics, the Anglicans and other "liberalist" groups. And yet they had 600,000 non-white followers to think of and all the other souls for whom they were competing. They adopted backstairs tactics and sent a deputation to Cape Town to express their anxieties to the Minister in person.

The result was a victory for both sides. Dr. Verwoerd

insisted on the principle of the clause, which remained untouched, but he introduced an amendment which made his power to place a church out of bounds to non-whites conditional on the consent of the local municipality. The Dutch Reformed Church then claimed that the Minister had no intention to overrule their autonomy (of which no one had suspected him in any case) and they retired discreetly from the encounter.

Dr. Verwoerd forced his Church Clause Bill through all its stages in Parliament with handsome majorities of Nationalist votes, the other Churches protesting to the last that they would defy the law if necessary. The Senate passed it too, and when Dr. Verwoerd emerged from the struggle, he was greeted in the lobbies by admiring women eager to shake his hand and congratulate him on gaining another victory for apartheid over the forces of a subversive liberalism.

By then the fog had passed from his eyes, giving place to a relaxed smile that melted over the contours of his face. You would never say that this was the man who had made so fanatic a defence of the need for sheltering whites from the proximity of non-whites when going to church on Sunday.

That 1957 session of Parliament was memorable for other things besides the emergence of Dr. Verwoerd as the Strong Man of the Nationalists. The Labour Party was still represented on the front benches of the Opposition—by Alex Hepple, Hyman Davidoff and Leo Lovell, all of them from the Rand and all of them doughty fighters of the terrier sort who were to be eliminated next year because the United Party wanted their seats.

"Apartheid is your god!" shouted Lovell at the rows of Nationalists facing him, and they became indignant at his onslaught. But Lovell repeated it because he saw he had touched them on the raw.

That Parliament still included the Africans' Members, four in the Senate and three in the Assembly, always fighting a rearguard action. But the Nationalists made no secret of their intention to evict all remnants of the African franchise from the House and they listened to their dogged debating with the indulgence customary to the doomed. The only ones who could rouse them to anger were the pugnacious Leslie Rubin (in the Senate) and Mrs. Margaret Ballinger, who used to be a lecturer in history at the Witwatersrand University in Jan Hofmeyr's time. Now she was one of the three in the Assembly (her husband, William Ballinger, a former Glasgow trade unionist, was in the Senate), and when she rose to speak, incisively, logically, the Nationalists opposite knew that she would not change their thinking, but she would make them smart.

Harry Oppenheimer was still in the House during that 1957 session, sitting among the United Party men for the Kimberley seat to which he had followed his father, Sir Ernest. He has since followed him to the chairmanship of the Anglo-American Corporation, and the De Beers group of companies, and of the Diamond Corporation, and therefore to his unofficial title of "The Diamond King".

Harry Oppenheimer, dark-haired and broad-shouldered, is not so impressive as his father was. In his manner there is a hint of diffidence suggesting, if you like, a sense of embarrassment at the wealth and power he represents. He was the only member of the Opposition to whom the Nationalists listened with continued attention. They had a respect approaching awe for the edifice which his father had created and the prestige which was descending becomingly on the shoulders of his son. They admired his know-how in command of millions, and they listened to his eloquence even when his economics was above their heads. He seemed to be the only man in the Assembly who had taken the trouble to learn how to speak in public, and to hear the clear stream of his sentences after hours of ragged debating was to listen willy-nilly.

Sir Ernest Oppenheimer, "last of the great magnates", was then in his seventy-seventh year, living in a great house in Parktown, Johannesburg. He received me once in a large, beautiful room that was hung with Renoirs, and talked of the Diamond Corporation's new headquarters he was to open in London on his next birthday, and then of the apartheid laws in South Africa.

"They are no trouble to us, you know ... I mean on the mines. We have all the native labour we need. You know why? The natives come to us because they know that on the mines they are sheltered. No Pass Law raids. No chivvying by the police. We look after them ..."

As the magnate explained, holding a long-stemmed glass, he spoke with a shrug and a smile.

"The Government's restrictive laws—apartheid and all that —don't touch them ... So we have no labour problems. That's how it works out for us ... That's how it is ..."

Seven months later Sir Ernest Oppenheimer died. The following year his son Harry, having succeeded to the Oppenheimer empire, announced his retirement from politics. In so doing he administered a damaging blow to his party and the liberal cause in South Africa. It was a declaration that big business in South Africa was washing its hands of politics, and it set an example which lesser men were glad to follow. It was a confession that the business of big business was business, and on that understanding, business was willing to play ball with the government.

When, three years later, Harry Oppenheimer made an appeal on the radio for South Africa to remain in the Commonwealth, it had no noticeable effect.

CHAPTER 16

Beauty and the Law

WHEN we moved back into our house on its half-acre in Auckland Park, the first person to telephone us was Tambula. Whether he had been calling the house regularly, or whether he'd got the news along some African grapevine I never discovered; but he knew we were back and he was coming to work for us again. That was how he announced himself. "The boss needs a general again. The boss come back, so I come back. How's the madam?" He was glad to hear the madam was fine and he was quite sure she would want him back too.

Tambula was then working in a boarding-house on the other side of town. Would his employer release him at once? He was quite sure she would, and anyhow he wasn't asking "that missis". I foresaw trouble there, and eventually Dora had to visit the boarding-house and plead with the disgruntled woman who ran it to let him go. What was the point of keeping an unwilling servant? Eventually the woman agreed when Tambula offered to forfeit the wages due to him. Then she relented and paid him half, and both were happy. That same day Tambula, having installed himself in his old 10 ft. by 7 ft. backyard room, was standing at the street corner and in his loud voice was re-establishing communication with the "generals" along the adjoining streets.

Actually the boarding-house keeper had no hold over him, though Dora tactfully did not press the point. It was apt to make some white folk angry. For by now Tambula was an "exempted Native", or as he put it, was " 'sumpted", which meant he was no longer carrying a pass. The story of

Tambula's "'sumption" went back a few years to the war period and was part of Tamula's rise in the world.

In Smuts's time, which in retrospect seems a time of easy-going live-and-let-live, the Government had begun to relax the Pass Laws. Every month tens of thousands of Africans were finding their way into the country's jails for petty infringements, and some way had to be devised of reducing the jail population and cutting the legal tanglewood in which the black folk lived and moved. A scheme was therefore introduced enabling an African of steady employment and proved character, vouched for by his employer, to obtain freedom from the curfew, the "specials" and the monthly pass-on-demand. It was intended mainly for teachers, clergymen and officials, but there was nothing in the regulations to exclude other classes of workers.

Tambula reminded me of this one pale morning after an encounter with the local police. It was after a late night session at the dance hall in Sophiatown, when I was awakened to find Tambula and a friend remonstrating with a Zulu policeman. Tambula was in starched shirt and dinner jacket, the friend in an outsize sports coat, and the policeman in a posture of truculence. I knew I had given Tambula his "special" the evening before, so I could see no immediate reason for the policeman's presence. But I soon understood. He had left it behind in his room, could not produce it on demand, and expostulation would not help. The policeman insisted on taking him to the charge office. There was nothing to do but accompany the trio to the police station a few blocks away and paying the fine.

In the morning the sorry-looking Tambula raised the matter of the "'sumption". It took me some time to equate "'sumption" with exemption, but eventually I saw the point.

The encounter with the policeman had been a humiliating end to a triumphant night, for Tambula had won another prize.

"What! For foxtrot again?"

"No! Foxtrot finish!" It was for something much better. "For best dressed!"

"Dressed as what?"

"Dressed as me. In a dinner suit!"

"First foxtrot, now dinner suit!" He laughed at the way I put it, and I laughed too. "Oh Africa! ... Oh Africa!"

It was the dinner suit that had started the trouble. In changing he had forgotten to transfer the special pass I had given him to the pocket of his lapelled dinner jacket. Or perhaps he thought the two did not go well together. The discovery of a "special" on him might even ruin his chances. The absence of it had cost him an argument with a Zulu policeman and £1 as admission-of-guilt fine.

"If the Boss gets my 'sumption, all this pass trouble is finish for me."

He had a good case. He had worked for me for ten years, and I could vouch for his good character.

"The Boss can type it." He had a great belief in the magic of the typewriter.

So I made the necessary application to the Native Affairs Department, supporting it with the necessary letters of recommendation. The Native Affairs Department took its time in making the necessary inquiries, and there was no response from there for some time. Tambula became sceptical about his chances. It now seemed to him that there was no good reason why the Government should give him an exemption when they could go on collecting two shillings a month from me for his pass, and twenty shillings from him every now and then when he was caught pass-less. But to his surprise and delight an official letter arrived one day asking for Tambula's photograph. There was no delay here. James had the picture ready, taken when he had won the prize as the best-dressed man, and this was duly sent to the Native Affairs Department.

Another few weeks passed and then Tambula's exemption card arrived. It had all his particulars on one side ... Native name, name known by, Chief and tribe. It had his photograph on the other, yes, in a black tie. And the whole was enclosed in a green folder.

To James Tambula that was more than a document. It was a release; it was his emancipation; it was his elevation to a higher order. It was pride, status and freedom all in one. Just as his change of name to "James" had raised him above the status of the witless primitive, so his " 'sumption" had raised him from the masses whose numbers were more important than their names, to the company of the acknowledged and the civilised.

He sewed that exemption card up in a cloth cover; he smoothed it and he stroked it; and he put it away in his newest sports jacket. But his pride was short-lived and his disillusionment was sudden.

Although he carried an exemption from the Pass Laws, a black man still had to produce his documents on demand. He still had to show his exemption card to a policeman to prove that he had no need to carry a pass. James knew this and was ready for it. It turned out, however, that the first young policeman who stopped him at night was less well-informed. He refused to accept the exemption and took James in all his Saturday night finery to jail. There he stayed till the morning, when a sergeant with more understanding examined his card and at once released him.

Tambula came home sorrowful and indignant. "I show him my 'sumption, but that white policeman don't know nothing. He say it's a driver's licence, and it's not a pass. I say what I do with a driver's licence when I never drive a car? He say it's no pass. I say I don't have a pass no more. I'm 'sumpted! But he never listen!..."

From then on both his exemption and his status seemed somewhat soiled. The white man's law was as rigid as ever and as humiliating.

Winter was the time when the black folk came knocking at the door, from house to house, asking for work.

In summer, the living was easy. If you didn't have a steady job you could still manage somehow, working now and then —in a garden if you were a man and had overcome your objections to the work; washing and ironing if you were a woman; getting a meal with friends and sleeping somewhere in a corner of Sophiatown. But in winter a man had to have regular food and shelter, for the winds of the Transvaal highveld cut like a knife.

Moreover, since the provisions of the Native Urban Areas Act and the Group Areas Act had been tightened up, a man had to be constantly on the watch for the police. If he was caught and found to be "habitually unemployed", he could be sent home and ordered not to return, or he might be sent to a farm colony, which in some places was run like a prison. A man had to hang on to his job, because if he lost it and had to go to another town he might never be able to return to his former home, even though it was his birthplace and he had grown up there. He had to have an employer to vouch for him and sign his monthly pass to show that he was needed and had a place in town. In that way a man could be sure of a roof over his head and something warm under his belt.

As the days grew shorter and the mornings colder, the work-seekers came slouching by. They used to stand at the garden gate till the white man or woman came out and shook a head, and they passed on to the next. That was how Christine came to us.

Tambula entered to say that there was a "gel looking for werk". And from the way he said it, he seemed to doubt very much that we'd be interested. We went out to see and there she was standing in the back garden, and at once we knew her trouble. And she knew it too.

She was wearing a faded cotton dress, a dilapidated jersey above the waist, and round her shoulders a blanket. Wrapped in the blanket was a baby sleeping soundly on her back, its nose snuggled against her shoulder blades. Standing next to her was another child, a girl of about three, and the group looked as hopeless and resigned as a piece of statuary.

She let us look at her knowing well enough what our answer must be. Tambula glanced from her to us, and shook his head. What could we do with a woman and two children in the house? She didn't even attempt to speak but just hung her head, and the child at her knee wrinkled its eyes. We sent her out some food. She stood in the garden eating, and feeding the child.

"She never get werk anywhere," said Tambula, and of course that did it. How could you turn a woman and two children from your gate knowing full well that no one would take her in? Perhaps that was why Tambula had put in his word.

So we engaged Christine at £5 a month and gave her the other little room next to the shower. She proved an excellent servant, working quite happily and briskly sometimes with the baby on her back or left sleeping in a cardboard box next to the kitchen table. The little girl was called Beauty, and she toddled after her mother round the house, looking a little frightened whenever any of the white folk entered the room.

But Beauty gradually lost her awe of us and came to life. Beauty for the first time in her three years was eating properly. She used to chew the top of a banana with a relish that made you wonder what rich flavours she found there. She put on fat quickly and her face turned a yellowish-brown. Instead of following her mother, she began to follow us from room to room, showing an intense curiosity.

One day she sat herself down next to my wife's mother at the sewing table, and a curious thing happened. She took hold of the old lady's hand and with her tiny black fingers vigorously rubbed her wrist. Then she compared it with her own. But nothing had happened. The white did not come off. She looked hard at both hands. The thought that held me at the time was that Beauty thought of her own colour as the normal, not ours.

Beauty was developing. In a short time she showed promise of becoming a person. It would have been an interesting experiment to let her grow up in a white household and see what sort of personality this child of the kraal might acquire. But of course that could not be under apartheid. That was just the kind of thing apartheid was designed to prevent. Trouble was waiting round the corner.

Those were the years, the 1950s, of the most stringent enforcement of the Pass Laws, when convictions, finings and jailings reached and surpassed 300,000 a year—or about a tenth of the whole African urban population.

Those were the days of the back-yard raids, when the police went in squads after midnight knocking up the backyard rooms and checking on their occupants. They did it, they said, to search out loafers, criminals and illegal lodgers. There were lodgers in plenty, of course, and they were all illegal.

Under the Urban Areas Act (another of the apartheid laws) a black man or woman could live on white premises only if employed there. But that did not include a man's wife or children, or a woman's husband. They had to live apart in the nearest location or township. Luckily, Tambula had no wife in town, and Christine as far as we could see had no husband. But they had frequent visitors, to whom the law applied with equal force. And what could a man do when visitors came to share his food and fire on a winter evening and stayed for the night? Tambula often had visitors, for he was a friendly sort, and I often heard their laughter at night. But by the morning they had invariably faded away, and by breakfast time all was quiet in the sunfilled back-yard.

When the police went raiding, they reached our block round about 2 a.m. We were awakened by loud voices and loud knocking at the back and knew what was afoot. Tambula had a lodger and we would have to get up and advance him £2 for the fine. Otherwise both he and his friend would be taken away to the police station and I should have to follow him there next day to get him out. In the course of a night raid of this sort, hundreds would be rounded up from the suburbs and sent to the cells for the night—or longer if they lacked the money to pay the fine.

Tambula, however, soon found a simpler way. He made sure he always had £1 on him against such occasions. When the police came raiding and found a temporary lodger, he at once offered them £1 in payment and all was quiet. In the morning he would tell me that the police had been round but —with a smile—he had persuaded them not to wake me. He had paid the fine himself.

But Christine was a different matter. I wondered how long

it would take the police to discover the presence of two African children in a white back-yard in a white suburb. It took about three months, maybe four, and then one morning we received a visit from two solemn men in uniform, one of them a sergeant. He asked me questions about Christine and her children, and then began reading sections of the Act out to me.

At this point Dora stepped forward. "Look, sergeant," she said, "that law was meant for adults. You can't apply a law like that to infants. It's absurd!"

But the sergeant knew his law. He had made sure of it before coming. He assured her that the Act did apply to Christine's children.

She appealed to him. "You can't expect me to turn children like these out of doors. You wouldn't do it yourself, sergeant, would you?"

He shook his head gravely without changing his tone. "But I didn't get myself in that position, and you did."

Nevertheless, her appeal had some effect. He was willing to overlook the younger child. It could be presumed that a babe in arms was beyond the terms of the Act. But Beauty would have to go. He gave me ten days "to remove her from the premises" as he put it. After that if Beauty was still "found to be residing on the premises" I would be prosecuted.

All this time Christine was about her work in the house. She knew what the police had called about, but with the fatalism of her sort she was resigned to whatever the white men would decide. She knew that she had no voice in the matter. I called her into the kitchen and Dora explained what the police sergeant had said. She nodded hopelessly as if she'd known all along it would come to this. She said she would take the child to its grandmother in the eastern Transvaal and leave it with her. We all knew what that meant for Beauty—running around in the dust of a mud-and-dung courtyard and living mostly on sour mealie-meal porridge. There seemed to be no other way.

But Beauty had been coughing. It was only something in the throat, said Christine. The child had had it before.

"Before she goes," said my wife, "she'd better get rid of that cough."

We took Beauty to the non-white hospital near Sophiatown. They gave her something to drink but insisted on our bringing her again. The report we ultimately got from the hospital was quite shocking. Beauty was suffering from TB and needed prolonged treatment. They were willing to take her in, but she would have to wait a while for a bed.

When we told Christine that Beauty would have to go to hospital, she showed a will and spirit of her own for the first time. She shook her head vigorously. "No, no!" She would not have anything to do with the hospital. She would not leave her child there. In any case Beauty only had something in the throat, and it would go away... She kept repeating that... something in the throat, and she would not leave her in the hospital. Christine had the primitives' fear of hospitals and she held to it with a stubbornness which astonished us.

It would be at least two weeks before there was a bed ready for Beauty. We talked to Christine almost daily and assumed that she would eventually agree.

When the police sergeant came again, we showed him the note from the hospital. He had nothing to say. He seemed relieved to find that the matter was now out of his hands. If the child was to be taken to a non-white hospital then the law could be regarded as satisfied.

We talked to Christine right up to the minute when the ambulance came. We told her plainly that unless Beauty received proper treatment in hospital, she would die. We kept repeating that Beauty would die... and that frightened her. Eventually she agreed and let Beauty be carried to the ambulance. She accompanied her to the hospital and returned to tell us reproachfully that she had left her there.

She went to see her twice a week for the next three months. She took the child sweets and toys we gave her, and she declared that Beauty was happy. But we never could make out from her whether she thought any better of hospitals. She had made a truce with the place, not an alliance. My wife went to see Beauty once or twice, declared that she looked fat and healthy, and on her third visit learned that the child would be discharged within a month.

Christine brought Beauty home in great joy one Saturday morning. Beauty stood at the open kitchen door and looked about her with satisfaction, as though she was entering on her own again. Then her mother gave her a large slice of bread and marmalade, and presently she had smeared it happily over half her face.

We kept Beauty for another three months. Then the inexorable sergeant called again. He said little. He merely made notes and told us that unless the child was removed within ten days, summons would be issued against me under the terms of the Urban Areas Act.

We made up a bundle of clothes for Beauty and her grandmother; we packed a box of food; and we sent Christine and Beauty away on the Lourenço Marques train. They'd have a three mile walk at the end of the train journey, but Christine was accustomed to that sort of travel.

She was back with us in a week saying that Beauty was happy and her grandmother was happy to have her. The law had been satisfied.

After that we asked about Beauty frequently, and Christine assured us she was well. There were no letters from home. Christine's family had not reached the letter-writing stage. News from Beauty came in a roundabout way through friends or relatives.

And then one day a letter did come. That was about three months after Beauty's departure, and we knew it must contain serious news. It was written by a headman, and the people in the reed huts in the villages did not go to a headman to have a letter written unless they had something to say. It stated simply that Beauty was coughing again. "Something back in the throat," said Christine, but the grandmother was apparently wiser.

"Go home," Dora told Christine, "and bring Beauty back. In your home she's not getting the right food. She's not eating well. Bring her back and we'll take her to the hospital again. Go home at once and bring Beauty back."

She appeared to agree and again we loaded her with parcels to take home. Then we waited to hear from her.

There was no word for a month or more. And then a letter came to Tambula. It said simply that Christine was sorry, but she had been unable to bring Beauty or even to come back herself. And Beauty had died.

So the law remained satisfied.

CHAPTER 17

Race and Register

THIS was the time when the Nationalist Government began to compile the South African "Stud Book"—the Population Register designed to keep the races pure, to keep the Europeans or whites of South Africa white, and the others their native black, brown, yellow or intermingled.

For years the Coloured population of South Africa—that is to say the half-castes, who are to be found mostly at Cape Town and the surrounding country—had remained more or less constant in numbers. The birth rate among them was always high—they had sound middle-class instincts—but they showed little or no increase. A Government commission appointed before the Second World War to inquire into their circumstances suggested that in certain districts there was a continual "passing over" of Coloureds into the white population. They also thought there might be some "passing" the other way. But in any case the report was little noticed and the reference to "passing" seemed to alarm no one. When the Nationalists came to power, however, after the war, and began forcing their apartheid policy, here was their hunting ground. They established the Population Register and began issuing identity cards to the entire population.

The Africans already had their passes, which were now in process of conversion into pretentiously named "Reference Books". In some respects this innovation was an improvement. It meant that instead of a man having to carry several documents on his person—Big Pass, Little Pass, Tax Receipt, Permit—he now carried them all together in one 96-page booklet with an identity card, permits to reside and work in a particular area, and many pages for his employer's monthly signature.

Now it was to be the turn of the whites and Coloureds. It became a photographers' holiday. Men with cameras toured the offices, workshops, factories, and in droves the white employees came to be photographed for their identity cards.

Government spokesmen argued piously that if the whites carried identity cards, the blacks would be less resentful of their Pass Laws. But that was not the reason. The purpose of the Population Register was to ensure that at birth registration or marriage, a person could prove his colour by production of his card. If he was white he could then be married as a white to a white, register his children as white, and claim the consequent privileges of a white skin for himself and his offspring. Conversely, if he was not entirely white, his identity card would show it, and there would be an end to "passing over"—an end to the clandestine insinuation of dark blood into white families—an end to the Coloureds who could point to distant relatives in the white suburbs of Parktown, Arcadia and Rondebosch, and sometimes did. The identity card was thus intended, in a very real sense, as a "race card" or a "certificate of race" to go with one's birth certificate.

This was the time of the blood hunt. As in Nazi Germany a Jewish grandmother could make a man "non-Aryan", so in South Africa a dark-skinned forbear could make a family Coloured for good. So this was the time when many a "borderline" household became apprehensive of any close examination of its ancestry. The Warden of the Cape Flats Distress Association, Dr. Oscar Wolheim, has pointed out that no old South African family can be sure it has avoided Coloured blood down the centuries. The stream of Coloureds leaving the Cape to "pass for white" elsewhere has dwindled. But in Johannesburg alone there are between 25,000 and 75,000 Coloureds who are happily living as white and have even married into white families.

This was the time when the less dark-skinned black men tried to scramble in among the Coloureds and so qualify for a better job and better pay ... and when a lighter-skinned

Coloured tried to pass for white and win the coveted race card that would make him white for good.

But it wasn't easy. The police and the Stud Book officials had their tests, probably not scientific but simple and workable. They were explained to me by a Coloured old grandmother standing at her garden gate in Coronationville near Sophiatown one sunny morning.

"Oh, yes, sir, it's not easy," she said, talking about the matter quite freely and without any sense of embarrassment. "If you're black and pretend you're Coloured, the police has the pencil test."

"The pencil test?"

"Oh, yes, sir. They sticks a pencil in your hair and you has to bend down, and if your hair holds the pencil, that shows it's too woolly, too thick. You can't be Coloured with woolly hair like that. You got to stay black, you see. And then they look behind the ears."

"What for?"

"That's only if you're Coloured and you try to pass for white. They turn you round and look behind the ears. That's where the colour shows most, and if you got it there, you just stays Coloured, sir. Nothing helps, no white powder, no face creams. Oh, no, sir."

I glanced down at the children standing with her, two little girls in pig-tails. They were both much lighter in colour than she was, and their hair was gingery.

"Yours?"

"My grandchildren."

"They're fair."

"Oh, yes, sir, very fair." She patted their heads and was happy for them. She knew that because of their light skins and reddish hair, they would have a better life, race cards or no race cards. They looked up at her, and she laughed. "Fair, fair."

She could laugh about it in a wry sort of way ... but not the 700 who came before the Race Classification Board to prove their white ancestry, and certainly not the hundred or more who failed and had to step back into the Coloured township with their Coloured identity cards.

The whole nation laughed when Mr. David Song of Durban, a Chinese business-man born in Canton satisfied the Board that he had always lived as white and had been accepted as white. They therefore declared him to be white although he was plainly yellow and was a pure-blooded Chinese.

Very hurriedly the Government in the 1962 session of Parliament altered the law making it impossible for a man to be declared white when he was obviously non-white in appearance and descent, no matter where or how long he had been accepted as white. This was "necessary for the preservation of the white race", declared the Minister in Parliament.

Nevertheless, Mr. Song having been pronounced white, stayed white. The laugh was with him.

Whatever might be said against apartheid, the Nationalists were determined to make it look logical. It was not enough to prevent whites from marrying Coloureds, or to prevent people, as they put it, from marrying out of their race groups. Nature went its way irrespective of the wedding ceremony and so did sex. What was the good of preventing the legitimate propagation of piebald-blooded children if the illegitimate propagation was allowed to continue?

Accordingly the Nationalists added a provision to the Immorality Act making it a punishable offence for white and non-white to have sexual relations, and so they hoped to set effective bounds to the strongest force in human nature.

Almost at once the police started to prosecute white men found with black or Coloured women, or white women found with Coloured men, and the newspapers began printing their sordid little stories as they came before the courts. Sometimes their affairs were not merely sordid. They broke homes; they wrecked families; they even drove men to suicide unable to face the scandal of a court appearance. The newspaper reports took on a monotonous squalor which involved both the people immediately concerned and the police who lay in wait, sometimes in back-yards and under beds, to catch them.

The law came into force in 1950. In the ten years that followed nearly 4,000 cases came before the courts, and no one pretended that this represented the full extent of the infringement of "the traditional way of life". On the contrary, it was generally accepted that the court prosecutions were no more than the "visible part of the ice-berg" and they suggested a moral attitude that filled the whites with shame and the non-whites with laughter.

Popular opinion began to demand the repeal of the Act, which instead of preventing "immorality" had only made it a familiar thing. But the Government was in a cleft stick of its own making. To repeal the law would be tantamount to giving a licence to miscegenation. They had to allow it to remain in force and hope that the newspapers would in time weary of these back-yard or back-seat stories of townsmen and farmers caught with their washerwomen or their housemaids. This is what nearly happened. The newspapers reduced their court reports to paragraphs—except when someone prominent in his community was the offender. Then they printed their columns and half-columns again. So here was the Immorality Law still bringing shame and confusion upon a nation.

Then something strange happened. The attitude to people prosecuted for "immorality" somehow changed from one of outrage to sympathy. Defiance of the Immorality Law became a kind of heroism. The young man who spent a night with a pretty African actress was regarded as no more than a naughty playboy who would have done better to plead guilty and so shorten the proceedings.

The man who lived with an African woman who had nursed him through a long illness, served a jail sentence in consequence, then married her and took her to England, was regarded as a man of honour and something of a hero.

The white girl who, when charged with a Coloured man, decided not to face the courts and fled the country, looked very much like the symbol of the freedom of the human spirit.

For the men who committed suicide, there was general sympathy.

And so human nature took its revenge on those who presumed to set bounds to it and make it subject to their laws.

CHAPTER 18

The Gathering Anger

THE 1950s were the years of gathering anger—the years when the Government accumulated more and more power into its hands, and when resentment grew among both the black and white populations.

As almost everywhere in the world, the flow of people was from the country into the towns—from the hungry Reserves and empty villages to the work and money of the cities. But the Nationalists professed that they could reverse the stream —back to the black "homelands", where the earth was eroded and starved, and back to the white farms, where pay was still only 30 shillings ($4) a month with daily mealie meal and some meat once a week.

The police were engaged in a constant check and hunt of Africans working in the towns. In one year, 1957, prosecutions under the Pass Laws system exceeded half-a-million. During the ten years, 1951–1960, they totalled more than three million.

The Suppression of Communism Act was used exactly as its critics had predicted it would be—against any active trade unionists or liberals whom the Government considered it advisable to curb. And it allowed them no appeal to the courts. It has been applied against people known to be Communists, and against people known not to be Communists but merely branded as such by the Minister of Justice. Since the Act came into force in 1950 nearly 1,000 people have been banned under its terms from attending public meetings and barred from all political activity. In addition, 120 African men and women have been banished to remote parts of the country on a Government allowance of £1 (less than $3) a month and left to eke out a living as best they can.

Among the banished are non-white organisers of trade unions (non-white unions are not recognised by law); men who have served sentences in jail for holding illegal meetings and then, as further punishment, banished hundreds of miles from their home; and tribal chiefs (like Albert Lutuli) who refused to conform to Government policy and were ordered to confine themselves to their tribal villages.

The long-standing threat to the universities now came into the open. The Extension of University Education Act was passed in 1959 solely for the purpose of excluding non-whites from the established universities and bringing non-white university students within the orbit of "Bantu Education".

The Nationalists had begun sharpening their knives for the excision of "mixed" education from the universities soon after the war. They had discovered that at the English-speaking medical schools, black students were allowed to work on white cadavers in the anatomy classes, and the Nationalist Members raised a cry of horror in Parliament.

The Nationalists regarded these "open" universities ("open" because they were open to all) and the many missionary schools throughout the country (except those of their own Dutch Reformed Church) with unconcealed abhorrence. Their principle, as expressed by Dr. Verwoerd in Parliament in 1953 was that "native education should be controlled in such a way that it should be in accord with the policy of the State". Education must train people in "accordance with their opportunities in life, according to the sphere in which they lived". In other words, education must proceed in accordance with the apartheid policy.

In spite of prolonged protests and demonstrations in and out of the universities, the Nationalists went ahead with enforcing their concepts of "Bantu education", designed to teach the non-whites to suit them to their station in a white-dominated society. For this purpose they established separate tribal colleges—for Suthos at Turfloop in the Northern Transvaal, and for Zulus at Ngoya in Natal. They took over Fort Hare for Xhosas, and they laid plans for a college for Coloureds at the Cape. The walls and "lapas" (tribal lounges) of Turfloop and Ngoya were scarcely dry when they brought the Extension of University Education Act into operation and closed the white universities to further admission of non-white students.

The establishment of tribal colleges was itself an ironic outcome of apartheid policy. Even the Nationalists, contemptuous of world opinion as they were, could not close the universities to non-white students without providing them with some alternative facilities. Hence plans had hastily to be drawn up for the provision of these "colleges in the veld", and money running into hundreds of thousands of pounds had to be provided for their construction. Twenty years before, any suggestion of spending money at this rate on African education would have been regarded with horror by the Nationalists, to whom the whole idea of educating black folk was loathsome. African education (except when discreetly administered by their own churches) seemed to them dangerously subversive, if not unnatural. Now they were ready to approve the expenditure of huge sums in the name of apartheid, and, of course, on the understanding that "Bantu education" was to be something inferior to education as they knew it, something designed "to keep the African in his place".

The Bantu Education Act of 1953 had already created the powers for bringing the mission schools within the Government plan. When in the following year these schools (hundreds of them) were ordered to accept the Government syllabuses and rules of conduct on pain of losing their State grants, only the Catholic Church as a whole refused and raised the funds it was thus deprived of by a country-wide appeal to adherents. In Johannesburg, the dogged Anglican bishop, Dr. Ambrose Reeves, resolved to close his twenty-three schools and use such of them as he could for parish purposes. But the Anglican Synod decided, as the lesser of two evils, to lease their schools to the Government, lest the teachers lose their jobs and the children be thrown into the streets.

The rules of conduct for the schools prescribed disciplinary action against any teacher for discourtesy or criticism. In practice, teachers have been dismissed merely on the grounds of "unsuitability". When African teachers' organisations protested against the new system, saying it was unrealistic to base an educational system on a tribalism that had already broken down, they were labelled as "subversive".

It is true that since 1950, the number of African children at school has more than doubled, having risen from 779,000 to more than one and a half million. But that is less than half the story. Most African children stay at school for no more than two or three grades or standards, and while the State spends about £93 ($224) a year per pupil on the 700,000 white children at school, it spends little more than £8 (nearly $20) per pupil on the African children.

Little wonder then that the average African school is delapidated, ill-equipped, staffed with under-trained, under-paid teachers and badly overcrowded (twice a day) with, to quote from an old school rhyme, many "seats on the floor". Little wonder too that the words "African or Bantu Education" have become two of the most hated words in the African's vocabulary.

Events in 1960 followed on one another as though towards an unseen climax. On January 20, soon after the opening of Parliament at Cape Town, Dr. Verwoerd announced that he would hold a referendum on the question of turning South Africa into a republic. That had been the Nationalist goal for years, but two earlier Prime Ministers, Malan and Strydom, had cautiously declared that a republic would be based on "the broad will of the people", though without ever defining what that broad will would be. It went without saying, of course, that the "broad will" would not include any non-whites. Only the white fifth of the population would have any say in the matter. But when the time came to define the "broad will", Dr. Verwoerd said that it was a simple majority and even a majority of one would suffice. So much for the broad will.

At that time the Stock Exchange was riding high. Gold shares had never been higher. Politics, it seemed, could never affect them or the confidence of investors, South African or overseas, in the Rand gold mines. Governments came and went, but the gold-producing companies kept finding new reserves of payable ore and pushing up their output. The announcement of a referendum on the republic sent a perceptible tremor through the financial houses around Hollard Street. But it was only a tremor, and the Afrikaans Press assured its readers that the announcement had had no effect on the market, which remained as firm as ever.

It remained firm because the investor was not for the time being looking at Johannesburg. He had his eyes fixed on Washington, straining for signs that America would increase the gold price, which still stood at 35 dollars an ounce. He had been waiting and hoping for a rise since 1950, and ten years later it seemed that America must at last give way, add a few dollars to the gold price and pile many millions on to the value of South African gold shares.

Then Macmillan came to South Africa and on February 8 gave his warning of "the wind of change blowing through the continent" and the "tide of national consciousness now rising in Africa"—the warning which so deeply offended South African business-men. Now there was more than a tremor. There was a shudder through all the board rooms, banking houses and building societies, and the share levels receded perceptibly from the high-water mark they had reached at the end of 1959.

During the week that Mr. Macmillan was travelling down Africa, the Cato Manor riots and murders occurred near Durban. Cato Manor was a slummy African township, where the police frequently sent raiding parties in search of illicit liquor, pass-less Africans and lawbreakers in general. That kind of raid was almost a matter of police routine. But this time the raiding party was attacked, and before it could send for reinforcements nine of its members (four whites under twenty and five Africans) were beaten and stoned to death. Echoes of Cato Manor were to be heard again and again.

CHAPTER 19

Sharpeville Monday

THE morning I was summoned to the room at the end of the corridor to meet the new editor of the *Rand Daily Mail* was otherwise a very ordinary morning in a newspaper office. The day staff were mostly out on early assignments; the discussions of the news, the page lay-outs and the prospects for the next edition had not yet begun; there was little to suggest that something quite important was happening in the history of the paper.

I went into the panelled office, was introduced and said some words of greeting. I added that I didn't quite know how to welcome a new editor, never having had to do it before. There was only one other person present looking rather reticent, and my attempt at flippancy made no ripple in the atmosphere. I left within a minute or so, feeling that my first meeting with Laurence Gandar had been disastrous.

But then I don't know of anyone who has not experienced a similar feeling of let-down on first coming into contact with him. A journalist in London once commented on his "glacial exterior". That was precise as far as it went. After that first meeting, I worked with Gandar as assistant editor for several years, but I never saw him fling a temper; I never heard him raise his voice ("not terribly good" was his strongest term of disapproval); and I rarely saw any change of expression in the cool steady eyes which kept contradicting the belligerent line of his mouth. But it was not long before I discovered that the exterior ice was really thin, and that beneath it there was a warm and even turbulent spirit.

Characteristically undramatic, Gandar announced no policy, made no quick innovations, and when he decided on staff changes they came suddenly and without fuss like a knife. It took him some time to get his seat in the editor's chair—he had before that been an assistant editor on another paper—and some time to get the feel of the powers he held and know the best way to use them. But he started to write analytical articles on the political situation under apartheid, and very soon people noticed that at last someone on an English newspaper in South Africa was giving the subject some cold, detached thought.

At first, strangely enough, not the Government but the United Party Opposition felt the sharper thrusts of his writing. Smuts's party, or what remained of it under Sir de Villiers Graaff, was dominated by land owners and businessmen, who often seemed to regret that they had been forced into the role of opponents of apartheid. They therefore took the line of patriotism, of "good South Africanism", which in practice meant "not rocking the boat" in the country, attacking the Government in Parliament because that was their job, but compromising when it would have seemed "un-South African" not to do so. Within the party, however, there was—in addition to the Babbitts—a group of liberal-minded and vociferous rebels, growing more and more restive under Sir de Villiers Graaff's benevolent "all-things-to-all-men" policy. I am sure that the *Rand Daily Mail* played a leading part in fanning their discontent, and finally fourteen Members of Parliament led by an Afrikaner, Dr. Jan Steytler (and including another old colleague of mine from the Reporters' Room, John Cope) broke away to form their own Progressive Party.

Gandar eventually gave the Progressives his newspaper's unequivocal support. He maintained it even when their representation in Parliament was reduced to one member, a woman, Mrs. Helen Suzman, and it seemed then that Gandar had backed the wrong horse. But he was backing principles not men, and in the principles of the Progressive Party, lying somewhere between the United Party and Alan Paton's radical Liberal Party (regarded by some people with Government encouragement almost as dangerous as Communists) he saw some hope of sanity and justice in the affairs of the country.

Of course right from the beginning, from that unexciting morning when he entered the *Rand Daily Mail* in Main Street—then a new building with a slightly pinkish hue that had not yet weathered—Gandar was never just an editor writing for circulation, or sensation or even popularity. He was as much aware of news values as anyone and understood that eventually a newspaper lived by its news not its views. But he found himself in a situation that presented him with a mission, and he accepted it—not impulsively, but deliberately and having a fair idea of where it might carry him. His mission was simply to plead for humanity in a society where humanism was being represented as weakness, justice as something adjustable, and civilisation as the white man's closed shop. In this sort of society to run a newspaper that devoted all its interest (and its great presses) to sport, crime, fashions, the courts and the mere froth of politics, the things that soothed people and kept telling them that this was the good life, like a beer advertisement, would have meant being cynical, and Gandar could never do that. There was nothing pretentious or affected in the way he applied himself to his work. He would stroll casually into one's office to discuss a leading article. Sometimes he would stop you in the corridor and do it there. (Later, when we had reason to believe that the telephone lines were "bugged", this became regular practice for any conversation of importance.)

When the calamity of Sharpeville happened, I don't think he was yet quite sure of himself, but we who were closest to him on the paper, A. B. Hughes and I, felt that the *Mail* was finding purpose and direction, and there was stimulus in knowing it. Hughes, a brilliant leader writer and a sparkling columnist, was at the start somewhat doubtful, perhaps because (as he once told me) Oxford had taught him the wisdom of doubt. But both of us were thoroughly stimulated by the knowledge that at last we were working for a fighting newspaper with a cause worth fighting for—and that does not happen often in the life of a newspaperman.

Sharpeville is a typical African location or township about thirty miles from Johannesburg and six miles from the town of Vereeniging, the centre of an industrial complex based on the coalfields adjoining the Vaal River. To the passing traveller it presents the usual drab and unchanging vista of streets and streets of huts, shacks and houses, and scattered trees. It was only one of several places where riots occurred on March 21, 1960, but it gave its name to all of them.

The Pan-African Congress had chosen that day for its demonstrations against the Pass Laws, and at the offices of the *Rand Daily Mail* we had received reports and warnings leading us to expect trouble. The Pan-Africanists had broken away from the African National Congress in protest against what they considered to be its too moderate policies and its alliance with various white organisations. They had become the militant wing of the African National Congress, were dubbed extremists, and they were led by Robert Sobukwe, a man of ability and courage in his thirties. He had been trained as a teacher at the non-white University College of Fort Hare and held the post of assistant in the Bantu Studies Department of the University of the Witwatersrand until resigning to devote himself to the anti-Pass campaign.

The Pan-Africanists had been in existence as a separate body for only about two years, and we were sceptical of their ability to carry out any effective demonstrations. Africans, from Clements Kadalie onwards, had shown themselves poor at organisation, and there was no reason to think that in two years the Pan-Africanists had overcome that weakness.

Early in March, Sobukwe announced what he said was to be a non-violent campaign against the carrying of passes, "the symbol of white domination", and he chose March 21 for the opening action. His plan was that on that day Africans would leave their passes at home, march to the police stations and give themselves up. If taken to court they were to accept the consequences.

His idea was obviously that the police would find it impossible to jail thousands and thousands of pass-less Africans, and the Pass Laws would thus be broken by the strength of mass non-co-operation. Sobukwe appealed to Africans to behave in a "spirit of absolute non-violence", and he hopefully appealed to the police to take no violent counter-action. He claimed to have 200,000 followers, but the real membership of the Pan-African Congress was probably little more than a tenth. Lutuli's African National Congress refused to support his campaign because they considered that it had no reasonable chance of success.

Little of all this appeared in the newspapers at the time, because anything we might print about African plans for strikes, demonstrations or even mass meetings could be interpreted as encouragement or incitement, and there was a law against that. All we could do was to gather all the information we could, wait for the day and be ready to report all that happened. We were not yet in a situation where it was unlawful even to report happenings, though such a day was not far away.

Sharpeville was on a Monday. Early in the day reports began coming in from the districts. Sobukwe and thirty followers had presented themselves at a township police station on the outskirts of Johannesburg and were arrested. But that was about the only place where Pan-Africanist action went according to plan.

Thousands congregated at Evaton, near Vereeniging, but were dispersed when jet planes flew overhead. At police stations near Cape Town crowds of men reported without passes and lined up to have their names taken, but no arrests were made. A few men surrendered to the police in Durban and Pretoria. But in other large centres there was no response to the Pan-African call, and it looked as though the day would pass off as expected—with inept demonstrations and a few arrests.

Soon after midday more serious reports started coming from Sharpeville. The information from our reporters was that large crowds were assembling near the police station and were in a dangerous mood. The *Rand Daily Mail* reporters and photographers on the spot (they gave evidence at the subsequent inquiry (have always maintained that the crowd was truculent. As evidence of this they could show that two of their cars were stoned. One also came close to the bullets.

Africans in the crowd afterwards insisted in affidavits to the Bishop of Johannesburg, Dr. Ambrose Reeves, that they had intended no violence; they had come "to talk not to fight" because they had been told there would be discussions about the Pass Laws, and they were in a good humour. The two views are not necessarily in conflict. For anyone who knows African crowds it is not difficult to understand how a mass of several thousand people can seem both good-humoured and threatening at the same time. The crowd had been gathering since early morning and by the afternoon it had reached a size of about 20,000 according to police estimates. But the Africans themselves maintained that there were never more than 5,000 of them. They pressed close round the police station.

The police version of the affair was that the crowd became so provocative that it was feared they would break down the fence surrounding the station. Men in the crowd were said to be carrying sticks, stones and pieces of iron. The police called for reinforcements by radio (the telephone wires being down) and more police arrived from Vereeniging in five "Saracen" armoured cars. Altogether there were 200 policemen at Sharpeville that day, two-thirds of them white, the rest non-white armed with batons.

Colonel Spengler, head of the Special or Security Branch, arrived at 1 o'clock, and Colonel Pienaar, senior police officer from the Witwatersrand, a short while later. Both were escorted in by Saracens which had to force their way through the crowds. Inside the station yard, Pienaar mustered his men on the spot, about seventy-five of them, and ordered them to line up facing the fence and the crowd.

Spengler and a sergeant were involved in a scuffle at the gates. As they were thrust back, Pienaar ordered his men to load five rounds, but gave instructions that "there was to be no shooting without an order to do so".

Jet aircraft flying overhead only had the effect of making the crowd more angry. The direction of the wind made it impossible to use tear gas to scatter the men and women pressing up against the fence.

The officers decided that they should try and bring the ringleaders into the station. They thought this might have a calming effect. They actually pulled three men in as they tried to clamber over. But as the police opened the gates to pull in another, about fifty men surged through and the police staggered back. Then everything happened ... Stones came showering down ... Two shots were heard from somewhere. Shouts of "Cato Manor!" rose above the din. Then the police opened up with their firearms.

The bursts of fire lasted from ten to twenty seconds, and were stopped by the commanding officers shouting at their men and waving their arms. No order to fire had been given. The police, or some of them, facing a huge crowd and fearing to be overwhelmed by them, had lost their heads and opened fire. The only warning came from an African policeman who shouted, "Run! They are going to shoot!" and then the firing started.

They fired 743 shots from the police station in bursts from Sten guns, rifles and revolvers. Only about half of the bullets found their victims, more than half of whom were hit from behind. Within seconds of the start of the firing the crowd had turned to run. They scattered leaving sixty-nine dead on the ground and 178 wounded.

When it was all over the crowds still stood at a distance looking on from the hedges, trees and houses. Police with rifles stood guard over the dead on a stretch of ground that, as everyone who saw it said, "looked like a battlefield".

Our reporters were not present during the shooting. They had been refused permission to enter the location by the superintendent. When at last they obtained permission from the police shortly after 1 o'clock they followed the route into Sharpeville taken earlier by the reinforcements. Then they heard the shooting.

Our crime reporter was Harold Sacks, a man in the best traditions of his craft, hard-living, hard-swearing, on the job all round the clock and on first-name terms with the senior police officers at any hour. He had with him our chief photographer, Warwick Robinson, another rugged but hearty character.

At the inquiry in May, Sacks described their journey to the police station. "When we approached the top of the hill, large crowds of Africans came towards us. Suddenly I heard the crack of a shot. It sounded like a hit on the car. There were three or four more shots—it seemed from small calibre firearms, and then the stones rained down. About eight hit the car. Later I found a length of beading on the car was missing, and I concluded it had been removed by the first bullet."

He thought the shooting lasted about fifteen seconds. "First there was a single shot. Then a pause. Then followed a burst lasting about three seconds, a shorter burst of about two seconds, and then finally three or four bursts of about a second each.

"When we arrived at the police station I told the driver to pull up behind a car on the side of the road because there were so many bodies on the ground. The scene was grim. They were lying next to the fence, on the pavement in front of the police station, on the road and across the road.

"At least half of the police at the station, white and non-white, came out to attend to the injured. They picked them up and placed them on the side of the road or carried them to the police vans.

"They appeared stunned. The whole scene was rather eerie. There was no sound from the crowd farther off, no moans from the wounded and no sound from the police station."

Then Warwick Robinson, ten minutes or more after the shooting, took the photographs that by next day had gone half round the world.

At the *Rand Daily Mail* office that afternoon, the first news we had from the Vereeniging district was of minor clashes between police and rioters resulting in one death by shooting, possibly two, and neither of them at Sharpeville. If that was all that was going to happen that day, we felt it was a small price to pay for the release of anger. But then the news began coming from Sharpeville, and though it came in snatches, it was shocking enough to show that the price for that day would be dear.

First reports spoke of a volley from the police into the massed crowd, leaving more than twenty dead and many more wounded. That was appalling. The floodgates of violence, it seemed, had opened. But the full horror of Sharpeville came about an hour later, when the number of dead was given as nearly seventy.

In a newspaper office one is inured to shocks—to those little slips of paper torn off from the telex machines carrying the most frivolous and the most dreadful news in uniform, grey, undiscriminating capitals. But these slips of paper seemed incredible. Something had gone wrong. Someone had surely gone mad. Or was it possible that the machine had gone electrically demented? But that kind of machine hadn't yet evolved. Every visit to the telex room merely confirmed the news, with later messages tapping out the grim details.

I stopped going to the telex room and rang through to the news editor. "Anything more from Sharpeville?"

"No. All quiet at Sharpeville," he answered, and then half-laughed uncomfortably as he realised he had used the language of a war zone.

A messenger brought us the telex slips pinned together. There were several of us in one room. We pulled them apart and passed them round. We wanted to discuss them, but there was nothing to say. Each one fingered a piece of paper and passed it on. The messages were terse, written in short, abrupt sentences. The big news always comes that way.

It was then the thought came to me, as though someone had just confided it to me, that the South African afternoon was over.

"It's over, boys. The afternoon is over . . . This country will never be the same again. They'll want their revenge for this. They'll want it, and they'll get it. And the world will be on their side. Now the black man in South Africa has been given a cause that the world can understand."

A few volleys of bullets, fired by a few policemen losing their nerve in the midday sun, had ended an era and given a new turn to South African history—a few volleys at a place with a name that the world had never heard before and which even few South Africans beyond the immediate environment had ever heard mentioned. Sharpeville—the name was now to stand for something bloody, sinister and indelible in the country's story, so that when Professor Arnold Toynbee, the British historian, speaking at the University of Pennsylvania a few months later, referred to "the whole of Africa" roused from "Sharpeville to Algiers" . . . he was sure that his audience would know what he was talking about and would understand.

It was dusk when six of us gathered in the office of Laurence Gandar to see Warwick Robinson's photographs from Sharpeville. We passed them round in silence for some minutes. They seemed to require no comment. They were the best news photographs ever taken in South Africa. They showed a field littered with dead and two policemen with rifles looking on. They were large full-plate prints, each nearly half the size of a page of the newspaper, and they recorded a stillness charged with atmosphere.

Very soon, as we passed them round, it became clear that we would not use these photographs. Gandar's face, normally grave, became darker in scanning them. Without saying it, we all knew that it would be no more than ordinary newspaper practice and courage to print these photographs; but more important than courage at that moment was responsibility. In that orderly wood-panelled office, hung with etchings and modern paintings, we knew the temper of the half-million black population which surrounded this white city of Johannesburg, and we could not print those photographs without being aware of their potentially inflammatory effect.

We argued about them. We were dealing with the best news pictures ever taken. All our instincts and training were for printing them. We considered various ways of reproducing them so as to lessen the impact of their horror and somehow turn aside the provocative effect they might have on the volatile population of the townships, already in a state of anger and excitement.

After much uneasy discussion we found ourselves unhappily using a selection of the lesser pictures, leaving the grimmest for later consideration.

And so it came about that the Sharpeville pictures, which went round Africa and the world, were not printed by the paper nearest the scene, the paper which had produced them. Thirty miles from Sharpeville, they looked too horrible to circulate in the streets, the shops, the houses and the buses.

Possibly it was a wrong decision. It is never wrong to print the factual news, and there can be nothing more factual than on-the-spot photographs. We were never sure that we had done right. We made plans to use the photographs omitted a day or two later when the atmosphere might be calmer. But there was to be no calm that week, and on Wednesday our reports from the townships persuaded us to put the Sharpeville pictures aside for good. If we had made a mistake, it was one that could not be retrieved. But if it was a mistake, it was an honourable one. The pictures were entrusted to me as assistant editor for safe-keeping, but as they had already been radioed overseas and to other South African newspapers, there seemed little point in that.

The night of Sharpeville also brought news of six deaths during demonstrations at Langa Location near Cape Town. Next morning the telex ticked out reports of thousands of Africans marching on Cape Town and reaching almost as far as the city before dispersing. There were to be similar demonstrations in Durban.

Both the African National Congress under Lutuli and Sobukwe's Pan-African Congress proclaimed a day of mourning for the dead of Sharpeville and Langa, and fixed it for the following Monday, March 28, when all Africans would be ordered to stay at home. Meanwhile the Commissioner of Police, Major-General G. I. Rademeyer, looking for a way to lower the tension building up in the towns and townships, announced that for the time being Africans would not be asked to produce their passes. When a short time later he rather surprisingly retired, this was generally considered the price he'd had to pay for his one act of wisdom in Sharpeville week.

CHAPTER 20

Sharpeville Week

MOST of the wounded were taken to Baragwanath, a large, rambling, multiple-unit hospital ten miles south of Johannesburg near the Orlando townships. It had been built by the British Army during the Second World War primarily for soldiers with lung complaints and afterwards sold to the Transvaal Provincial Administration. Then it was developed as a hospital for the non-white population, and under its medical superintendent, Dr. Isidore Frack, it grew to a great institution of 2,300 beds. By 1960 it was widely known to the African population, near and far, for the help they could receive there, and to medical men in other countries for the unusual cases and treatments it enabled them to observe.

The first news of the slaughter at Sharpeville reached the hospital at 2.30 p.m. in a call from the police at Vereeniging, thirty miles away, alerting the officials to prepare for casualties. The number to be expected was given at about fifty, but it soon began to mount. By about 4 p.m. it was given as 150 and eventually it turned out to be only a few less.

Dr. Frack, a man weathered like an oak and possessing great humanity and ability, immediately gave orders for the necessary wards to be cleared. The hospital was accustomed to dealing with a rush of casualties from accidents and brawls at the week-end, but this was "Operation Disaster". The ambulances began to arrive from Sharpeville at 4.30 p.m. and Dr. Frack himself supervised their distribution in the wards and the clearance of the operating theatres.

At about 6 p.m., Dr. Frack, harried and helping in the

wards, heard to his astonishment that the police had arrived. What astonished him even more was to find, on going to his office, that they had taken possession. A colonel of police was sitting at his desk surrounded by his junior officers making themselves comfortable. The wounded were still being wheeled in down the long corridors.

Dr. Frack is a mild-mannered man, but the sight of the policemen making free with the Medical Superintendent's office filled him with an anger he had some difficulty in keeping under control.

He went up to the colonel-in-charge. "This happens to be my chair."

The colonel at once apologised and gave up his seat.

Someone else made room for him and Dr. Frack sat at the head of the table. "Now, gentlemen, what is it?"

"I want you to understand," said the colonel, "that the wounded coming in here are all under arrest."

"Under arrest!" The doctor was amazed. "But, gentlemen, may I remind you, this is a hospital not a prison."

"Nevertheless," insisted the officer, "you must regard them all as under arrest."

"But, colonel," said Dr. Frack as steadily as he could, "I want you to remember that I am in charge of this hospital and it is I who give the orders here."

That somewhat checked the colonel, but at this moment a sergeant entered the office carrying ink-pads and sheafs of printed documents. The colonel explained that he had given instructions that finger-prints of all the wounded should be taken, and he was about to send his men into the wards for that purpose.

Dr. Frack declared that he would never permit it. He repeated, "This is a hospital, gentlemen, and I want you to remember that. . . ."

The colonel replied with another demand. "I still say the wounded are under arrest and in accordance with practice I intend to place two men at each bed."

This was when Dr. Frack nearly did lose his temper. "Oh no! . . . Over my dead body! . . ."

When the effect of this remark had been absorbed, he

appealed to them, addressing the police familiarly in Afrikaans. "Kerels! (Fellows), wees barmhartig... as u blief! Have some pity... please! There are some people out there who are dying. Others are going to lose an arm or a leg. How can we carry on treatment in the wards if there are two policemen standing at each bed?"

He finally agreed to allow two policemen to stand outside each ward. "But please bear in mind, there are to be no finger-prints. This is a hospital...."

Dr. Frack had his way, and the colonel accepted his way of doing things grudgingly.

That night sixty-six surgical operations were performed at Baragwanath. Many of the bullets extracted were in the back, and many of them were of .45 calibre copper-sheathed, a fact which subsequently gave rise to the rumour that the police had used dum-dums.

Later in the evening, Dr. Frack realised that many of the wounded needed more than physical comfort. They had families who had to be cared for. This was something he could not cope with himself, so he sent for a friend, a priest at the Community of the Resurrection, not far away. Next morning, the Bishop, Dr. Ambrose Reeves, came to Baragwanath.

The police resented the presence of the Bishop even more than the firm attitude of the Superintendent. Dr. Reeves was in the wards, talking to the wounded, comforting them, taking statements. They suggested that his presence was unnecessary. Dr. Frack answered that there could surely be nothing wrong in having a priest in the hospital.

They asked Dr. Reeves to leave. He replied that he would do so only if requested by the Superintendent. Dr. Frack said that he had no objection to the presence of the Bishop. Relations between the doctor and the police remained formal but strained.

None of this was known publicly at the time. It was all pieced together later. What we and the public heard came on Saturday with the news that Dr. Frack had been suspended from his post on orders from Pretoria. No reasons were given either to him or to anyone else. He was told to hand over direction of the hospital to a deputy who had himself to deliver the letter ordering Dr. Frack to leave. He did it with tears in his eyes.

The suspension of Dr. Frack shocked the world almost as much as anything that had happened that week. But Dr. Verwoerd's Government had frequently shown an unhappy capacity for compounding one wrong with another. I remember Dr. Frack next morning sitting in his lounge on the north side of town, surrounded by half a dozen newspaper correspondents who had flown in from London and elsewhere since Monday. They were eager to probe the reasons for his suspension.

He looked weary and perplexed. He talked about the wounded and the severity of their injuries. To all the world it seemed as if he had offended in showing excessive concern on behalf of those who had escaped the mortal bullets at Sharpeville.

The following day, Monday, the Government realised that someone had blundered. It was probably the Minister of Justice, as head of the Police Force, who had demanded the doctor's removal. What the police resented most was the presence of the Anglican Bishop in the hospital.

Dr. Frack was summoned to Pretoria to see the Administrator, and he was reinstated in his post without any explanation being given for his suspension. The staff welcomed him back with unconcealed relief.

That was the week-end when Chief Lutuli publicly burned his Pass Book at a demonstration in Pretoria and was photographed doing so. He called upon all Africans to do likewise and destroy "this symbol of slavery". Not many followed his example, however. The average African could not believe that passes had been abolished in one day. He knew too much of the severity of police methods to believe that pass-burners would get away scot-free, and he mistrusted the ability of his own leaders to protect him. He was in fact caught between two fears—the fear of the police and the fear of his own agitators who were exhorting him to resist. When Lutuli was later prosecuted and fined £100, that was the signal to all that the hated symbol of the pass still stood.

The week advanced to the climax of the Day of Mourning. Next Monday would show whether Sharpeville had sparked off a still greater explosion—whether African anger had passed into desperation—whether the police would be able to hold their fire. The African population was sullen or afraid. You could see anxiety in your African employees who lived in Orlando. On Monday, if they disobeyed Congress orders and came to town, they would be met by retributive gangs on their way home in the evening.

On Sunday night, one of the African messengers on my floor, Joseph by name, came to me and begged, "What I do tomorrow, sir? ... I can't come to the office. I afraid to come. When I go home they kill me. They come to my house ..."

He was a family man and wanted only to be left alone to do his work (mostly running with proofs) and to bring up his children. There was nothing warlike about Joseph. I could see him happily carrying proofs for the rest of his life. He was not under my orders, but he came to me for advice.

"You stay home," I said, "and keep out of trouble."

His apprehension turned to the light of gratitude. "I not lose my job, sir?"

"Your job tomorrow is to keep out of trouble and not get hurt ... Hamba Kahle ... Go in peace."

He laughed and was off.

Next day was strangely quiet, and so was the city. Never before had a hundred thousand workers stayed away, and their absence gave us a vision of what Johannesburg might be like without its African labourers. Not all of them were absent. Those who were employed at houses in the city and those who had found it possible to stay in town overnight, went about their work much as usual. But the masses of absentees left great gaps in offices, factories and workshops, and the streets looked slow and half empty.

Early in the day there was no knowing what the quiet portended. Reports from the townships suggested that they were as calm as the city... with lots of people about but little overt activity. The test would come in the later afternoon when those workers who had dared to ignore the stay-away call had to return home. They had been promised police protection, and that was the danger. Every terminus, railway train or bus-stop became a possible clash-point.

The calm continued throughout the afternoon, and when shortly after five we wrote our editorials for the *Rand Daily Mail*, it was on the comforting assumption that appeals for steadiness had had some effect, and the day had passed off peaceably. But we wrote too soon.

When I returned to the news room after dinner, I was greeted with alarming reports of widespread violence. Trains returning to the townships had been stoned. Cars had been ambushed at the entrance roads and pelted. Police on duty at railway stations had been defied by the crowds and attacked. A Dutch Reformed Church mission had been set on fire. Police stations had been stoned. Murder was on the roads, and a man had been found beaten to death beside his car. An African policeman had been killed.

We waited for the reports to come in with the full toll of death and destruction, so that the story could be pieced together. Meanwhile we held back the editorial page in the composing room.

Things looked worse at about 9 o'clock. The fires were spreading. They were springing up at distant points in the townships. Attempts had been made to set a police station on fire. The roads were under watch and at least one of our cars had stopped some stones. "It's war in the townships," said one of our men. The night's story began to look like another tale of horror.

And then it stopped. An hour later it was all over. Anger had flared up and died in a matter of hours. Our reporters returned to say that the fires were out or under control; the rioting had petered away; all was quiet in the townships. What had apparently happened was that the returning workers had managed to scramble or fight their way home, and once indoors they were safe.

"It's as quiet as a morgue," said one of our men. "No one will put his nose out."

Sitting at the top of the news room, I re-wrote the column of editorials. There were times when one could work better in a crowd. The main leader expressed a sense of relief that the day had been no worse and that the police had exercised restraint. The leader page was sent away while the front-page banner line was being written:

MOURNING DAY'S VIOLENT END
... Sudden outburst, then quiet

Joseph, our floor messenger, was back at work next afternoon. He came into my office with a sheaf of galley proofs over his arm and a grin on his face.

"How did you manage, Joseph?"

"They did come to my house, sir." It was not necessary to explain who "they" were. "They" were the A.N.C. or the P.A.C. organisers.

"They come to my house ... They look round me ... They see I'm not gone to work ... They go away ... Say nothing. I say nothing too ..."

"And your pass?"

"Oh I tell 'em I got no pass any more ... I throw my pass away."

"And did you?"

"Not me! I hide it in the lavatory. I know they never go to look there."

He went away laughing.

CHAPTER 21

The Ugly South African

For twelve years apartheid had ruled in South Africa as a principle and a policy. Now it was suddenly exposed as something in guns and jackboots, and from now on almost everything Dr. Verwoerd's Government did was to strengthen that aspect of it to South Africa and the world.

Robert Sobukwe, leader of the Pan-Africanists, who had been arrested on the morning of Sharpeville, when he had presented himself to the police at Orlando with fifty followers, was charged with the crime of violence. A man of great courage—any black man in South Africa who is ready to challenge the laws must be endowed with courage in a high degree—he followed at his trial the rule he had urged on his followers, "no bail, no defence, no fines". He refused to plead, declaring that the laws under which he was charged were made only "for the white man", were administered by white men, and he could not recognise their justice or validity.

He was sent to prison for three years, and 160 others tried during the same period, were sentenced to like or lesser terms. They refused to recognise the authority of the courts and refused the alternative of a fine.

Parliament was in session at Cape Town during Sharpeville week, and the shootings were discussed in the Assembly on the disastrous day and those immediately following. The Nationailsts' first concern was to shift the blame.

Mr. G. P. van den Berg, a Member from a Transvaal country town, attributed the disturbances to the fact that "people like Mr. Macmillan toured through Africa and made the sort of speech which he made in Cape Town", and to Opposition speeches in Parliament which were "subtle attempts to incite the Bantu to revolt".

Another country-town Nationalist, J. E. Potgieter, said that the main cause of racial tension was the propagation of "ultra-liberalist" doctrines by the Opposition.

Inevitably there came the usual charges against the Press (always the English-language Press), and an exhortation, again from a Nationalist country Member, that the Press should be denied parliamentary privileges.

Though Dr. Verwoerd said he did not favour any inquiry because it could provide "a platform for agitators", he ultimately appointed two one-judge commissions to inquire into the events at Langa and Sharpeville on that eventful Monday.

The man who really shocked his own people, however, as well as the Opposition, was the Nationalist Member for the Vanderbijlpark division, where a crowd of 4,000 had gathered at the police station on the morning of Sharpeville and one African had been shot dead. Vanderbijlpark was only ten miles from Sharpeville and its representative in Parliament was Dr. Carel de Wet, later South African ambassador in London, a medical practitioner by profession, a fist-shaking politician by habit, and a baiter of the English Press by choice. He rose in the Assembly in the afternoon before Parliament had heard the news from Sharpeville.

"It is a matter of concern to me," said the young doctor (he was in his forties), "that only one person was killed."

During the sensation and hubbub that followed, the Opposition Members were loud in their protests:

"A terrible remark to make!" exclaimed the courtly Major Piet van der Byl of Cape Town.

"Nothing in all my Parliamentary career has shaken me more," said Marais Steyn, one of the United Party's captains from the Transvaal. "Does he mean that the police should use more violence than is necessary to restore order and that the shedding of blood should not be limited?"

Thus challenged, the doctor defended his standpoint: "On behalf of the voters of my constituency, on behalf of the white people of South Africa, and on behalf of the Bantu, I wish to say that when it becomes necessary to use force it must be used in such a manner that it makes it clear to everyone that there is no place for murder ... I say that because the whites in this country also have the right to protection."

Dr. Verwoerd intervened to defend his henchman, saying that all he had done was to plead for order and firm action where necessary before more lives were lost. No one had the right to interpret the words as meaning that more force had to be applied.

"What else could he have meant?" demanded Marais Steyn.

"It is shocking," answered the Prime Minister, "that one Christian should attach such a meaning to the words of another Christian."

But it was apparent that the Prime Minister himself had some difficulty in appreciating the benevolence of the doctor's sentiments. From the Nationalist Party caucus the following day, it was reported that Dr. Verwoerd had rebuked the ebullient Dr. Carel de Wet and warned his Members not to indulge in "wild and irresponsible statements".

The phrase, "only one person was killed", had by then, however, been written into the history of Sharpeville. It takes something as little (or as much) as this, at a time like this, to fix the image of a party or a people.

The State of Emergency proclaimed on March 30 applied to all the main cities of South Africa and many of the smaller towns. Several days later the Unlawful Organisation Act was pushed through Parliament, and as soon as it became law on April 6, the Government banned the African National Congress and the Pan-African Congress. Now began the big season of pre-dawn raids and arrests. During the next few weeks nearly 2,000 people (100 of them whites) were arrested in various parts of the country on orders from the Minister of Justice. In addition, 21,000 Africans were jailed in a new and more stringent round-up under the Pass Laws. The emergency regulations prohibited the publication of names of the "detainees" until they were officially released, and as this did not happen for weeks, the names became the subject of rumour, surmise and guesswork.

It was known that Chief Lutuli had been arrested; so had Professor Z. K. Matthews, Walter Sisulu (former secretary-general of the now-banned A.N.C.), Philip Kgosana, Mrs. Z. Gool (a Coloured member of the Cape Town City Council), Mrs. Helen Joseph (president of the South African Federation of Women) and others who with her had been among the original accused at the treason trial. The detainees included trade union officials, an Anglican clergyman, some university lecturers, lawyers and journalists connected with liberal or Leftist organisations, and Cecil Williams the producer of my play *The Kimberley Train*. (Subsequently placed under house arrest, he escaped and fled to Britain.)

No charges were brought against the detainees. They were merely held on orders from the Minister and would be held until "investigated"—which for some would mean the end of May and for most the middle of July. In Johannesburg they were kept at The Fort. They were allowed to receive periodic visits from relatives and to accept books (after scrutiny by the prison authorities), but they were not allowed to see any newspapers or to listen to radios. It was common knowledge, however, that both papers and radios were at various times smuggled into prison, and Cecil Williams was reported to be holding readings of Shakespeare for the entertainment of his fellow detainees.

Under the emergency regulations the circulation of any statement likely to subvert authority, or to incite the public or cause any hostility, was prohibited under pain of a £500 fine or five years' imprisonment. Newspapers were prohibited under threat of suppression from printing anything of a "subversive character". The prohibition was made wide and vague, placing the onus on editors to determine what was "subversive" and unpublishable. The Afrikaans papers were not troubled because they tended to regard all criticism of the Government as subversive. But we were anxious to publish as much as possible, and so we were in constant consultation with our lawyers (sometimes late into the night) deciding what were the limits of the law and how close we could get to them without unreasonably risking suppression of the paper. Many were the threats and demands in Parliament from Nationalist members to take action against the "English Press" and so demonstrate the Government's "strong arm" or "kragdadigheid", as they loved to call it. The Cape Town correspondent of the London *Daily Herald*, Myrna Blumberg, was among the first detained under the emergency laws, and on April 12 the Government ordered the expulsion of Norman Phillips, the hard-hitting correspondent of the Toronto *Star*, who had arrived in Johannesburg a day or two after Sharpeville.

Suppression of any of the English newspapers would have been a victory for the Government not for the Press, and was therefore to be avoided. Nevertheless in their anxiety to keep going and their reluctance to challenge the Government, some of them undoubtedly erred on the smug side of caution. In those days Bishop Reeves's accusations of timidity might have been applied to more than one of the English dailies, and it applied to all of them on "The Day of Whips" when, I maintain, the English Press in South Africa failed its public and fell below its own standards of courage.

In Johannesburg, the first news we had of "the whips" in the streets of Cape Town was a report from Parliament on April 4 which quoted one of the Opposition front-benchers, Harry Lawrence, saying that "an African clergyman had been beaten with a sjambob (a heavy whip) by a policeman in the street", and another African, a university lecturer, had been struck in the face. He expressed concern for what was going on and pleaded (the House was then discussing the Unlawful Organisations Bill), "Do not apply the law of the jungle!"

When we asked our correspondent in Cape Town (the *Cape Times* and the South African Press Association) for more details of these extraordinary occurrences, none were forthcoming. When we pressed for information we found that Cape Town lawyers had ruled that to print the full story could amount to incitement and would be an infringement of the emergency regulations. Obviously this was a borderline case where it would have been honourable for the newspapers to take a risk. But we never got the full story for publication and had to wait to read an account of the Day of Whips in an air edition of the *Daily Telegraph* from London :

"The Africans attacked, both in the main streets of Cape Town and in the streets of the outer suburbs at Pinelands, Claremont and Woodstock, fled screaming from their uniformed police assailants. Their screams horrified the peaceful white citizens in the streets. Under the emergency regulations these citizens thought it useless to make formal complaints. But they telephoned in their scores to local newspapers and journalists from abroad, to voice their fear, horror and disgust at the police action."

CHAPTER 22

"The Polecat of the World"

On April 9, 1960, Dr. Verwoerd was shot in the face during the opening of the annual Witwatersrand Agricultural Show in Johannesburg, this year called the "Union Exposition" as part of the festival to mark the fiftieth year of Union. For two weeks at least, the future of South Africa rested on a razor's edge.

The would-be assassin was an English farmer, David Pratt, an unpolitical type but the kind of unbalanced character that is often thrown up in times of turmoil and stress. (He ultimately committed suicide while under detention in a mental institution.)

It was at once announced that the Prime Minister's injuries (under the right ear and in the neck) were not "very serious", but for the next few weeks he lay in hospital recovering from his wounds.

There seemed little doubt at the time that had Dr. Verwoerd been shot dead, a new wave of violence would have broken out in South Africa. The temper of the moment was such that his assassination must almost certainly have touched off an explosion. Instead, while the country waited for him to recover, it seemed that the opportunity had been created for a new spirit to take hold of South African politics and race relations.

The reason for this was not merely that Dr. Verwoerd, the chief banner-man of apartheid, was for the time being out of action, and his complete recovery was uncertain. Within the Nationalist Party there were also moderates who were now emboldened to speak out and voice their misgivings. Some of them had already come out in the open in the party's newspapers less than a week before.

On April 4, *Die Volksblad,* an Afrikaans daily in Bloemfontein and official organ of the Nationalist Party in the Orange Free State, had shown that even among the *"baasskap"* (or white-boss) Nationalists who were thick in that province, there were those who saw that the "old times" were over. It went so far as to admit in a leader that nobody could expect the country to return now to the "normal times" of before.

But it was the still more authoritative *Die Burger* of Cape Town which voiced the fears that now began breaking through Afrikaner self-satisfaction. In what was subsequently referred to as "the polecat leader" (or editorial) and was headed "The Overseas Catastrophe" on April 7, it said that South Africa's external relations in many political, commercial and cultural spheres were in acute danger. It pointed boldly to the evil effects of apartheid, the word and the policy, on South Africa's standing in the world :

"It is clearer than ever before that the word *apartheid* has irretrievably come to grief because of its exclusive association in overseas minds with negative actions.

"South Africa cannot any more and in any degree afford this word in respect of our overseas relationships.

"If we want to build up those relationships out of the ruins, we must expedite all positive aspects of our race policy in time with the haste of history . . .

"We must give all our overseas friends reason again to hold their heads high, we must give grounds for fair-minded foreigners to move to our side, and we must try to cripple our chronic enemies.

"If we are not able to do this with our internal policy, we must look forward to a permanent status as the polecat of the world, with all the catastrophic political and economic implications of such a position."

It became obvious that within the Government there were serious differences between the moderates (who were mostly down at the Cape) and the extremists, personified by Dr. Verwoerd, in the Transvaal North. Ten days after the shooting of Dr. Verwoerd, when the Prime Minister was still in hospital and reports (some of them from high places) suggested that his incapacity might be of some duration, it seemed that the moderates had found a spokesman and a leader. He was no less than Mr. Paul Sauer, the Minister of Lands and senior member of the Cabinet, who presided at Cabinet meetings in Dr. Verwoerd's absence and acted as Leader of the House.

Round-faced, bald and amiable, Paul Sauer stood up at a small place significantly called Humansdorp (part of his constituency near Port Elizabeth) and delivered what soon became known as "The Humansdorp speech" or the "new deal speech," in which he advocated a new attitude and a new spirit. Sharpeville, he said, was "the turning point" at which "the old book" of South African history was closed. For the immediate future South Africa would have to reconsider "in earnest and honesty" her whole approach to "the Native question".

"We must alter the conception of *baas-skap* in the areas which will be made available by the Government to the Bantu ... There should be absolutely no reference to *baas-skap*," he pleaded.

The African felt that he was being chased around. He must be given "hope for a happy existence" and "pinpricks" which had prepared the African for A.N.C. and P.A.C. propaganda must be removed. Mr. Sauer urged adjustments to the Pass laws, the liquor laws, the wage rates ... and he wanted "healthy contacts" with the Africans in the towns.

Words like these had not been heard from any head or acting head of government in South Africa for years, and for the moment it looked as if a new book of South African history was indeed to be opened by the rotund little Minister of Lands who for the time headed the Cabinet.

But within hours the party whip had cracked from Pretoria. Dr. Verwoerd's private secretary announced that Mr. Sauer had not consulted the Prime Minister before making his Humansdorp speech. The next day, April 21, Mr. Sauer was openly ordered to toe the party line when Mr. Eric Louw, Minister for External Affairs, informed the House of Assembly that only the Prime Minister could make any important announcement on basic policy. His statement was greeted with cries of "Hear! Hear!" from the Government benches.

Mr. Sauer himself was not in the House. He was still on his way back from Humansdorp, 400 miles away. Until he returned and made clear his position, there was still a chance that the moderates among the Nationalists had a leader ready to challenge the strong arm of Dr. Verwoerd. But they were not left long in hope or doubt.

The amiable Paul Sauer, whose appearance gave the impression of a man who wanted nothing more than to be left alone, was not the one to lead a revolt or a crusade. When he returned to Cape Town later that day and he was asked to what extent his speech reflected Government intentions, he answered, "It was a statement of my opinion, and that is all."

So Paul Sauer toed the line, and from his bed in Pretoria Dr. Verwoerd held his grip firmly on the Government and on party policy. And though Sauer retained his position in the Cabinet, he commanded little prestige either there or in the country.

Die Burger too must have regretted the burst of candour in its "polecat leader", which was hotly criticised within the party and prominently quoted in the English Press. The English newspapers would never have dared to attach such a term to South Africa. In their columns it would have been regarded as treasonable. But they seized upon it when uttered by the Government's most respected mouthpiece, and they made good use of it. The "polecat" voice was never again heard from the Afrikaans Press, but it has echoed and echoed —as a cry of alarm which, though repudiated by the Nationalist Party, betrayed the fears at its heart.

From this time dates the South African Government's rejection of the term "apartheid" as the label of its policy. Malan had raised it as a slogan on his banner and carried it to victory at the polls. Strydom and Verwoerd had made it ring round the world. The Nationalists, much as they resented the English language, boasted of having given it a new word. But now they cast about for ways of shedding a symbol that had served its purpose and had become unsavoury and embarrassing.

Dr. Verwoerd had already put forward his Bantustan plan. This was to be the positive side of apartheid and was announced in such a way that it could mean anything the Government wanted it to mean. It was a plan for the development of the African reserves, eroded, parched, poverty-stricken and scattered in many parts of the country. It was to be a plan for consolidating them where possible, making them self-supporting and giving them eventual independence under their own Territorial Authorities—or so it was proclaimed. But like so much enunciated by Dr. Verwoerd's Government in policy and legislation, the real purpose of the plan was left vague and ambiguous. The Government never defined with any certainty what "independence" for the Bantu territories would mean. Speaking to the English Press and for overseas consumption its spokesman talked of Bantu states within South Africa that would have "independent self-government". In the Afrikaans Press, where it would be read by the white Afrikaner population, this became merely "self-government". But when talking to the Africans themselves, to the Xhosa of the Transkei for instance, the Government used the word "inkululekho", the Xhosa word meaning "freedom from bondage".

No one in South Africa, least of all the Nationalists, believed that Dr. Verwoerd's Government intended creating any African states with more than a semblance of independence. The African reserves exist in hundreds of scattered fragments as impossible to put together into coherent wholes as the proverbial "Humpty-Dumpty". No one believes that the Government is able or willing to spend the huge sums of money that would be necessary to make the reserves self-supporting, another of the professed aims. In 1955, the Tomlinson Commission estimated that the money required to do this would be at least £104,000,000 (about $300,000,000) spread over ten years. That same commission would probably put the cost much higher now. But the Government showed no inclination to spend more than fractional amounts of the Tomlinson requirements, and the Bantustan plan remained a scheme for giving the African the forms of self-government while denying him the substance.

The Government established a Territorial Authority in the Transkei, the only one of the African homelands which exists as a continuous extensive area. A territory somewhat larger than Wales, it has over a million people living on agriculture and the remittances of its men-folk, most of whom work as migrant labourers in the white areas. It was in the Transkei that the Xhosa branch of the Bantu peoples, advancing down the east coast in the eighteenth century, first met and clashed with the whites coming from the south-west, and here they remained "across the Kei River" as a subject nation.

Here the Government set up a council for the "self-government" of the Transkei made up of the Chiefs who, as paid officials, were willing to co-operate with the Government. At its head was Chief Kaiser Matanzima, the Government's choice as first "Prime Minister" of the Transkei, an astute man whose philosophy has been well summed up by one of his followers: 'Ask for what you want; take what you can get; use what you have to get what you want". He was strongly challenged by Paramount Chief Sabata Dalindyebo, who gained a majority in the subsequent popular elections. But the other Chiefs, holding allocated seats in the assembly, dutifully gave their support to Matanzima and made him Chief Minister. Meanwhile the burly backveld M.P., Hans Abraham, had been appointed Commissioner-General of the Transkei and he allowed himself to be photographed taking his top-hat off to Chief Kaiser Matanzima. This was good for overseas propaganda. But how the South Africans (including the backveld Nationalists) laughed at the picture of "the Hon. Hans" displaying the "positive" side of apartheid in a top-hat!

The Government clearly revealed its real intention about the Transkei when it stated that Port St. Johns would never be part of the self-governing Transkei. Port St. Johns is the only harbour in the territory and the only outlet to the sea;

but it would never be controlled by the Chiefs. Moreover it maintained "emergency" rule over parts of the territory and promulgated a set of regulations for the Bantustan towns, limiting residence by lodgers, prohibiting gambling, and preventing the holding of meetings or assemblies except by permission and, possibly, under police control. The Transkei Assembly was given power over roads, health, education, and agriculture; but control over defence, security, foreign affairs, finance and the judiciary would be retained by the South African Government. So much for "independence", "self-government" or "freedom from bondage".

Before any "self-governing homelands" were created, and before any Territorial Authorities could be established, Dr. Verwoerd's Government passed the Promotion of Bantu Self-Government Act in May 1959, the immediate purpose of which was to clear the way for the removal of the white representatives of the Africans from Parliament. Since 1936 there had been seven—three in the Assembly and four in the Senate—and for more than twenty years they had been the severest and best informed critics of Government policy towards the African. But the Nationalists made no secret of their aim to rid themselves of this troublesome presence in the House. Now it was accomplished, and the process started under General Hertzog of destroying African representation in Parliament was complete. The first fruits of the newly proclaimed policy of Separate Development (alias apartheid) was thus, not the extension of African rights, as the Government and its Ministers professed, but their diminution.

The referendum on a Republic was held on October 5, 1960, and produced a majority of 74,580 in a poll of 1,653,772 in favour of a republican form of government. Dr. Verwoerd announced that South Africa would become a republic the following May, and at once the continuance (or otherwise) of its membership of the Commonwealth became a question of practical politics.

It had all along been understood that if South Africa became a republic, it would have to apply for "approval to remain a member of the Commonwealth", and the general opinion was that it would not be rejected. But as the time for the next Commonwealth Conference in London approached, the issue became more and more doubtful. In Canada, Malaya and India, the opinion was openly expressed that South African racial policies were incompatible with membership of a multi-racial Commonwealth, and the truth was of course that Dr. Verwoerd's Government felt that way too. The Nationalists actually resented their association with non-white states and had never been at any pains to conceal their dislike. Dr. Verwoerd's own reference to the "younger and less developed black states" who were members of the Commonwealth scarcely covered up his scorn.

When the time approached for him to go to London to attend the meeting of Commonwealth Prime Ministers in March 1961, Dr. Verwoerd made it clear that he would make no concessions on racial policy to please any Commonwealth member, and that was the intransigent note on which he departed—"no concessions". The Nationalists had all along avowed that they would remain in the Commonwealth only as long as it suited them and now their leader was to show that they meant it. Any concessions would be interpreted by his party as a surrender to the pressure of the "black states".

He was accompanied in London by Mr. Eric Louw, and the question of South Africa's membership came before the Commonwealth Prime Ministers on March 13. By the end of that day it became apparent that the matter was not being treated merely as a formality and South Africa's membership was not to be taken for granted. As the discussions dragged on into the next day both factions in the country became apprehensive. Both began to realise that they had badly underestimated the antagonism to South Africa's racial policies in the Commonwealth as they were to continue to underrate it in the world. The Commonwealth countries, particularly Britain, Australia and New Zealand, were anxious to keep another "founder member" in "the club"—but not at any price. And that was a shock as much to the pro-British South Africans as to the anti-British Nationalists, a shock to their common self-esteem. The Boers found it hard to believe that Britain would not do anything to keep them, would not stretch any principle and agree to any compromise to hold them within the association into which it had brought them by conquest sixty years before. The English-speaking section were equally dismayed to discover that for the sake of principle Britain was ready to jettison its million or more people of British stock in South Africa.

Actually more than South African membership was at stake. The three-day discussion was a test of Commonwealth ideals. Was the Commonwealth merely a trading association ready to do business under any conditions? Or was it bound by aspirations of internationalism that could hold ten nations of many creeds, colours and races in comradeship across half the world? What, in short, was paramount in this straggly Commonwealth of Nations that history had linked in a seemingly haphazard way? Was it business, or was it humanity?

What was actually said and done across the table at Lancaster House, London, on March 13, 14 and 15, 1961, may not be known for a long time. What has been related has amounted to little more than official summary designed to make the break that occurred as civilised and as little rancorous as possible. But in South Africa what we understood had happened was this:

There was no line-up of the black states against the white. Such a ganging-up was the very thing that Nehru of India, Tunku Abdul Rahman of Malaya, and Ayub Khan of Pakistan wished to avoid. True to the undertaking to his Nationalists at home, Dr. Verwoerd refused to make any concessions that would show the slightest departure from his race policies. To make such concessions would amount to "the humiliation" of his country. A nation with an inferiority complex is easily humiliated.

Both sides in South Africa feared the break that was looming as the London discussions went into a second and a third day. The Afrikaners, for all their vaunted pride, feared it for economic reasons, the possible loss of markets for their agricultural products; the English in addition feared it for sentimental reasons, reluctant to see the severance of ties with the great country of their origin and kin.

There were no direct reports from Lancaster House, only rumour, suggestion and conjecture... from correspondents, lobbyists and observers. At last, on the afternoon of the third day, it looked as though the matter had been resolved. The Prime Ministers were willing to issue a statement agreeing to South Africa's membership of the Commonwealth as a republic and setting forth certain Commonwealth principles which South Africa as represented by Dr. Verwoerd was able to approve.

No one was happy with the solution. After three days of debate it seemed that there was far too little that Dr. Verwoerd was able or willing to approve. The resulting statement was accordingly more remarkable for what it evaded than for what it contained. It apparently left out everything that really mattered. Nevertheless, it looked like an acceptable if tenuous compromise, to which all the Prime Ministers were willing to put their names.

Although there were no official releases from the Conference, news emerged quickly. We knew in South Africa on the afternoon of March 15 that agreement had as good as been reached. The country was preparing to go to bed that evening heaving a sigh of relief. People going home from work saw a poster in the streets put out by *Die Vaderland,* the Afrikaans afternoon paper in Johannesburg, announcing: "Ons is in—We are in—Unofficial".

In the offices of the *Rand Daily Mail* we had to answer telephone calls from people in the suburbs asking us if it was true. We answered that we were still waiting for the official announcement, but we thought that it was true.

We were all wrong. The break at the Prime Ministers' conference in Lancaster House, London, came just when it seemed that South Africa's membership had been propped up again and all formal differences had been overcome.

No doubt one day someone will describe the scene in the conference room. For the time being one has to picture it. There they were round the table in Lancaster House, down a classic London street—the strained white faces of Macmillan (for Britain), Diefenbaker (Canada), Menzies (Australia), Holyoake (New Zealand), Verwoerd and Louw (these two looking deeply dejected in a photograph taken soon afterwards on their departure); the uneasy, sallow faces of Nehru, the Tunku, Khan and Mrs. Bandaranaike (Ceylon); the dark critical faces of Nkrumah (Ghana) and Tafawa Balewa (Nigeria)—none of them satisfied with the patched-up arrangement, all of them aware of its inadequacy.

There was a pause ... a break for that traditional interrupter of English ceremonial, a cup of tea ... and time for a little more thinking ...

And then someone raised the question of the acceptance by South Africa of diplomatic envoys from the new African states, the other African members of the Commonwealth. It would be an appropriate manifestation of friendship.

That was when the breach came.

It was not Dr. Verwoerd's rejection of the suggestion that did it ... but the contemptuous way in which he had treated it. The excuse afterwards given in Pretoria on his behalf was that he could not have the capital crowded with so many foreign embassies.

It was the proverbial straw on the camel's back.

It now became apparent that if South Africa could not agree to even this formal manifestation of friendship, then Commonwealth membership would indeed be an empty thing.

Dr. Verwoerd and his advisers withdrew, and when they returned it was to announce the withdrawal of South Africa's application for admission into the Commonwealth as a republic.

The official announcement we had that evening, round about nine o'clock was not "We are in!" but "We are out!"

Among the Nationalists of South Africa, the "withdrawal" from the Commonwealth was represented as a great victory for Boer principles. Elsewhere, South Africa's "expulsion" was regarded as a vindication of Commonwealth, international and humanist ideals.

To do Dr. Verwoerd justice, he had never undertaken to keep South Africa in the Commonwealth, to which neither he nor his followers had any sense of attachment except in the way of trade. He had said more than once that he would do all he could to retain Commonwealth membership, but he would make no concessions. In other words, if South Africa remained in the Commonwealth it would be entirely on his own terms: "granite" was his watchword, and granite does not budge. That sort of attitude was hardly promising. It even raised a suspicion that he would look for a pretext to break with the Commonwealth, or he would not avoid one. And of course that is what happened.

On the other side there was genuine anxiety to keep South Africa "in the club", especially among the older members—Britain, Australia, New Zealand and even Canada. Their motives were partly sentimental, partly economic. There was also among them the belief that they could better influence South African policies within the Commonwealth than out. But as the conference proceeded it must have become more and more obvious that it was going to be extremely difficult for anyone to be South Africa's advocate. From the days of the Kruger republic, Afrikaners have had a fatal genius for antagonising their friends, and now it was concentrated in the tormented personality of one man.

To the representatives of the other countries, his arrogance must have felt not just intolerable, but also deeply inimical. There was no living with it. The break had to come.

For Britain it was a more violent wrench than for any other country. It ended an association that had lasted for a century and a half and had in some ways become closer with the passing of years. But Britain could not insist on what would have looked to all the world an unprincipled partnership. Whichever way you look at it, the final separation was accomplished in the most enlightened traditions of British statesmanship.

CHAPTER 23

U.N. and After

THE plane that carried us north through Africa in September 1961 carried almost a full load of passengers, almost entirely white. As we moved westwards for Dakar, the general complexion of the passengers changed. At each step one or two white faces disappeared and dark faces took their place.

It was not merely a change of colour but also a change of attitude. A plane gives one little opportunity to admire the natural scenery; one's attention rests on one's fellow travellers.

These Africans from Brazzaville, Monrovia and Lagos were different from the few who had joined us in the south. They were free and easy in their ways, uninhibited, and showing no tendency to merge into the background. They were officials, business-men, journalists. This was Africa, their world, and they were on the move. Hopping from state to state was for them like travelling on a suburban route and picking up acquaintances on the way.

When the sleek Pan-Am plane reached New York next morning, I found myself in the company of two Nigerians, one a trade union official from Lagos, the other a wiry, alert little man, Xrydz-Eyutchae, editor of a newspaper in Port Harcourt. The patient representative of the U.S. State Department who met us at Idlewild, was relieved to see me on conversational terms with the Nigerians. His job was to see us off to Washington, and he seemed glad to think he could place them under my guidance. In the south-bound plane the conversation ranged from Verwoerd in South Africa to Tafewa Balewa in Nigeria—they were a little astonished to find that I knew the name—and in a very short time they had sized me up. By the end of the journey we were firm friends, and during my week in Washington I was seldom without one of them at my side.

I was one of an international party of journalists, to which Eyutchae also belonged. The trade unionist had attached himself to us only because our paths had crossed. Eyutchae, like me, was travelling on a specialist grant from the State Department that kept us in the States for more than four months. Others in the party, also converging on Washington during that first week, were from India, Pakistan, Korea, Norway, Poland, Argentina, Sierra Leone, Egypt, Burma, the Philippines and Cyprus—about twenty in all.

Those four months travelling from east to west and south through an American fall—I prefer the word to "autumn"; it says so much more—gave me a broad and sometimes intimate view of American society, the opportunity to take a backward view of my own, and the experience of living with men of other nationalities and colours that was the most memorable of all. For six weeks the whole group lived on the beautiful campus of the University of Indiana, and from the windows of Ernie Pyle Hall, the Department of Journalism, I watched the trees in the street change colour with a wonder that only one long absent from northern skies can understand.

American society seemed to contradict everything that I had learned from books, newspapers and films, especially films. The most impressive fact, once you left New York, was the normalness of American life and its basic sanity—its family life, its work, and its leisure—bigger and more extensive than anywhere else no doubt, but never freakish or in any sense monstrous. If the streets of New York, with their millions of trudging feet, confront you as an enormous treadmill, and if the wheeling expressways of Chicago swallow you as in another kind of satanic mill, you think of the great hinterland of the West and the South as the ultimate corrective to the fantastic outgrowths of the cities.

Not places so much as people gave me an enduring picture of America ... Not the Collegiate Gothic of the Indiana campus, but men like Floyd Arpan, Chris Savage and John Stempel, who ran the Department of Journalism and made me understand why the Press has so much more prestige in the United States (if not more vitality) than in Britain ... Not the glitter of the *Time-Life* offices in Rockefeller Center, but the somewhat untidy news room of *The Record* of New Jersey across the river, where the genial Donald Borg presided over a few million dollars' worth of newspaper, men and material by day, and watched the "bang-bangs" (with me) on television at night ... Not the flashy hotels of Florida, but Mrs. Eleanor Roosevelt, at seventy-seven, addressing an audience of 3,000 at Miami on the work of the United Nations and holding them hanging on her every deliberate word for forty astonishing minutes. When I said to her, on being introduced to her afterwards, "That was a wonderful speech!" she smiled like a little girl ... Not even the classic architecture of Washington, but the black man who stopped me in the street to ask the way, and then chatted as man to man.

For a South African to meet black men on an equal footing was a singular experience. Practically all my life I had been accustomed to thinking of men of colour, whether deliberately or casually, as in some way or other inferior, and often as I tried to tell myself that inherently they lacked nothing the white man could claim, their own attitude placed a gulf between me and them. They were always obsequious, servile or afraid. Once when I asked a Zulu messenger at our office in Johannesburg to demonstrate the Zulu handshake with me, he trembled as he took my hand in his. It then occurred to me that he had probably never held a white man's hand in his before.

I had been warned that on this tour of America I might have to room with other men. And so it happened. In various places my room-mates were Kjell Amdahl of Trondheim, Wieslaw Gornicki of Warsaw, Xrydz-Eyutchae of Port Harcourt, S. Santanam of New Delhi, K. A. Batalvi of Lahore, Julius Cole of Freetown. When I shared a room and a bath with Eyutchae (I think it was in the Biltmore at Atlanta, "integrated" for the occasion), I watched myself far more closely than I watched him. The white man's habits so easily betray him. He was an independent little man, sometimes surprisingly simple in his reactions but accustomed to exercising authority. (The first part of his name, he told me, was the Nigerian version of "Rex".)

When he came out of the bathroom sporting striped pyjamas, I was already in bed, reading. Through the corner of my eye, I watched him get into the other bed. He also took up a book. What a situation for a South African, I thought to myself! Back home this would be not only impossible, but it would be illegal, punishable under I don't know how many laws. But as he stretched himself in the bed, I noted mentally that the heavens did not shake at this conjunction, and the walls showed no awareness of this flagrant breach of the South African way of life by one of its nominal adherents. I kept looking at the same printed page and quoting to myself, ". . . But the architrave and the battlements stood fast . . . !"

Even Communism took on a different look as seen through the always questioning eyes of Gornicki of Warsaw. "The difference between Poland and Jugoslavia," he would say, "is that in Jugoslavia you may criticise Moscow, but never Belgrade. In Poland you may criticise Warsaw, but never Moscow. I think ours is the better situation, no?" I told him that the out-flowing Polish soul, as he showed it to me, was probably the best hope for Poland whatever its situation.

All the way through America I kept looking back at South Africa, and the farther I went the more unreal our "South African way of life" became to me; the more distorted and falsified it seemed. Here in America there was no equality between rich and poor; there was no full equality between black and white; there was no complete acceptance of the one by the other. But it was not the law that made differences and antagonisms. They were made largely by the heritage of history and largely by the preferences and prejudices of men. The function of the law was to even them out—not as in South Africa to define and to confirm them, to set them up as the statutes of the land, to make prejudice and inequality the rules of judgment and appoint judges to apply them in the courts.

In America, "Two-four-six-eight...We don' wanna integrate..." shout the students of Georgia..."I am against integration," said a girl student of Emory. "My parents are southerners and they've always been against it."

In South Africa, "Kaffir op sy plek!" (The Kaffir in his place), shouts the Afrikaner..."White man Boss!" echoes the Englishman.

But in America, the law is still on the side of humanity and individual dignity. In South Africa it is on the side of humiliation and makes humanity a thing to be slandered.

In America that year, South Africa's spokesman at United Nations was Eric Louw, Foreign Minister, he of the crabbed manner and the rasping voice, whom our cartoonist Bob Connolly always depicted with a tall hat (for the rising cost of living in his days as Minister of Economics) and a sheaf of newspaper cuttings (for his constant carping at the English Press). He had been at the United Nations for several years before, a regular visitor in fact since Lake Success days, and won himself no enviable reputations. He was one of the least liked delegates at U.N., and his diplomatic parties were largely avoided. If South Africa ever had a case, he had damaged it irreparably. Now he was there again defending "onse mense" against the accusations and the hostility of the world, which to him were inexplicable. After all, "we had come to the aid of the West in two great wars" (although he was a member of a Government comprising men who had opposed both wars, had pleaded the cause of Nazidom and called Belsen a piece of British propaganda).

"We have," he protested, "sent one and a half million African children to school" (without mentioning that 90 per cent left in Standard or Grade 2, and if they hadn't, there would have been no one and no place to teach them because the amount spent on non-white schooling was a fraction of that spent on white schools).

He claimed that the word "apartheid", which had "become almost a swear word in many countries", was only an abbreviation of the term "aparte ontwikkeling" (separate development), though he was well aware that "aparte ontwikkeling" was only an afterthought and the idea must therefore have been abbreviated before it came into existence.

All these things I read in newspaper reports and in booklets circulated in America, and commonplace as they had become in South Africa from boastful repetition, presented here as righteous fact to a world assembly they were outrageous. I think I was down in Georgia when I read a report of the speech he had given in the Assembly on October 11, painting an idyllic picture of the way the African was living in South Africa. All he asked for, he said, was "that we be permitted to carry out our policy of looking after the interests of our Bantu and other non-white people without interference from outside". To describe apartheid as a policy of "looking after the Bantu" was indeed a topsy-turvy description of the situation, of which only a South African Nationalist could be capable without fear of ridicule.

He argued that if the system of "differentiation practised in South Africa is to be regarded as discrimination", then it was practised also against the whites. No whites were allowed to enter Bantu areas without a permit, or to trade in Bantu townships, or to own land in Bantu homelands, or to be represented on the Bantu Authorities. That was another perverse argument that so obviously made nonsense of the truth. The fact is that whites have no need to enter Bantu areas or townships except as commercial travellers or sightseers; they do not need land in the Bantu homelands because they already own 86 per cent of the land in the country; and they do not need to participate in the Bantu Authorities, which do not govern them. It was like telling Americans in the U.S. that they were being discriminated against because they were not allowed to live in the Indian reservations. All this Mr. Eric Louw was well aware of, and yet he chose in an international assembly to turn the truth "agterste-voor" as his own people say, "back-to-front".

I must confess that I hoped for an opportunity to answer him; if one voice could speak so equivocally, another voice could denounce the deceit. It seemed to me as simple as that. But no occasion arose until I was back in New York in

November for a few days before leaving for San Francisco. And then it came unexpectedly.

During the last week of November the resolution calling for sanctions against South Africa was to be debated in the General Assembly. I was due to leave for the west coast on Wednesday, November 29, and did not expect to be present either for the vote (which that year failed by a narrow margin) or for Mr. Louw's answer to the debate, which was far down in the week's agenda. So when I walked down to the U.N. building from Times Square on Tuesday afternoon, it was merely to see one or two friends in the Press Room and listen to some snatches of the debates.

At the Press table I found David Friedman of the South African Press Association who covered U.N. for the South African newspapers, and I met Rene de Villiers, a member of the staff of the Johannesburg *Star*, who was on a short tour. Very soon I learned to my surprise that Eric Louw was expected to speak early that afternoon, and I was glad I had come. David Friedman went to listen in one of the soundproof chambers; but Rene de Villiers and I took seats in the Press section directly behind the delegations. We watched the South African officials nervously preparing themselves for a great occasion. When an Indian delegate rose to speak they ambled out of the hall, but came hurrying back when he sat down, in fear lest they might be missing South Africa's big chance.

There was some complicated balloting that afternoon, and we sat for more than a tedious hour waiting for the result. It was about 5.30 when at last the South African Foreign Minister was called to the rostrum. As he left his seat, the other members of the delegation moved one up to get a better view of their spokesman. Then I noticed among them Carel de Wet, the Member of Parliament for Vanderbijlpark, who on the day of Sharpeville (which happened to be in his constituency) had expressed concern in the House that only one man had been killed (before he had heard of the rest). I felt indignant that this man (who also happened to be on tour) should have been allowed to roost among his cosy colleagues in the U.N. Assembly. I looked from one to the other—from the self-righteous Louw now facing us at the rostrum, to the self-satisfied bulk of Dr. de Wet a few yards in front of us.

Mr. Louw spoke across the hall in our direction. What he said mattered little. It was an evasive reply to the charges made against South Africa, and rested mainly on a denial that the policies of the South African Government were a danger to international peace. I had in mind all that he had said before and the kind of South Africa he was defending, and it seemed to me monstrous that he should speak at a world assembly and meet with no protest. In South Africa I knew protests were of no avail. But a protest made here, however feeble, would not be ignored. They would have to pay attention to it in South Africa.

I knew the state of mind there. They would say the protest was made in the wrong place. But when protests made in the right place go unheard, one seeks other places. And the place where the Foreign Minister was speaking so insolently and arrogantly was the right place. So here was my opportunity to show that the spirit of protest was still alive among the easy-going, lotus-eating South Africans, and if I missed my opportunity I would never forgive myself. There might never be another like it.

I knew I would not get much time to speak. As it turned out I had less than I had expected. I could see none of the U.N. guards to right or left. That was enough for me. Mr. Louw's voice went grating on ineffectually ... What I would say would not matter beyond one word, "half-truths". That was the thing to throw at him. And that was the word I shouted as I stepped up to the barrier just behind the delegates..."Half-truths! ... He's telling you half-truths. He's been telling you half-truths all the time ... Don't listen to him ..." There was time for little else.

I saw Mr. Louw stagger, as it were, in his speech. I saw Carel de Wet's padded face turn round at me in dismay. Then two broad-shouldered guards in plain clothes, whom I hadn't noticed before, came up from behind and held me by the arms. As they drew me away I saw Rene de Villiers holding his head down and apparently wishing that the floor would open and swallow him.

In the Assembly itself there was apparently no ripple, but the general feeling was described to me some time later by a U.N. official. "There was many a man there who would have liked to run round and hug you."

My own feeling was that I had muffed it all. I had not prepared anything. I should have noticed the burly guards near the door behind me. But I had uttered the right word. It would ring round to South Africa. It was enough.

The two guards led me down to a small room in the depths of the building. "Fancy a gentleman like you doing a thing like this!" said one of them.

"Why? Don't I look as if I've got the guts?"

He only looked at me. I think my use of the word "guts" surprised him as much as anything. "This is going to be serious for you."

"How serious?"

He made me wait in the little room while he spoke on the telephone. He took away my Press card. "Who was the man with you?" he asked.

I realised they must have questioned the innocent Rene de Villiers. "He had nothing to do with it. I met him here for the first time."

They appeared to be awaiting instructions.

"How long are you going to keep me? I've got an appointment down town at six." It was already close to the hour.

It took about ten minutes for instructions to come. Then the senior guard said, "You may go. But we'll keep this." He dropped my U.N. Press card into a drawer. "We'll see you out."

They accompanied me to the Press Room, where I had left my coat. Then to Reuter's office, where David Friedman had his desk. He was not there. But I left him a message with Reuter's man, who asked what had happened. I told him.

The guards led me to the front door of the U.N. building and shook hands with me. "Don't come back," said one..

"Not this time. But . . . see you again."

They looked at me oddly as though trying hard to understand me, and not quite making it.

Next day, Wednesday, November 29, I took a plane to San Francisco, hoping that the storm would not break before my departure. It held off till the following morning when a call from Professor Floyd Arpan at Bloomington, Indiana, let me know that the fat was in the fire. Some time later he told me how he had received the news. It was either from U.N. or the State Department, and when he heard it he turned to his colleagues at Ernie Pyle Hall and said, "Until now the Journalists' Project has gone fine. But the day before yesterday the roof fell in. Only none of us heard it."

Over the telephone he was kindness itself. He told me that the South African Embassy in Washington had made an immediate approach to the State Department demanding that my tour in the U.S. be terminated—it had about six weeks to run—and that I be returned at once to South Africa. He hoped this would not be necessary and suggested I send him a full report. I did it within the hour or so, and then tried to forget it. But I was not allowed to do so.

Apart from a mention in the *Herald-Tribune* and the *Washington Post,* the incident had received little attention in the American Press, whose men were probably accustomed to "crackpot" interruptions at United Nations. But in South Africa, the clamour burst in Press and radio. The English newspapers (including my own) reported it briefly and factually, but the Afrikaans newspapers gave it headline treatment with pictures, and Radio South Africa (now going full blast as a propaganda machine for the Government) gave it prominence in its principal newscasts on two mornings running. More was to follow.

The morning after reporting the "ousting" of a South African journalist from U.N. on its front page (why the word "ousting" I never understood), the *Rand Daily Mail* printed a front-page leader written by Laurence Gandar dissociating the newspaper from my action. (I still don't think that was necessary, even though I was not there to gauge public feeling.) The *Rand Daily Mail* also announced my suspension from the post of Assistant Editor. The Afrikaans papers went rather more hysterical in type face and cartoon. My wife received threatening telephone calls at the flat calling me a traitor and promising to meet me with a "reception committee" on my return. Most of this I learned in telephone calls from correspondents in New York asking for my reasons and comments. All I could say was that I wanted to demonstrate that the spirit of protest was still alive among South Africans and this was the place to show it. The *Rand Daily Mail* printed two pages of letters both approving and condemning my behaviour.

My wife's letters were alarming. They even raised the question whether it was safe for me to return, suggesting that friends had raised it too. All this indicated to me a state of opinion that was astonishing. While South Africans sneered at United Nations, and Government Press and radio lost no opportunity to belittle its membership and councils, an incident like this sent them into storms of indignation. According to the popular view, it was all right for Mr. Louw to appear at U.N. and use half-truths to defend the odious practices of his country; but it was all wrong for me to disconcert him there. That was the so-called sporting attitude which turned to indignant complaint when Coloured spectators at a rugby match cheered the visiting side. So unsporting of them, what! So unsporting of me!

From Indiana campus, the staunch Professor Arpan kept sending me bulletins. The South African Embassy was making daily calls on the State Department demanding my expulsion from the country and the cancellation of my visa. It showed itself, in Arpan's words, "angry, determined and vindictive". But he was insisting on the right of free speech in a free country and he was hopeful that the State Department would resist the pressure from Pretoria (all of which was officially denied in South Africa).

From the journalist students at Ernie Pyle Hall came a communal letter gently scolding me and commending me at the same time. From other members of the Multi-national Journalists' Group, now scattered in various parts of the

States, came applause and congratulations. I was in New Orleans when a letter came from Floyd Arpan to say that the State Department had decided to ignore the South African demands (which the Embassy then thought it best to deny ever having made).

By now I had also made up my own mind. I would return to South Africa. That seemed to me the right thing to do, as showing that I stood by what I had said and done. After a final meeting with Professor Arpan and the Group at Bloomington and a few more days doing the Broadway shows, I flew back to Johannesburg in January. At Jan Smuts Airport the reception was as friendly as it could possibly be seeing I was met by my wife and A. B. Hughes, who drove us to town.

At the office that same afternoon my meeting with Gandar was entirely cordial. I think I understood the complex state of feeling that made it necessary for him to disown me one day and welcome me back a few days later. In certain quarters, particularly the Afrikaans Press, the opinion was held that my "head would roll". Afrikaans newspapermen confided as much to Dr. Argus Tresidder, Public Affairs Officer at the U.S. Embassy in Pretoria, who had originally nominated me for the tour. But no such disaster overtook me in any sense. Gandar let me know as gently as he could that I would not be restored to the position of Assistant Editor. I think I took it stoically. What made it easy for me was that I was in fact to change places with A. B. Hughes for whom I had the greatest respect. I had worked under him before; he had worked under me; now I was to be under him again. Neither of us foresaw any difficulty; and there was none. For the sake of appearances I was given the title vaguely of "Production Editor" and told that I would not be expected to write any political matter. As I had no desire for exercise in the cynical science, I had no regrets—though I knew it would really be impossible to assist in the running of a daily newspaper like the *Rand Daily Mail* without being involved in its political work.

As soon as it became known that I was back, the Afrikaans papers telephoned me for interviews. I declined to answer their questions, but that did not prevent them from printing interviews of the "no comment" variety. One of them even issued a street bill, "Sowden of U.N. fame is back—interview", and suggested that I had made a secret re-entry into the country. As I had returned in a passenger jet of the South African Airways and passed through the usual immigration and customs offices, that seemed hardly likely. Another stated that I could expect "police action".

It took a few days before officialdom became aware of my presence in the country. Then I received a telephone call from the Chief Passport Officer in Johannesburg telling me of a letter he had for me from the Secretary of the Interior. I could guess its contents. He offered to call on me next morning—and would I have my passport ready? Instead I said I would call on him the same afternoon. This "action" I had expected and wanted as little fuss over it as possible.

When I entered his office about an hour later, the Chief Passport Officer shook me by the hand and motioned me to a chair at his desk. He showed me the letter from the Secretary of the Interior, for which I had to sign an acknowledgment. Transfer of the passport across his blotting-pad took no time at all. He thanked me for my co-operation. I said it was good of him to offer to call on me, but I thought this would be the simpler way. Whereupon he shook my hand again and it was all over. Not a word passed that the Secretary of the Interior would not have approved of. But I am not sure about the two hand-shakes.

At the time I could not see what "police action" could possibly follow. But it did about two weeks later. It came in the form of a letter from the Commissioner of Police demanding the return of my Press identity card. This was a document issued by the police entitling the holder to be in any area under police control for the purpose of obtaining information. As I had had little contact with the police for years, it was of no practical value to me, and I knew I would not miss it. After it had been sent in, Gandar wrote a letter of protest to the Minister of Justice asking for the matter to be reconsidered, such procedure being provided for under the original terms of issue. This merely gave the Minister an

16—LOA

excuse for stage-managing a mention in Parliament, and on May 1 the letter was made the subject of a question in the House from one of the Government's Members.

The answer of the Minister of Justice was that "under no circumstances was he prepared to accede to the request" for the Press card to be returned.

His announcement was greeted from the Government benches with the remark "... traitorous behaviour ..."

All of this simply demonstrated that the "Sowden episode at U.N." as it was called, or the Sowden protest against government by evasion, prevarication and double-dealing, had not gone unheard. It had been noticed and felt precisely as I hoped it would be, and it had hit home.

During the weeks and months that followed, I found myself inevitably tempted with the thought of leaving South Africa for good, getting a "one-way permit", and finding newspaper work in some other part of the world. Before leaving America I had been offered a job there if I was thinking of staying, and in 1962 through the good offices of Floyd Arpan of Indiana my inquiries brought another offer from Massachusetts. When it came to the point of making a decision, however, I found that I had sent my roots deeper into South Africa than I thought I had. It took me weeks to make up my mind, and when I turned the offer down I did it most regretfully. But this country was still my home, with all the emotional tug of a place and people that I knew with most of the years of my life. I found it too difficult to break.

There was another consideration. Gandar, in his undramatic, unspectacular way, was running the paper like the captain of a fighting ship. We had to steer it among Laws of Incitement (preventing the printing of information that could be interpreted as inciting non-whites against whites)... past regulations for the banning of people (who thereupon might not be quoted except with the Minister's permission)... past the Prisons Act (preventing the publication of information coming from the jails)... past accusations of "smearing" if we published details about starvation in the African villages

... past charges of "liberalism", "pro-Communism", "humanism", "subversion" and, most heinous of all, "un-South Africanism" if we continued to criticise the Government and damage the "South African image abroad"... past restrictions, regulations and edicts behind which the Government still pretended that South Africa had a free Press.

But there was a challenge in editing a newspaper under these conditions—conditions which obliged us to please no one, and to consider no one but humanity and the facts about people and things as we could best establish them.

We developed a distant contempt for the other newspapers, Afrikaans and English, whose main purpose seemed to be to apologise for the Government's rigours, stupidities and perversions, and who regarded it as their patriotic duty to depict apartheid as the best of all possible systems, in the best of all possible countries, in the best of all possible worlds—for the white man. But the public, showing that it still had a conscience, bought the *Rand Daily Mail* for its news, its views and apparently also for its advertisements, which showed no diminution.

It was still worth staying here to help in the editing of a newspaper like that as long as it could make itself heard above the din of women's pistol clubs, business-men's back-slapping and the new South African jingoism.

But how long could we do it? How long would we be allowed to run a free newspaper among a people that so obviously did not want to be free?

CHAPTER 24

Exit

THE next general elections were due to be held in 1966. The elections of 1961 had shown white emotion in South Africa running true to form. The echoes of the Mau Mau of Kenya were still ringing in people's ears as they went to the polls, and the results showed the expected swing to the Nationalists of further English-speaking opinion, which meant both English and Jewish. Since then the Congo had replaced the Mau Mau as the Big Fear with which to inflame the public mind. "Look at the Congo!" was the cry hurled at the "sickly humanism" of the liberals (a favourite ministerial phrase taken direct from the Nazis), and however irrelevant it might be, we knew it was going to work for the Nationalists even better than the Mau Mau had done. We considered it fairly certain, therefore, that the 1966 elections would further strengthen Dr. Verwoerd's position, and give him all the justification he needed for placing his clamps on the Press, as he had long kept threatening to do. In this context, "the Press" meant "die Engelse Pers" (the English Press), and that meant first and foremost the *Rand Daily Mail*.

Through the early 1960s, Gandar had a free hand, though there were indications of uneasiness among some of the directors. He and Hughes were at the top of their form in the daily editorial columns (with an extra page on Saturday), and even I, supposedly restricted to non-political writing and the theatre, was not muzzled. But the signs of rising hostility closing in on us were unmistakable. Even while admitting that the Saturday edition of the *Mail* was the best paper in the country, readers were becoming restless. Worse still, some of our advertising men were going about with long faces. "Our policy! Our policy!" they kept whispering in the corners. To them it was a disaster.

The police were closing in on us too. We had good reason to believe that they had informants in the building. The day after an important editorial conference had taken place in Gandar's office, our man on the crime round reported that Marshall Square appeared to have inside information on it, though nothing had happened there that could possibly have interested the police at any normal time. After this it became standard practice to hold any discussions, whatever their purpose, well beyond range of a telephone receiver, and Gandar's conferences in the corridor became more frequent.

Nevertheless, the uncomfortable sense of being under hostile observation continued, and suspicion soon centred on a member of the reporting staff. The police had in fact planted an agent in the Reporters' Room, and by the time we had been able to track him down, he had done his work.

A few months previously we had engaged a reporter who professed to have come from a training school run by an afternoon newspaper group at Cape Town. He proved to be neither very capable nor very bright and little credit to his school whatever it was, but perhaps he was pre-occupied with his other assignment. He turned out to be a spy for the Special Branch and his real headquarters were with them two blocks up the street at the top of a building that went by the name of a grocery firm, "The Grays". The grocers still had their liquor store in the building. This was one of the odd details about our secret police. They did their work from a nondescript building in the middle of town and had their sinister interrogation rooms on the sixth floor, from which an Indian suspect had jumped to his death a year before.

At his subsequent appearance to give evidence in court, our spy tried to pose as a James Bond type bent on audacious exploits. He was anything but dashing—a sallow-faced fellow in fact, who walked shoulder-first down a passage or into a room. When our News Editor's suspicion's fastened on him, he was already out of the office, having presumably completed his mission. By now several young men were behind bars—

one of them from the staff of a companion journal of ours; another a reporter who had worked for us for a short time and then left; the third also a reporter pulled in for examination under the "90-day clause". He was released after about five weeks, during which he had undergone repeated interrogations, once for thirty hours continuously.

The other two journalists were ultimately sentenced to terms of imprisonment for two to three years. And what was their crime? They had been proved to be connected with the remnants of a Communist organisation, to which the under-cover man had followed them, attending meetings with them. The Communists of South Africa, even in the days when they were free to operate, were about the most inept lot of plotters in the world. This surviving remnant, from the evidence given in court, appeared to be about as potent as a tricycle.

Throughout 1956 we felt we were moving from one crisis to another, never sure when the climax would come, but meanwhile trying to do a decent job of reporting, giving a good coverage of the news, and at the same time keeping the public mind aware of the things that mattered. Prosperity was back. Verwoerd's ban on the export of capital had sent our reserves up again. Not knowing what to do with their money, people simply had to re-invest, and the Stock Exchange was booming again. That new building in Hollard Street was not too grandiose after all. It displayed its fountains in the forecourt like a prosperous business-man displaying his golden watch-chain. In this sort of atmosphere, white South Africans consider it their first duty to be good to themselves, and they dislike any intrusion on their sense of wellbeing. They resented the occasional items of news we printed reminding them of the "police state" conditions which hemmed in the lives of the greater part of the population. Now and then there was news about the people banished to remote parts of the country; they were non-whites, so it didn't really matter, but it was disturbing to hear of them. There were people under house arrest, like Mrs. Helen Joseph (restricted for another five years) unable to leave their homes after dark, if at all. But they were (it was all too readily assumed) Communists, so it didn't really matter. Helen Joseph's crime was that she had been visiting the people in banishment, trying to make their lives a little less dreary and keep them in touch with the forbidden world. It was, of course, misguided to carry on such humanitarian work; it was wrong to keep them in touch with anyone, and it was wrong of the *Mail* to keep the public aware of them.

We found occasion to remind them now and then of Chief Albert Lutuli, banished to his home in Groutville, Natal. One of the Cabinet Ministers had described the award to him of the Nobel Peace Prize in 1961 as "grotesque". He was living in a little African village which had been established in 1836 as a mission station by the Rev. Alden Grout of the American Board of Missions. Until 1962 Lutuli's voice was still heard in South Africa, for it was possible to report and quote him at times, and he used to contribute a column to the Johannesburg *Sunday Express*. Under the Sabotage Act of 1962, however, it became an offence to quote any "banned" person. It then became illegal to print anything he said; the newspaper had to stop his column; and a man who had come to represent to the world the voice of sanity in South Africa was silenced in his own country. All we could do now was to quote what others said about him, and we occasionally did so when the opportunity arose.

We also kept reminding the public in various ways of the plight of the political prisoners in the jails of Pretoria, Johannesburg and the offshore Robben Island at Cape Town. We did it not merely because they were "politicals", but because we knew that the political prisoners were far worse treated than the ordinary thieves, crooks and other criminals who had not offended against the Suppression of Communism or the Unlawful Organisations Act. The prisoners were visited in jail by clergymen, certain of whom occasionally confided in us without running the risk of alarming their congregations. But there was little we could do about it unless we could get direct information from "inside". There was a law, one of the creations of Mr. Vorster, Minister of Justice, which prevented the printing of any descriptive material about the prisons (even a photograph taken from the street) unless we could be quite certain of our facts. That sort of information was very difficult to obtain, but early in 1965 a mass of it came our way in the form of testimony from former prison officials and former inmates. Among the first was an Afrikaner called Van Schalkwyk, and among the others a Scotsman called Strachan. The information was taken down by one of our reporters, Benjamin Pogrund, and written by him after many consultations with the editor and our lawyers, who also scrutinised the completed stories, and cross-examined our informants.

One day in June I was asked to provide space in the paper for a "jail series". Allocating space for features was one of my daily unpolitical jobs. The articles appeared during one week and they created all the impact we had expected. They were well written; they were packed with fact and detail; and though some of the more horrid revelations had been deleted from Pogrund's original copy, their disclosures of dirt and torment in jail made grim reading.

We scarcely had to wait for official reaction. Police entered our office in Main Street on the morning the first article appeared (they used to station two men on the top of the staircase on such occasions) and demanded documents, reporters' notes and copies of the articles still to be printed. We gave them what they wanted, under protest. They could not prevent the appearance of the remaining stories (all in type by now) and they were merely practising their customary methods of intimidation. The affair became the talk of the town.

We felt quite sure that our "jail stories" presented a faithful picture of conditions in the prisons where politicals were kept, and we had done no more than expose an evil in our midst—which is the duty of any newspaper if journalism is to have any meaning in society or if newspapermen are to be anything more than Government toadies.

Gandar had done the right and courageous thing in authorising the articles, and yet it turned out that he had played right into the Government's hands, as the Government no doubt felt he would inevitably do sooner or later. They now had Gandar and the *Rand Daily Mail* in their power, for no matter how correct and how true Pogrund's stories were, the police and the prison authorities were confident that they could bring all the evidence they needed to refute them, and they could call any number of witnesses to swear that there was no maltreatment of people in prison. That is what eventually happened.

The first of the prosecutions, which followed a month or two later, at once revealed the police tactics. It was a prosecution not of the newspaper but of a man who had given us information, the young prison warder Van Schalkwyk. The *Rand Daily Mail* was not called, was not allowed to give evidence and Gandar had to write a formal letter contradicting the public prosecutor who had told the court that the newspaper had paid its informant, which was demonstrably untrue. The prosecutor, a man called Yutar, took up an attitude that could not have been more melodramatic had he been appearing in a suit for breach of promise. He sanctimoniously quoted the Bible; he appealed to principles of patriotism; and reduced the man in the dock to tears of remorse.

Van Schalkwyk chose to plead guilty, having been led to believe that if he did so he would get a suspended sentence. But he got the maximum of three years. The other cases against our informants were to drag on into 1968. The newspaper management gave the defendants all the legal assistance that was possible, but the trials all ended the same way. Though Gandar and the *Rand Daily Mail* were not in court (yet), everyone understood that it was the *Rand Daily Mail* that was really on trial, and the cases all went against us. Long before they were over, however, something else had happened. The climax we had been expecting in the office had broken over us.

One morning in November 1965, Gandar walked into my office next to that of his secretary, and told us that the owners had decided to act. We had always thought of the owners as some remote syndicate whose members were seldom named and whose whereabouts were slightly unreal. But the owners were real enough and apparently not so remote. Until now they had left the paper by and large to the appointed board of directors who, to be fair, had backed Gandar, though not always with enthusiasm. But the paper was beginning to lose ground both in revenue and circulation, though neither to any serious extent. It was still packed with advertising; people who were afraid to be seen with it still read it; and commercial firms were still contributing to our annual Christmas fund, though not as generously as formerly. Anyhow, the owners thought that the signs were serious enough, and that the time had come for changes. Accordingly, the directors told Gandar that he would have to go. There was apparently a limit beyond which a daily newspaper could not continue in opposition both to a government like ours and to popular white opinion. A newspaper was after all a big investment, and investments had to be protected. Nobody would be more highly pleased than the Government if the paper failed and had to close down. It was not difficult therefore to see the owners' point of view, however much we might deplore it.

What exactly was to happen now was not quite clear. There was apparently some face-saving to be done. But meanwhile Gandar was asked to give his advice on the appointment of another editor. I told him at once what I intended doing. I had long made up my mind that when the inevitable change of tone or of policy came, I would leave the *Mail*, and now was the time. I considered that I could still reasonably look forward to ten years of working life, and I would not spend them working for a newspaper that I felt was about to join the chorus shouting for White-Man-Boss, the white man's dividends and the good life under apartheid in South Africa. As a British national I had obtained a British passport, but as a South African national I still needed a permit if I wished to leave the country. I had been to the passport office and got the necessary form of application five months before. Next day I went again and handed it in.

It took the directors a few weeks to find a suitable formula. Gandar had reasoned with them, arguing that this was the wrong time to make what would be seen as an out-and-out surrender to the Government. In the first place, they would be publicly passing judgment on him and the *Mail* in the prisons issue even before the courts had finished doing so. Secondly, with the general elections due in a few months' time, they would be crippling whatever chances remained to the Opposition, the *Rand Daily Mail* being regarded as the principal Opposition mouthpiece. The directors listened and finally produced what seemed to us an extraordinary arrangement. They accepted one of Gandar's nominees for editor—Raymond Louw, who until now had been a capable news editor—and they announced the appointment of Gandar as editor-in-chief. This looked very handsome to the public, or that section of it which approved of Gandar. Only we on the staff knew the real meaning of it. Gandar was no longer to be in control of the news columns; he was to preside only over the columns of editorial opinion.

The directors (or owners) had the odd idea (as it seemed to us) that editorial writing did not matter much. They were worried mostly about the news columns, and they disliked the prominence given to what they considered "negative" news. From now on, I felt sure enough, the *Rand Daily Mail* was to be as other dailies—playing up any news that bolstered or enhanced white South Africanism, and playing down (in back pages preferably) anything that might embarrass it. Gandar accepted this arrangement because it still left him with a voice and a large measure of freedom. But I was confirmed in my conviction that for me to stay would mean to acquiesce in a state of affairs and a state of mind that were both odious.

So the *Rand Daily Mail* was made to capitulate—ironically just when it was being hailed overseas as the champion of newspaper integrity. The previous year Gandar had been awarded the Gold Medal of the Institute of Journalists in Britain for his fight in defence of the independence of the Press. We were all proud of this honour and felt some satisfaction in its glow. Later the same year, the American Newspaper Publishers' Association Foundation was preparing to make its World Press Achievement Award for "The pursuit of truth, freedom and justice", and the *Rand Daily Mail* was asked to prepare a dossier.

All this was going on when independence and freedom were already being compromised, but the *Rand Daily Mail* won the award together with an eloquent citation and an invitation to send someone to America to collect it. The announcement, made at about the same time as that of Gandar's promotion, looked impressive in print and many of our loyal band of readers sent their congratulations. Gandar had already been deprived of his passport, and so the Managing Director went to America to receive the prize.

That was no longer in my time, however. After keeping me waiting two months (and after an interview with the Special Branch at the Grays), the Government had at first flatly refused to give me any passport or permit to leave. But I pressed my claim, remembering that Vorster had said that one way of getting rid of "sickly humanists and liberalists" and "other such vermin" was to let them run when they wanted to. About two weeks later I received a letter from the Department of the Interior informing me that if I wished to apply for a "one-way exit permit" I was free to do so, at the same time warning me that if I left with such a document, I would be treated as a prohibited immigrant if I ever returned and would then be liable to a term of imprisonment of anything up to two years.

I applied for the document and received it in the middle of February. It was accompanied by the strange instruction that if I ever lost it, I was to report to the nearest South African consul. Someone with a sense of humour (or entirely lacking in one) must have framed that morsel of unnecessary advice.

On March 17, 1966, I boarded a plane for Israel. The only man to come and see me off at Jan Smuts Airport was Laurence Gandar. I had advised most of my friends against coming because the Special Branch had a way of taking names on such occasions. Gandar and I had little left to say to each other by then; all had been said. And the rest was expressed in a final handshake. I still think that the six or seven years I worked with him on the *Mail* were the most exciting and the most satisfying of all my years on newspapers.

When I left there was a new cry ringing through South Africa. The Rhodesians had made their Unilateral Declaration of Independence in November, and South Africans suddenly found that they had brothers in faith on the other side of the Limpopo. For years it had been uncertain which way the Rhodesians would jump. For ten years South Africans had watched the experiment of "Partnership" going to pieces in the ill-starred Federation of Rhodesia and Nyasaland (1953–1963), and then rubbed their hands in satisfaction when the Federation crumbled. They had said all along that partnership between whites and blacks could not work, and now it was plainly proved to them. But all that the Federation had really proved was that the white Rhodesian, like the typical colonial overlord, hated the very idea of partnership, and would not budge an inch to make it work. The only partnership he would tolerate was, as it was said, that of the horse and its rider. That was what the South Africans applauded when Ian Smith declared for U.D.I., and in his defiance of Britain, the Western world and Africa, they saw their own heroics mirrored on the other side of the river. Had Rhodesia been willing to accept majority rule or any arrangement affording a prospect of it, black Africa would have moved so much nearer to the Republic. That was how South Africans saw it. But the Rhodesians had opted to become a buffer state, and South Africans were at no pains to conceal their joy. Forty-five years before, the Rhodesians had said "no" to Smuts and had turned their backs on Boer nationalism and its language (they still rejected Afrikaans officially), but now they had shown that white blood was thicker than the waters of the Limpopo and the Republic could stretch its strong arms northwards.

So they cheered Ian Smith. Soon they were calling him "Jan" like a true "boetie". They shouted for petrol to keep the wheels of Rhodesia turning and they sent their convoys of tankers tearing up the roads to Beit Bridge. They applauded every item of news that apparently showed Smith successfully thumbing his nose at Britain and the U.N. And anyone who dared to suggest that Britain could never agree to the emergence of another apartheid state in the north, another minority regime built to keep the black man down, was looked upon rather pitifully as a fool or, worse still, a traitor.

Moreover, South Africa was arming—no longer with bush-carts or even Saracen armoured cars. Millions of pounds were going into jet planes, submarines, tanks and more. If anyone dared to inquire where was the enemy against whom we were arming, the answer given was "security", a word which was made to cover a multitude of offensive weapons. Look at America! Every time Negroes rioted in an American city, the South African felt he was getting his money's worth in his country's arsenals. He would put his trust only in force and the show of force as the shield of his civilisation and the only means he knew of postponing Nemesis.

Looking back from the blue, if troubled, skies of Israel, I soon saw South Africa as something unreal and unaware—a land forced into a tortured pattern and the people in it boasting of their achievement. Contrary to the white man's belief, the newspapers abroad were not bristling with hostile and biased reports from the Republic. The newspapers in Israel and—as I was to find later—in London, printed surprisingly little news from Pretoria or Johannesburg, and what they printed was factual and detached. There was no need to stress or "angle" the news from South Africa. Such as did come from correspondents or the agencies was sufficiently grotesque in itself—a schoolgirl from a white family being declared Coloured and then re-declared white; the allocation of separate bathing beaches (out of town of course) to Coloured people; and white women being warned again that one day they would have to scrub their own floors—and this in the land "in which it seemed always afternoon"!

But when the big news came it was the most grotesque of all.... On September 6, 1966, it must have been a newspaperman's instincts which drew me to a newspaper office. At about 4.30 in the afternoon I turned into a side-street off the Jaffa Road, near Zion Square, to get to the offices of *The Jerusalem Post*. As I approached the front door, I was met by a staffman, Joe Blumberg, a former colleague of mine in Johannesburg. He was sure that I had heard the news. But I hadn't. That morning, the South African Prime Minister, Dr. Verwoerd, sitting in his front bench in Parliament in Cape Town, had been stabbed by one of Parliament's messengers. And this time the assailant had made sure. Verwoerd was dead.

A few minutes later I was upstairs reading the cables. The details, as they came to light, made the affair more and more astonishing. That a man of the assassin's dubious background and record should have been engaged as a messenger in the House of Assembly, in proximity to the heads of government, was in itself almost incredible. But it was true, and to be understood only in the light of that streak of amateurism that runs through South African administration. Verwoerd's bodyguard had apparently learned little from the first attempt on the Prime Minister's life in 1960.

It was easy, for anyone familiar with the interior of the House, to picture the gruesome scene—the burly messenger walking along the carpet between two rows of front benches; Verwoerd leaning back in his seat near the golden mace; Verwoerd leaning forward as the man approached to accept what he was bringing ... then a knife plunged into his neck. And so pandemonium with newspapermen looking on twelve feet above. It must have been as quick and sudden as that.

Still more grotesque was the course of the subsequent trial. The assassin, Tsafendas, pleaded that he was possessed of a demon tape-worm which had driven him to the deed. The court found that he was insane, and that was the end of the trial. Then South Africans breathed a sigh of relief. It was not after all a political murder! One gathered that had it turned out to have been political, they would have been much more deeply upset. But it was only the act of a madman, and somehow they found that to be a consoling thought. So there was nothing to be done about it but to find another strong man to take Verwoerd's place at the helm, and all would be right in the state of South Africa again.

They had in fact already found their strong man. John Vorster, who had been imprisoned during World War II as a Nazi sympathiser, was already Prime Minister. The choice was logical and even inevitable, fully consistent with Nationalist thinking. Ever since coming into power in 1948 the Nationalists had put their trust in extremists ... Malan,

Strydom, Verwoerd... and now Vorster... each one more of an extremist than his predecessor. Moreover, as Minister of Justice, Vorster had been responsible for much of the fierce legislation passed under Verwoerd—the banishments, the "90-day law", the house arrests. He had in fact been Verwoerd's big stick. What more natural than that they should now appoint the Big Stick to take his place?

So the South Africans who, in the words of Leo Lovell, M.P., had made Apartheid their god, now enthroned Force as its Chief Apostle. Thus they proclaimed once more that in South Africa there was to be no reasoning, only compulsion; no humanity, only dogma; and no dialogue with one's neighbour, only a wall.